Why Do You Need This New Edition?

6 good reasons why you should buy this new edition of *The Psychology of Blacks!*

1. New opening chapter entitled Building for Eternity

2. New chapter on spirituality

3. New chapter on coping with racism and oppression

4. New chapter on African-centered psychology and the juvenile offender

5. New chapter that looks beyond 2010 to the future

6. Updated chapters on African-centered psychology in the modern era; identity development, using contemporary figures like Barack Obama and Michael Jackson as referents; the African American family; education; and mental health issues among African Americans

Fourth Edition

THE PSYCHOLOGY
OF BLACKS

CENTERING OUR PERSPECTIVES IN THE AFRICAN CONSCIOUSNESS

Thomas A. Parham, Ph.D.
University of California, Irvine

Adisa Ajamu
Howard University

Joseph L. White, Ph.D. Professor Emeritus
University of California, Irvine

With contributions from

Roslyn Caldwell, Ph.D.
California State Polytechnic University, San Luis Obispo

And

Kenya Taylor Parham
California State University, Northridge

Prentice Hall
Boston   Columbus   Indianapolis   New York   San Francisco
Upper Saddle River   Amsterdam   Cape Town   Dubai   London   Madrid
Milan   Munich   Paris   Montreal   Toronto   Delhi   Mexico City   Sao Paulo
Sydney   Hong Kong   Seoul   Singapore   Taipei   Tokyo

No part of this manuscript can be cited or reproduced without expressed written consent of the first author

Executive Editor: Susan Hartman
Editorial Director: Craig Campanella
Project Editor: Kara Kikel
Editorial Assistant: Laura Barry
Marketing Manager: Nicole Kunzmann
Production Manager: Fran Russello
Cover Director: Jayne Conte
Cover Designer: Suzanne Behnke
Cover Image Credits: Fotolia: Collection of vintage African masks different styles © poco Fotolia: The African © Robert Mroczek Fotolia: Child © Miroslav
Project Manager: Niraj Bhatt, Aptara®, Inc.
Composition: Aptara®, Inc.

Credits and acknowledgments borrowed from other sources and reproduced, with permission, in this textbook appear on relevant page.

Library of Congress Cataloging-in-Publication Data
Parham, Thomas A. (Thomas Anthony)
   The psychology of blacks : centering our perspectives in the African consciousness / Thomas A. Parham, Adisa Ajamu, Joseph L. White; with contributions from Roslyn Caldwell.—4th ed.
      p. cm.
Includes bibliographical references.
ISBN-13: 978-0-13-182773-8
ISBN-10: 0-13-182773-1
   1. African Americans—Psychology.   I. Ajamu, Adisa.   II. White, Joseph L.
III. Caldwell, Roslyn.   IV. Title.
   E185.625.P355 2011
   155.8′496073—dc22
                                                                        2010036773

10 9 8 7 6 5 4 3 2 1

Allyn & Bacon
is an imprint of

ISBN-10:   0-13-182773-1
ISBN-13: 978-0-13-182773-8

CONTENTS

DEDICATION

This fourth edition of *The Psychology of Blacks: Centering Our Perspective in the African Consciousness* is dedicated to Dr. Asa G. Hilliard III and Nana Baffour Amankwatia II. Baba Asa transitioned to be with the CREATOR and Ancestors in the Summer of 2007, while attending the annual meeting of the Association for the Study of Classical African Civilization, which was held in Kemet (Egypt). For all of us, he continues to be sorely missed. Yet, in acknowledging his loss and absence, we recognize how blessed we were to have known him, worked and interacted with him, and learned from him. He was truly one of the twentieth century's best thinkers, whose penetrating insights continue to resonate in our minds, hearts, and spirits, and in the spirits of so many culturally conscious people all around the world. Dr. Hilliard's love of African people was deep and profound; and during his life, he was able to achieve maximum congruence between that emotional and spiritual connection to his people, and specific behaviors he engaged in to advance and facilitate our mental liberation. For that, we are especially grateful and hope that this text is a fitting, albeit small, tribute to his life and legacy.

ACKNOWLEDGMENTS

In writing this book, each of the authors owes a debt of gratitude to so many people in our lives who support our professional and personal endeavors, and give us the strength and encouragement to "keep on keep'in on" in both the face of life's adversities and in navigating the intellectual sea of cultural sterility that continue to plague the discipline of psychology.

For Dr. Parham, he writes:
Thanks are extended to my wife Davida and daughters Kenya and Tonya, who continue to be a source of strength and sustenance. Through your individual life pursuits, you all honor me for the husband and father I pride myself on being. Thanks are also extended to my colleagues in the Association of Black Psychologists who continue to inspire me with their commitment to serve the academic and mental health needs of African-descent people, and clients of all colors, who benefit from the culturally specific ways African-centered teachers, researchers, administrators, and clinicians come to do what they do. I also owe a special thanks to my elders, mentors (Dr. Joseph White, Dr. Horace Mitchell and Dr. Janet Helms), and teachers in the discipline of African psychology, in graduate school, professional life, and beyond, whose investments in me I hope will be repaid through my commitment to "pay it forward" and serve my community within and beyond the boundaries of academia, mental health treatment centers, professional organizations, urban cores, and suburban enclaves. I thank you, Dr. White, for loving me and all of your students enough to integrate that truth into all that we do. I also want to acknowledge my partners (mostly, but not exclusively men of color) from Daniel Murphy High School, Cal State University Long Beach, University of California-Irvine, Washington University, Southern Illinois University-Carbondale, Philadelphia, and the greater Los Angeles, California area who have blessed me with friendship over the years and whose presence in my life, whether past or present, has taught me the value of brotherhood and family beyond that which I share with my own siblings (Pamela, William, & Gerald), who I love dearly, and who continue to love me unconditionally. A "shout out" is also in order for my Uncle Tony Fitzsimmons, who even as an 81-year-old man, and after giving me my first baseball glove at age 10, continues to teach lessons in opening up his heart to share with others. I also owe a special thanks and appreciation to my assistant Dorothy, whose steady hand and attention to detail helped to produce the draft and final versions of this manuscript. Thanks and profound respect are also extended to my colleague and intellectual teacher Dr. Na'im Akbar, who graciously agreed to write the forward to this fourth edition. Lastly, I give honor and praise to the CREATOR, who has blessed me in ways that are lasting and abundant, as I ask He/She to continue to watch out over the soul of my late mother Sadie F. Parham, whose voice and spirit continue to guide my life.

For Dr. White, he writes:

I want to give thanks to my wife Lois who continues to be a life partner in all that I do. I thank you for your love and support. Thanks are also extended to my children Lori, Lynn, and Lisa, all beautiful and accomplished women in their own right. No father could be more proud. I also wish to thank the many students I have taught, trained, and influenced (either formally or informally) over the years. It is their thirst for knowledge and desire to make the world a better place that continues to encourage me. I am also cognizant of the fact that in the twenty-five-plus years since I authored the first edition of *The Psychology of Blacks*, much has changed in the world. And yet, the most important lesson we can continue to provide in our work on a Black or African psychology is less about the technological advances we now take as commonplace, the academies in which we articulate our theories, or the centers where we assess and treat our client populations. Rather, that lesson is reserved for the authenticity of the human condition and that connectedness to others, and the hope that we will ultimately learn, as Dr. King reminded us, to live together as brothers and sisters, before we perish as fools. How long . . ., not long!

For Adisa, he writes:

Love and loss; life is lived in the space between those words. The space between the third edition of this book and this fourth edition has been marked by the loss of several loved ones, who now reside in the community of ancestors: My father, John L. Mackey, Baba Jacob H. Carruthers Jr., and Baba Asa Hilliard III—Giants in a world too small to fully accommodate the enormity of their being. (Iba'ra torun)

To be an African man is to be born into a world in which African women's love surrounds you like water around a fish. In that spirit, I offer my love to my mother, Evelyn Mackey, and my sister Ca-Trece Mas'Sey for their inspirational examples of good character, strength, and determination. Also, I offer my love to Zakiya Fulami, Karyn Brooks, Dawn Onley, Karima Deadrick, Kishere Mbuya, Asteria Hyera, Omiladé Adédìran, and Sia Stewart—strong sisters who provided me with both sunlight and shade along the path to completing this book. I also extend my love and gratitude to Baba Wade Nobles and Iya Vera Nobles, Baba Vulindlela and Iya Nozipo Wobogo, Baba Cliff Stewart Jr., and Iya Omitadé. Every person needs a home, and I have been blessed with two: The Institute for the Advanced Study of Black Family Life and Culture, my intellectual home, and Ìjo Òrúnmìlà Àti Òrìsà, my spiritual home. I am because we are and because we are therefore I am: I pray that my godsons Bakari and Daniel come to appreciate the quality of this truth.

Dr. Joseph L. White, "the God Father" of Black Psychology—his love for and commitment to African people continues to show us the way forward. And lastly, Dr. Thomas A. Parham—"Dr. P," as he is affectionately called by his students—one of those rare people who actually strive to achieve a *"Maatian"* balance between his words, thoughts, and actions. He is a model husband, father, scholar, and teacher. In this spirit, no person could ask for a better friend, and certainly no student has ever had a better example to follow.

FOREWORD

Beginning with the first edition in 1984 of *The Psychology of Blacks: An Afro-American Perspective*, penned by Dr. Joseph White, each revision of this valuable discussion has provided an insightful commentary on the evolving description of the definitional autonomy taken by Black psychologists of our people. This definitional prerogative was formalized with the establishment of the Association of Black Psychologists in 1968 and concisely articulated by the "emancipation treatise" by the Elder Writer, Joseph White of this fourth revision, in his classical manifesto: "Towards a Black Psychology," initially published in *Ebony* magazine in 1970. With each of the three previous editions of this book that have reviewed the evolution of the field of Black psychology, the particular approach of this book has continuously "trumped" other similar texts with a winning hand of "Four Aces" that make *this* commentary uniquely valuable. Each revision has remained consistently a winning document with these "Four Aces" by an expanding network of contributors from the seminal volume by White in 1984, co-authored with his student Thomas A. Parham in 1990 and eventually including his student's student Adisa Ajamu in the Parham, White, and Ajamu joint authorship in 2000.

The "Four Aces" that have distinguished these volumes and rendered them uniquely significant are: *"Affirmation, Advancement, African-centeredness, and Awareness."* The first of these "Aces", *Affirmation*, is the principle for a positive approach to discussion of the Black experience that is (in this edition) as it has been in the previous editions, a cardinal rule that has guided the thought and approach of this readable and important volume. As Joseph White clearly stated in his seminal "treatise" (that actually was expanded and further articulated) in the first edition of *The Psychology of Blacks*: "The distinguishing role of Black psychology was to be positive about Black life and to move away from the deficiency, deprivation-focus and pathology orientation of traditional Western Psychological discussions of Black behavior and expression." This fourth edition has remained true to that declaration in that it remains thoroughly *Affirmative* about Black life. The ideas in this volume do not deny the reality of distinctiveness and difficulties confronted by Black people in their mental adjustment, but the current authors have persisted in their *Affirmation* of the value, dignity, and significance of Black existence.

The second "Ace" in the "winning hand" of the current revision of this important work is its review of the evolving *Advancement* of the field of Black psychology. This edition as each of its three precursors has been definitive in acknowledging that the field of study is in a state of growth and adaptive evolution. The authors themselves have contributed from their own scholarship and have critically surveyed the continuing research, theory development, and expanding conceptualizations in the field. Consistent with the stipulation of the "Affirmative Ace" from above, this review of the *Advancement* has not been regressive, dogmatic, or restrictive, but has been thorough in surveying the progressive thrust of the field. They have been able successfully to *Advance* from the *deconstruction* of the early concepts that were rooted in deficiency to the constructive analysis now characterized by Parham in this volume as an agenda to *"build for eternity."* The longevity and continued usefulness of this volume through nearly thirty years and four revisions is because of its commitment to review and renew the *Advancement* of studying the "Psychology of Blacks." The field itself, according to their description, certainly has not been static but has advanced as have these scholars who have developed their research and conceptualizations in synchrony with this commitment.

The fourth revision of this text has maintained a relevant contextualization for the "winning pair of Aces" of *Affirmation* and *Advancement* from a paradigmatic perspective of *African-Centered Thought*, which is the "Third Ace" that has distinguished this particular treatment and analysis. Parham, White, and Adisa have been unapologetic and clear that the only possibility for conceptualizing Black behavior accurately is to do it within the appropriate context of an African-centered understanding of life. Cultural clarity is the only perspective that informs the indigenous origin and richness of Black life as an expression of authentic African being and its implications for all of humanity. As Parham clearly asserts by his dedication of this edition in celebration of the dedicated scholarship and genius of the brilliant African-centered thinker/scientist/psychologist, **Dr. Asa G. Hilliard III** reaffirms that the context of these ideas is not for a transient periodical but for all eternity. The lesson taught to us with such vigor by Dr. Hilliard is that the Ancient Africans devoted their scholarship, science, and thinking to building for a timeless context. The permanence of such a perspective is preserved and recorded in the ancient monuments and structures that have continued to simultaneously mystify, critique, and inform more transient approaches and fleeting perspectives for thousands of years, as they continue to give testimony to the timelessness of such eternal thought with their presence as sentries in the African deserts of the Nile Valley. Even when the personal identity of the actual builders has been obscured, the accuracy of their perspective speaks to the validity of this lofty context.

The "Fourth Ace" displayed in the "winning hand" of this current edition is *Awareness*. It is *Awareness* that is the ultimate objective of human inquiry or search for knowledge. The Ancient Africans declared that the singular path to being fully human and manifesting our ultimate essence was to acquire knowledge or as they concisely stated: "Know Thyself." As the sustained scholarship of Dr. Thomas Parham so well typifies, the arena that is most fruitful for the student of the human mind in general and the Black mind in particular is found in the elaboration of the concept of "identity." The hallmark of Dr. Parham's scholarship that has also evolved over the years has been in pursuit of the golden grail of human self-knowledge that is contained in an understanding of Identity. "Identity" is undoubtedly the contemporary manifestation of this principle that has been handed to us from the Ancients directing us to "Know Self" as the portal of all knowledge. The idea of "cultural competence" as another critical arena of Parham's scholarship and another key concept in this volume is intimately connected to this particular "Ace" of *Awareness*. It is through the lens of appropriate culture that we gain insight into knowing people who always exist in a milieu of culture that informs identity.

The student, scholar, or seeker who encounters this fourth edition of *The Psychology of Blacks* has certainly been dealt a "winning hand of Aces" containing *Affirmation, Advancement, African-Centered Thought, and Awareness* that will bring enlightenment to those travelling the path of unraveling the persisting questions of Black life and the enigma of human existence in general.

                                                            —*Na'im Akbar, Ph.D*

PREFACE

African teachers who want to teach [and treat] African people, young and old, must have an agenda for the transformation of African people based on sound information. . . . We must be poised to rescue African ways from oblivion. Before the old people die, before the traditional schools are crushed or abandoned, the historians, ethnographers, philosophers, psychologists, physicians among us must preserve our cultural wealth. It is the ignorant African, continental and Diasporan, who craves the approval of their alien masters. It is the dying African who is ashamed of his or her own deep thought and profound tradition because of anti-African scholarship and media.

(Asa Hilliard, 1997, p. 17)

Healing is work, not gambling. It is the work of inspiration, not manipulation. If we healers are to do the work of helping to bring our people together again, we need to know such work is the work of the community. The work of healers is work for inspirers working long and steadily, in a group that grows over the generations, till there are inspirers, healers wherever our people are scattered, able to bring us together again.

(Ayi Kwei Armah, *The Healers*)

It is a profound understatement to note that much has changed in the world, in American culture, and by extension in psychology, since the publication of the first edition of *The Psychology of Blacks* in 1984—some of those changes carrying profoundly Orwellian undertones. To get a grasp on just how profoundly the culture has changed, one need only consider that 1984 saw the first Apple Macintosh go on sale and Dell Computers was founded (as PC's Limited); the United States Marines pulled out of Beirut, Lebanon; Indian Prime Minister Indira Gandhi was assassinated; Desmond Tutu was awarded the Nobel Peace Prize; and the Democratic National Convention nominated Walter F. Mondale for U.S. President and Geraldine Ferraro the first woman nominated for Vice President; a phenomenal college junior by the name of Michael Jordan lead the Olympic basketball team to a gold medal; it was the year of the first MTV Video Music Awards in New York City, Miami Vice (the television series, not the movie) premiered; a basketball star named LeBron James was born; and soul singer named Marvin Gaye died.

When the first edition of this book went to press, African Americans were merely twenty years removed the Civil Rights Act of 1964, barely nineteen years removed from the Voting Rights Act of 1965, which had enfranchised them, and thirty years removed the *Brown v. the Board of Education Supreme Court decision* of 1954, which had overturned the *Plessy v. Ferguson decision*, which had provided the legal basis the separate but equal doctrine that had given Jim Crow much of its motive force. That same year, Dr. Joseph L. White was a professor at the University of California-Irvine, Dr. Thomas A. Parham was an assistant professor at the University of Pennsylvania in Philadelphia, and Adisa Ajamu was dreaming about a future bright with possibilities as a young adolescent. As we go to press with the fourth edition of *The Psychology of Blacks* in 2011, the nation's economy, while in recovery, is the worst it has been since the Great Depression, pop and R&B music is still recovering from the loss of perhaps its all-time greatest icon in Michael Jackson, and the country has elected now some two plus years ago the first African American as its president with the most votes in American history.

Quite naturally, just as much has changed in American society, much has changed in psychology in general, and in African-American psychology in particular in the nearly two-and-a-half decades since the publication of the first edition of this book in 1984. Consequently, our efforts over the years have to larger and lesser degrees attempted to reflect some of the salient social and cultural trends, the important changes and challenges within the field, while attempting to offer new interpretations of some of the old realities that lie at the intersections of both fields: culture and context have become critical variables in psychology.

Each of the previous editions welcomed the addition of a new voice—a psychological thinker from an ascending generation: Thomas Parham in 1990 added his voice as a co-author for the second edition, while Adisa Ajamu added another voice to the chorus in 1999. The addition of second and third authors helped to usher in the jegna tradition, where Dr. White was a professor and mentor to Dr. Parham, while Parham, in turn, was professor, advisor, and mentor to Adisa and Dr. Roslyn Caldwell (whose contribution appears in Chapter 9), and parent to Kenya Parham, whose voice is heard in the Afterword. The inclusion of ascending generations was not only in keeping with the African tradition of intergenerational dialogue and development that undergird this effort, it has also provided multiple vantage points from which to view, think about, and discuss old intransigent problems in new ways. And with the ensuing intergenerational dialogues emerged subsequent nuances, which ultimately were mirrored in the books' evolving perspectives—from Black to African American to African-centered.

These evolving perspectives have been more than merely nominal or superfluous nods to the culturally fashionable. Rather, each new perspective has been the outgrowth of social, cultural, and historical forces in the African world at large (both on continent and in the diaspora), their influence on us and our work, the ongoing intergenerational dialogue among ourselves, and within the field of African American psychology more broadly. The evolution to an African-centered perspective was/is informed by the plethora of new evidence as well as new interpretations of old evidence that has enhanced our understanding about African/African-American life and longing across numerous domains of knowledge.

The African-centered perspective, which both characterized the third edition and animates this fourth edition, is to some extent emblematic of the fact that we as scholars have consciously favored a more Pan-African model of psychological scholarship, one which explores both sides of what sociologist Paul

Gilroy calls the *Black Atlantic* over the more proximal American-centric one in vogue: A wider lens invites more into the frame. The result has been that while our efforts remain multidisciplinary in scope, we have also remained engaged in a reflexive dialogue with the African world community—its histories, its cultures, and its psychologies—in search of useful psychological knowledge that lies on the African side of the African-American hyphenate. This has had the added benefit of not only allowing us vantage points that make it possible for us to keep the material contained in the books relevant in both a contemporary and heuristic sense, but, of equal importance, it has also placed us in a position to anticipate unfolding trends.

There is a tendency in this postmodern age of ours to oversimplify complexities and make simplicities complex. As such, there is often a propensity to search for the one book—Psychology for Dummies—that will tell us succinctly (and quickly) what can only truly be accrued by long hours toiling in the fields of knowledge and augmented by lived experience. We seem to be perpetually on a quest for the one book that allows us to say confidently: "I know." The readers in search of that book, the one that will satiate fully their quest for understanding of African-American psychology, will not find the rewarding echo of knowledge in this volume. However for the readers who view this effort as a beginning, an apercus to begin to think deeply about the life and longing of a critical segment of the population, they will find the effort and the rewards in reciprocating harmony. For while this book carries the authoritative and seemingly omniscient title *The Psychology of Blacks*, we are cognizant that LIFE does not consult academic disciplines for how it is to be lived, nor do people live or experience their lives as a series of successive, discrete academic moments. We are clear that life exists as an organic whole that more often than not defies tidy typologies, and that the social sciences' best understandings about human behavior arrive not as immutable, objective truths but rather as contingent spasms of lucidity and insight informed by the culture and context that produced them.

Thus, no single book, no matter how well intentioned in its ambitions, comprehensive in its scope, or multidisciplinary in its reach, can ever really hope to capture within its frame the totality of any peoples in all of their full, dynamic, and variegated complexities. To suggest as much about African Americans is to deny them the very adaptive vitality, experiential nuance, and lived complexity that is characteristic of all members of the human family. And no such effort is attempted here. What we have attempted to do in the preceding chapters is not so much to provide the reader with answers (even though there are some), but rather to provide a wider prism through which to view the conditions of possibility for new areas of exploration and discovery in African-American psychology, to identify some salient issues that are timely (in a contemporary sense) as well as of enduring psychological significance for the continued understanding and growth of African-American communities, and in the best tradition of scholarship, hopefully inspire future deep thinkers to ask better and better questions.

We begin this fourth edition with a Forward by famed psychologist, author, and lecturer Dr. Na'im Akbar, whose deep-structured thoughts and penetrating insights are always food to nourish one's intellectual appetite. Following that is a brand new opening chapter, which discusses the concept of "building for eternity," in seeking to synthesize the apparent opposites of ancient wisdom and contemporary relevance. That chapter is followed with an analysis of African psychology in the modern era, where those new and familiar faces to the instructional aspects of this field of study can learn about the intersections between the passions of a committed group of scholars and practitioners, and the organizational dynamics which anchored their position and posturing within the discipline of psychology. Next is another completely new, albeit brief, chapter on the concept of spirituality and our thoughts about the necessity to include this construct in every aspect of our work as African psychologists. There have also been significant updates to the chapters on the Black family, identity congruence, educational issues, and advances in mental health. These chapters are bolstered by some new thoughts on coping with oppression, the application of African-centered psychological principles to the juvenile offender, and a look beyond 2010 to the year 2020. The chapter discussing issues with the juvenile offender and the criminal justice system is a particularly welcome addition, not simply for the timeliness of the topic, but for the inclusion of one in our field who is quite a rising star, Dr. Roslyn Caldwell. We are honored to have her with us on the fourth edition journey and hope that you the reader will find her contribution noteworthy. Finally, we hope you will enjoy this fourth edition and that the information contained within these pages will quench your thirst for knowledge, inspire your intellects with wisdom, and ignite your passions to better serve the mental health needs of African-descent people.

ABOUT THE AUTHORS

Thomas A. Parham, Ph.D

Dr. Parham is assistant vice chancellor for Counseling and Health Services as well as an adjunct faculty member at the University of California, Irvine. Dr. Parham is a past president of the National Association of Black Psychologists, where he also holds the title of distinguished psychologist. He is also a fellow of both the American Counseling Association and the American Psychological Association, and a proud alumnus of the Minority Fellowship Program. He is also past president of the Association for Multicultural Counseling and Development (a division of ACA).

Adisa Ajamu

Àdisà Àjàmú is the founder and executive director of the Atunwa Collective, a Community Development think tank in Washington, D.C. He is a research fellow at the Institute for the Advanced Study of Black Family Life and Culture in Oakland, CA. Currently, he is completing three books, an intellectual history of Black psychology, a collection of essays on African-American life and culture, and a book of short stories.

Joseph L. White, Ph.D

For the past forty-nine years, Dr. White has enjoyed a distinguished career in the field of psychology and mental health as a teacher, mentor, administrator, clinical supervisor, writer, consultant, and practicing psychologist. He is currently professor emeritus of psychology and psychiatry at the University of California, Irvine. Affectionately known as "the Godfather," Dr. White is one of the contemporary fathers of the Black psychology movement. He is also currently a member of the Board of Trustees of the Menninger Foundation in Houston, Texas.

1

▪ ▪ ▪

Building for Eternity

In the first, second, and third editions of this text, the authors sought to advance a position that there exists a coherent, workable, understandable, and enduring perspective of the human condition that is uniquely African. This perspective or worldview illustrates and illuminates more than just the attitudes, emotional tones, values, and behaviors of a people. It highlights the spiritual essence of the people that permeates every aspect of their being. This fourth edition in *The Psychology of Blacks* series is intended to be in harmony with those assertions.

We begin this edition by introducing a construct Parham (2004) calls "Building for Eternity." For some of us, building for eternity is a strange concept, particularly because the lives of people in America and around the world are often built around what is temporary and fashionable in the moment. Even the discipline of traditional psychology is vulnerable to such fleeting intellectual ideas, both because of the cultural biases that permeate many of its theories and because it often employs a "democratic sanity" process of deciding what is normal and healthy (Akbar, 1991). The discipline of African psychology then must be careful not to replicate these shortcomings, even as it moves into another decade of scholarship, teaching, research, and social advocacy.

Ironically, The Association of Black Psychologists (ABPsi) celebrated its forty-year anniversary in 2008, and it begs the question, within the concept of building for eternity, about how it has survived over these many years? Many have heard the stories of Black psychologists' frustrations with the American Psychological Association (APA) and their attempts to seek a redress of their grievances in both regional meetings and national conventions during the mid- to late 1960s. Many more may remember those turbulent 1950s and 60s in America and the struggle for civil rights led by such leaders as Dr. Martin Luther King, Whitney Young, A. Phillip Randolph, Rosa Parks, Fannie Lou Hammer, and Malcolm X. Still, others understand the psychic struggle Black people navigated in seeking to balance the "integrationist" and "nationalist" ideologies as a strategy for social change. Each of these elements and many more accounted for some percentage of the variance in explaining why that group of fifteen to thirty courageous men and women decided to separate from the APA, and by extension, the discipline of "White" psychology. Records provided by Goddard and Nobles (2008) indicate that the Founding Mothers/Fathers of the ABPsi were: Calvin Atkinson, Ronald Brown, Ed Davis, Jim DeShields, George Franklin, Reginald Jones, Roy Jones, Robert L. Green, George Jackson, Mary Howard, De Lorise Minot, Leon Nicks, Lonnie Mitchell, Bill Pierce, Joseph White, Shirley Thomas, Samuel Winslow, Joseph Akward, J. Don Barnes, Harold Dent, Russ Evans, Bill Harvey, Al Goines, Luther Kindall, Thomas Hilliard, Mel King, Walter Jacobs, Jane Fort Morrison Wade W. Nobles, Sylvia O'Bradovich, David Terrell, Charles Thomas, Robert L.Williams, and Mike Ward. Goddard and Nobles (2008) also suggest that in their infancy as an organizational body, these courageous men and women were guided by the principles of self-determination, agency, and mutual self-interest. These women and men set out to build a professional organization through which they could address the long-neglected needs of Black people and Black professional psychologists. They pledged to see themselves as Black people first and psychologists second.

In recalling the history of the ABPsi, we have read about the need for a psychology that was strength based as opposed to pathology oriented (White, 1972). We have read about the betrayals of objectivity represented in the theories and constructs of Euro-centrically oriented psychology when they were applied to persons of African descent (Thomas & Sillen, 1972; Nobles, 1972, 1986; Parham, White, & Ajamu, 1999; Dent, 2008). We have read about the bias in mental testing that severely disadvantaged Black children (Williams, 1972; Guthrie, 1976; Williams & Mitchell, 1980; Thomas, 2000) and the resulting California court case that led to the injunction against testing Black Children (Larry P. *vs.* Riles and the State of California) and placing them in EMR classes solely on the basis of IQ scores. But that may not be the entire story. The founding of the ABPsi and the foundation of the discipline of African/Black Psychology was more than just a group of frustrated professionals reacting to the ideological inflexibility and racist attitudes and behaviors of their White psychologist counterparts and the APA. The founding of the association ABPsi and the contemporary discipline of African psychology, in Parham's (2009) opinion, was really about a cultural war. A war in this case refers to the conflicting values and dogma that become the source of tension, disagreement, and protracted struggle between two or more opposing forces. In this case, the combatants are the disciplines of Euro-centric and African-centered psychology, and the battlefields have been the academic classrooms, mental health treatment facilities, hospitals, schools, corporate board rooms, private therapy offices, conference sessions, and community activities that represent their practices. Indeed, there has been and continues to be a cultural war. There has been a "war of ideology", a "war of values", a "war of self determination", and a "war of cultural relevance." Details of this cultural war will be further outlined in the next chapter.

But in thinking about the concept of building for eternity, we are reminded of a trip Thomas Parham took to Ancient Kemet (Egypt) just before the turn of the new millennium with the brilliant Dr. Asa Hilliard. There, he had a chance to witness the genius of our ancient African ancestors, and marvel at their cultural legacy.

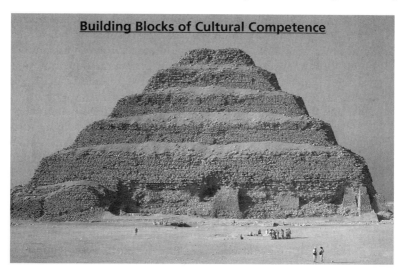

IMAGE 1-1 Step Pyramid, Building Blocks

In viewing the complex at Saqqara, outside of Cairo for example, where the step pyramid designed by Imhotep and built for the Pharaoh Djoser still stands after nearly 5000 years, it provides us with a model from which to view the real origins of psychology. That structure is the oldest monument on the planet. Having seen the magnificence of Queen Hatshepsut's Temple in the Valley of the Kings; the Pyramids on the Giza Plateau; and the temples at Dendera, Edfu, Komombo, Philae, and Abydos, they all stand as a testament to the cultural richness of the people and civilization that has lasted over time. And so, it leaves one to ponder how the psychology of a people and culture influenced both what was produced and built, as well as how they engaged their ancient reality.

In ancient times, when an individual became ruler or was crowned Pharaoh, the builders, masons, stonecutters, and other artisans immediately went to work on building his/her tomb and temples. This practice was designed, among other things, to ensure that everything that the ruler did was chronicled on the walls of his/her tomb for people across generations to see. In that regard, building for eternity was not simply about chronicling one's life, but more important a way of disciplining one's behavior to align it with proper conduct, because it was recorded for all time. And look at how those structures have lasted, as have the inscriptions and images that were carved onto the walls of the temples and tombs to form the reliefs. For example, in a visit to the Temple at Dendara, which was a monument to the Goddess Haythor, one can see the images of her with symbolic "cow ears" carved onto the walls of the temple column structures. Further south of that structure in the Valley of the Kings is the Tomb of Ramses VI, depicting images of Ramses with the God Osiris and the scales of Ma'at and twelve witnesses. Here, reliefs on the wall illustrate the Pharoah Ramses VI hoping that the witnesses would serve as testament to his aspiration to live a good life.

Just south of that location is the Temple at Abydos, which was dedicated to the God Osiris. Here, images on the wall reflect the first Holy Trinity, with God (Osiris), attended by the Mother (Isis), and the Son (Heru). Indeed, this holy trinity magnifies the trinity of God the Father, God the Mother, and God the Son. In this same temple complex, on a different sanctuary wall, is an image of a pharaoh who during his reign came to seek the blessing of the Gods. In performing the ritual of cleansing with the water, the image reflects that ruler being showered with the waters of life and eternity, symbolized by drops fashioned in the form of the ancient Kemetic ankh (the symbol of life and eternity). But perhaps the most astounding and magnificent relief, which exists at both the Temple of Queen Hatshepsut and the Temple at Luxor, is the scene depicting what many come to know as one of the cornerstones of Christian theology. Here, one can readily see a relief depicting the Annunciation (where God reveals to the Virgin that she will conceive a child), the Immaculate Conception (where the virgin immaculately conceives through the power to the Spirit), the Divine Birth (where the baby savior is born), and the Adoration (where wise men come to honor and adore the infant baby). More fascinating than the images themselves is the time period in which the temple was constructed. In the case of Hatshepsut's Temple and the reliefs, history records its construction around 1473 B.C., suggesting that the basis of that Christian theology is in fact a cornerstone of African mythology as well.

But to view those ancient structures as simply monuments to the glorification of a particular pharaoh is to misunderstand their parallel intent. Clark (2005) reminds us that each of these structures was constructed in ways that paid homage and respectful tribute to the DIVINE FORCE in the universe. In many temples throughout Kemet, the structural layout is similar, with most having an entry, a courtyard, a hall of columns, and one or many sanctuaries for the deity that was being honored or worshipped. If one began the journey from the entry, through the courtyard and columns, and back to the sanctuary of the "Holy of Holies," each step progressed in elevation. Symbolically, the further back one proceeded toward the sanctuary, the closer to Heaven one would be. In essence, their height and meticulous construction were intended, among other things, to create a stairway to heaven. Thus, their building required a synthesis between preparation and construction on one hand, and an aspiration to harmonize with divine intent on the other. This is an important point that will be emphasized later, as we consider the implications for building an African-centered psychology that will last for eternity.

In thinking about the conceptual anchors, assumptions, strategies, and techniques we use to construct our psychology and the standards of competence we use to evaluate our work and that of other professionals, it is important that we adhere to that basic premise. Accordingly, this text, and by extension, the discipline of African psychology, begins with a few basic assumptions. The first of these suggests that if the foundation of our psychological theories and constructs, and schools of thought is not anchored in values that contribute to the cultivation of the human spirit, then what we build as a theoretical base will not sustain itself over time. If, however, the psychology we build is reinforced by the granite walls of truth; if what we build is constructed from the limestone quarries of righteousness; if what we build is framed by the wooden planks of elevated human consciousness, and is strength-based; then we build our psychology and psychological practices for eternity.

The second assumption we make is that the identity of a truly competent professional, that is the definition of who they are in their essence and character, can never be anchored in the notion of material acquisition. Possessions, like degrees and certifications, feel good to the ego, but are materials that do not fundamentally support and affirm our humanity as helping professionals. They are not always good for the soul. Depending on where degrees and certifications are obtained, and the foundations of those didactic and experiential learning opportunities, the training may merit certification from that learning institution, but may be less than functional when applied to populations that are culturally different than those on which the theories taught were based.

The third assumption we make, like our ancient Kemetic Ancestors, is that building a psychological foundation for the instruction, research, and practice of African psychology that will last for eternity requires a synthesis between preparation and construction on one hand, and an aspiration to harmonize with divine intent on the other. Essentially, this means that the training we are exposed to throughout our education, be it in graduate school or professional development seminars, will have its structural integrity compromised if it is constructed without reference to what will be most beneficial to the clients we serve, and not simply to the professionals who serve them. We adhere to the philosophy that in serving our clients, we are serving God's creation. Thus, as you the reader seek to integrate this new perspective with the traditional training that you have received, it will require that you, much like our colleague Derald Sue (2003) recommends: free yourselves from traditional definitions of counseling and psychotherapy, expand the boundaries of professional practice, expand and utilize alternate helping roles, and learn from indigenous models of healing. That is what this text seeks to do. In essence, this text is your intellectual permission slip to reorient your thinking to a more culturally congruent worldview.

In advancing this notion of "building for eternity," we are also reminded that no one book will ever fully equip one to engage in the practice of an African-centered psychology. Those lessons require years of coordinated study and practical experience, coupled with good supervision and continuing education. Thus, while other training opportunities create the illusion of competence, a more thorough education will require you the reader to have an expanded repertoire of awareness, knowledge, and skill that encompasses both what you know and what you don't know and still need to learn. In speaking of competence, we are reminded of Parham's (2002) text *Counseling Persons of African Descent*. In the subtitle, he asks the profession "*How* do we raise the bar of what passes for competence?" Parham argues that competencies are skills or attributes that allow psychologists, counselors, or therapists to respond effectively to the demands of a particular situation or circumstance. This definition centers around the idea of belief and conviction, in asking each of you, and others who might read this text, what have you really learned and what is the utility of your knowledge and skill in addressing the needs of African-American clients who desire your services?

Fundamentally, these definitions force us to question: *Can we acknowledge the authenticity of the education and training you have received?* When clients look to you for answers to the culturally tainted dilemmas they are confronting, but they are nowhere in your repertoire, *can you acknowledge the authenticity of the education and training you have received?* When clinical situations create frustration and despair, because you have difficulty conceptualizing client dynamics from a culturally appropriate frame of reference, *can you acknowledge the authenticity of the education and training you have received?* When you just don't seem to know what you need to know to be effective, and your confidence has been shaken, *can you acknowledge the authenticity of the education and training you have received?* If your answer to these questions is an unqualified or even a qualified "NO," then you are in danger of being labeled what A.J. Franklin (1971) once called being "Young, gifted, and Black [ethnic] with inappropriate professional training." And if you suspect that the training and education you have acquired thus far is insufficient, then your rock of competence on which you build your academic endeavors, professional practice, and program of research cannot be feeling very steady.

This issue of an unstable rock of competence forces us to confront the question of what do we really believe? And as you struggle to find an answer to that query, this text invites all of you to remember what Parham (2004) has previously argued that "belief is an invitation to discipline one's behavior in ways that aligns it with the principle of truth." In essence, we are suggesting that your beliefs, your convictions, indeed the very foundation of the principles you the reader (be you student or professional) hold as most salient, are the conceptual anchor points from which all other activity in a professional's life should emerge. We say this because in our opinion, too many professionals claim to believe in certain truth and principles, when we sit for doctoral comprehensive or post-doctoral licensing examinations, yet fail to move beyond those immediate anchor points to operationalize those principles and truth into their counseling and clinical work, instructional practices, or research endeavors. The problem here is not simply one of definition, but one of the beliefs in possibility. Essentially, the progress in developing greater levels of cultural competence we all seek to make is sometimes seen as a plateau, rather than a process in need of constant innovation. Thus, once we achieve some measure of progress (i.e., attending a workshop at a conference, or reading a particular book on some aspect of Black or African psychology, or obtaining an endorsement of the competencies from a professional association), those acts in and of themselves are often times assumed to be the ultimate goal. Therefore, our strength in the convictions we learn becomes stagnant in those initial outcomes.

Unfortunately, it is our opinion that a stagnant belief system is a direction that is a little bit off center from what the architects of the African-centered movement in psychology were really talking about in their writings and presentations (Akbar, 1992, 1994; Ani, 1994; Fu-Kiau, 1991; Grills, 2002; Hilliard, 1997; Jackson, Gregory, & Davis, 2004; Kambon, 1992; Myers, 1988; Nobles, 1986; Parham, 2002; Parham, White, and Ajamu, 1999; Phillips, 1990; White, 1972,

1984). In considering then, the development of a psychological perspective, it naturally begs the question of what do the principles and practices of an ancient Kemetic civilization teach us about the consciousness of a people, and a psyche that allowed that civilization to survive, thrive, and prosper for thousands of years, and through more than twenty-five dynasties? What lessons can we take from their prior work that informs us about the need to build for eternity?

The first lesson suggests that we need to build an African-centered competency and proficiency base of knowledge that is conceptually sound, culturally congruent, compelling, and practically relevant. This latter factor is particularly important in that we need to identify and support those people whose passion for helping would create a reciprocal pathway back into the communities from where they came. In short, the architects of the African-centered competency movement, in turning to us, are not simply trying to secure the endorsement of this generation of scholars, professionals, and students. Rather, it is our position that they seek to inspire us with the vision that our awareness, knowledge, and skills could be used to build a competent professional practice that would last for eternity. In the struggle to change the cultural sterility in our profession, the authors and scholars who have contributed and continue to do so are essentially asking each of us a question about where are we building our intellectual, emotional, behavioral, and spiritual structures, and on what rock are academicians, clinicians, and researchers alike standing?

And so, if we are to build for eternity, how do we properly orient this generation of diversity-minded students and professionals to create a set of competencies in African psychology that will endure? What are the ingredients and materials necessary to prepare and nurture your professional competence into eternity? **First**, we need a building block composed of sound conceptual anchors.

Building Blocks of Cultural Competence

- Strong belief in the possibility of human transformation
- Strong foundation and belief in theoretical and conceptual models of helping
- Knowledge of culture at the deep structure level (difference between surface understanding and deeper insight)

IMAGE 1-2   Conceptual Anchors, Building Blocks

Remember that a theory is nothing more than a set of abstract constructs that we use to make sense out of data that we see. Once applied, however, the theories of African psychology should address questions regarding the nature of reality, sources of psychological strength and resilience, the etiology of African people's distress, systems of human interaction, mental health, the role and task of the healer, how and why people's psychological debilitations change, and what is a successful outcome in the context of mental health service delivery. In addition, this text asserts that theories of African psychology must include:

- A strong belief in the possibility of human transformation.
- A strong foundation and belief in theoretical and conceptual models of helping.
- Knowledge of culture at the deep structure level.

The clients we treat everyday have real issues of identity confusion, drug use and abuse, family violence, poverty, educational challenges, relationship drama, depression, anxiety, etc. And yet, so much of what we do helps them adjust to their circumstance rather than helping them to change it (Parham, White, & Ajamu, 1999). Thus, it is our task, as competent professionals, to also develop and acquire information about individuals we teach, treat, and study, which is free of the contamination, that blinds us into believing that the condition of African people is so bleak, that there is no hope of transformation. It is our contention, as Parham (2002, 2004) rightly chides us, that we cannot be healers without a consciousness that believes in the possibility of people's elevation to rightful places of rulership and mastery over their own circumstances. We must have faith and a strong conviction if you want to be competent. In short, culturally competent people will have to help others transcend their feelings of frustration, rise above their cognitions of powerlessness, in order to access not just the cognitive, affective, or behavioral dimension of our personality, but the spiritual dimension in which resonates the power to instigate change and transform a particular circumstance or experience.

Second, we need building blocks composed of our values. Among the values we should include are:

- Aspirations to harmonize with divine intent.
- Cultivation of the human spirit and elevated human consciousness.
- Strong ethical standards that are culturally based.

We must teach ourselves that we are not the sum products of our degrees, certifications, licenses, but rather are seeds of divinely inspired possibility. We must teach this generation of individuals who come to our halls of academia that the gifts they have been blessed to acquire are not intended for their own personal ego gratification. Rather, those who have been blessed with talent and degrees will not be judged by the level of prominence they achieve or by the income they accumulate, but rather by how they use their educational gifts to serve their people, their communities, and humanity in general.

In a similar fashion, professional conferences that are becoming yearly forums for discussing culturally general and specific content like The WINTER

Building Blocks of Cultural Competence

VALUES
- Aspiration to harmonize with divine intent
- Cultivation of the human spirit and elevated human consciousness
- Strong ethical standards that are culturally based

CONCEPTUAL ANCHORS

IMAGE 1-3   Values, Building Blocks

ROUNDTABLE, THE MULTICULTURAL SUMMITS, or even the NATIONAL CONVENTION OF THE ASSOCIATION OF BLACK PSYCHOLOGISTS will not be judged ultimately on the degree to which they achieve a level of prominence in the psychological or counseling conference circuit. Instead, they will be judged on the degree to which they generate new knowledge; inspire and equip new generations of professionals with better tools to inform how they operationalize their work in psychology and counseling, and use their sphere of influence to make a difference in the profession; and advocate for those things that require a voice, but are rarely heard.

If we come together each year as a community of scholars; spend several days exchanging ideas, feeling good, and being inspired; and then return to our professional places and spaces without having delivered a message to the profession from our collective voice, then we abdicate our responsibility as the caretakers of this culturally centered flame that burns deep inside of us. Our profession of African-centered psychology needs to know that we have concerns; our clients need to know that we are advocating for them; and our communities need to know that we have not lost our ability to care. Children who continue to be assessed in schools all across this land, and are placed into special education classes, are in need of some competent assessment. Clients of African-descent who submit themselves for psychological assistance continue to be misdiagnosed everyday and are in need of competent clinicians. Students of African-descent who continue to be taught in outmoded theories and techniques are in need of some competent instruction. Where is our voice? Where is our outrage? Where is our commitment to change this state of affairs? Indeed, students and professionals alike who are committed to promoting an African-centered psychological perspective must ask themselves about the strength of their beliefs, and the clarity of their convictions.

A **third** building block is composed of the competency dimensions that have been articulated in the psychological and counseling literature for over a decade. These include:

- AWARENESS of self, awareness of our biases, awareness of socially oppressive phenomenon, and awareness of dehumanizing MAAFA experiences.
- KNOWLEDGE of a group's history and culture; knowledge of within group variability and between group difference; and the cognitive, affective, behavioral, and spiritual dimensions of the personality.
- SKILLS in connecting with clients, conducting proper assessments, facilitating awareness and insight in clients, setting therapeutic goals, taking action and instigating change, and feedback and accountability.

Here, we ask ourselves what must we teach this current generation of students and professionals? Our answer to that query is we must teach them to study the great works of wise and learned persons, rather than works that emanate for what some have called the conceptually constrained scholars of the world. And so, the belief in our capacity to become wise, and not just knowledgeable, is an essential element in our ability to build the solid rock and a strong foundation for our cultural competence. And so, we must instruct and socialize our students, professionals, and the people we deliver services to that someone should emerge from these yearly conference interactions with the resolve to teach from the writings of Joe White, Robert Williams, Reginald Jones, Robert Guthrie, Asa Hilliard, Na'im Akbar, Wade Nobles, and Linda James Myers, and not simply the book of Freud. They should resolve to teach from the works of Janet Helms, Bell

Building Blocks of Cultural Competence

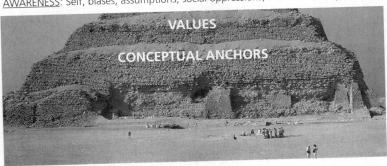

COMPETENCY DIMENSIONS

SKILLS: Connecting with clients, competent assessment, facilitating awareness, set goals, take action and instigating change, feedback and accountability.

KNOWLEDGE: A group's history and culture, within group variability and between group differences, cognitive, affective, behavioral, dimensions of personality.

AWARENESS: Self, biases, assumptions, social oppressions, and MAAFA experiences.

VALUES

CONCEPTUAL ANCHORS

IMAGE 1-4   Competency Dimensions, Building Blocks

Hooks, James Jones, Harriet McAdoo, James Jackson, Gail Wyatt, and Bill Cross, and not simply the theories of Jung. Students and professionals should learn to understand the teachings of Kobi Kambon, Marimba Ani, Roderick Pugh, Chet Pierce, and Cheryl Tawede Grills, and not simply the works of Skinner and Watson, or Ellis, or Perls. They should also learn to teach from the books of Belgrave and Allison, A.J. and Nancy Boyd Franklin, Helen Neville (along with Tynes and Utsey) and not just the generic theories of counseling and psychotherapy. Indeed, building for eternity requires a strong foundation with deep structure cultural knowledge that is the composition of your rock.

Building for eternity also requires personal action, and an engagement of a professional ethic that extends beyond the boundaries of the classroom, mental health clinic office, or breakout session, into the communities in which the clients we treat reside. The knowledge dimension of competence has to address the need to develop more positive relationships among men and women, so that we can help them build strong families. The skill dimension of competence has to address the needs of children who require a spiritual and not just a psychological assessment. We need to help them build their self-esteem. The knowledge dimension of our competence must address the needs of those who struggle with substance abuse, and help them find a way out of that affliction. We must help them adorn the psychological and spiritual armor that can help them rebuild their lives. The skill dimension of our competencies must teach us to address the needs of +the poor and economically disadvantaged, so that they can build the pathways to productivity and success. The awareness competencies must assist us in confronting our own biases and prejudices, such that we can engage in the healing and reconciliation of ethnic divisiveness that plagues our communities. Indeed, we must build strong coalitions. In addition, the awareness competencies must help us shed our fear of challenging systems of oppressions, so that in the spirit of our ancestors, we can continue the legacy of advocacy and struggle against those social forces that diminish the dignity and humanity of certain segments of the population.

Our **fourth** building block of competence is composed of commitments to access the domains of advocacy. These include interventions at the: *Individual* level, *Institutional* level, *Organizational* level, and *Societal* level.

And, building for eternity requires individual efforts that compel us to maximize the congruence between what we preach and what we practice. We must extend ourselves, as professionals committed to African psychology, to offer a kind word or an arm of support to our colleagues we meet. We must resist the temptation to gossip or say unkind things about professional colleagues, especially those whose work we find it necessary to challenge, or even find objectionable.

We must have more than sensitivity to African-American issues; we must advocate to our academic department and professional association leaders for changes in policies and practices that continue the institutional racism, sexism, and so on that have such a strong foothold in our profession. We must be more nurturing to our students and not so critical of their imperfections or abusive to their spirits. That's the only way we will break the cycles of intellectual and emotional abuse that is plaguing our academic communities, and creating casualties out of the ranks of our students and trainees.

Building Blocks of Cultural Competence

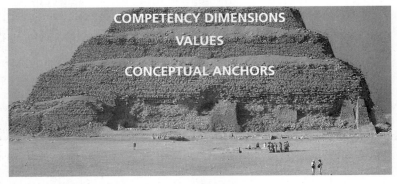

IMAGE 1-5   Domains of Advocacy, Building Blocks

In addition, we must learn to honor each other as brothers and sisters, respecting and celebrating the diversity we individually and collectively represent, and not just denigrating those who differ from us on some criteria that only have meaning within your own individual psyche.

Building Blocks of Cultural Competence

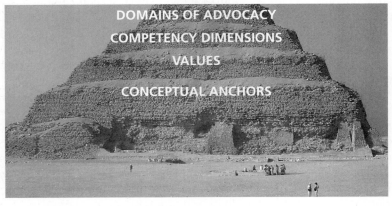

IMAGE 1-6   Liberation, Building Blocks

The **final** building block of cultural competence is ready to be placed once we have:

- Conceptual anchors
- Strong values
- Competency dimensions
- Domains of advocacy

Then, we as professionals and students can achieve some level of **liberation** at the intellectual, emotional, behavioral, and spiritual levels. We can discard the mental shackles that keep us conceptually incarcerated. We can throw off the chains that keep us emotionally repressed and afraid to push the boundaries. We can dislodge ourselves from those comfortable categories of behavioral apathy that keep us locked in stagnate places. And, we can break out of the malaise that keeps our spirits from experiencing the true synthesis between positive and negative polarities. Indeed, once these building blocks of cultural competence are in place, then students and professionals are more prepared to engage in a course of implementation where interventions in the classroom, counseling offices, or community centers are likely to be more substantial, more beneficial, and more likely to promote positive and lasting change for persons of African descent. This is what our psychological theories must help the discipline of African psychology produce.

2

■ ■ ■

African-Centered Psychology in the Modern Era

DEFINITIONS

Those who have not had the benefit of reading the first, second, or third editions of *The Psychology of Blacks,* or who are otherwise unfamiliar with the concept of a Black psychological perspective, may be asking themselves "What is this discipline called Black or African-American psychology?" As such, perhaps the most logical place to begin this fourth edition is with a definition of the construct (psychology of Blacks) and with a discussion of why an African-centered psychological perspective is necessary.

Nobles (1986) reminds us that in its truest form, psychology was defined by ancient Africans as the study of the soul or spirit. He writes:

> A summary reading of our ancient mythology reveals that ancient Egyptian thought can be characterized as possessing (1) "ideas of thought" which represent the human capacity to hay "will" and to invent or create; (2) "ideas of command" which represent the human capacity to have "intent" and to produce that which one wills. Parenthetically these two, will and intent, are the characteristics of divine spirit and would serve as the best operationalization of human intelligence. (Nobles, 1986, p. 46)

Nobles further asserts that the psychology that was borrowed from Africa and popularized in Europe and America (so-called Western psychology) in some respects represents a distortion of ancient African-Egyptian thought. What the ancients believed was that the study of the soul or spirit was translated by Europeans into the study of only one element of a person's psychic nature, the mind.

In a similar vein, Akbar (1994) has persuasively argued that the Kemetic (so-called Egyptian) roots of psychology bear little resemblance to the modern-day

14

constructs. Akbar explains, for example, that the term *sakhu* represented in its original form illumination and enlightenment of the soul or spirit. However, this perspective lost its meaning when the Greeks reinterpreted it to mean behavior and created a discipline to quantify, measure, and materialize the construct objectively.

Thus, the term "psychology" (in a Western context) is constructed from the words *psyche* (meaning mind) and *ology* (meaning knowledge or study of) and is generally assumed to be a study of human behavior. What is fascinating to see, even as we write this fourth edition text, is how little has changed in traditional psychology's coverage of its African psychology roots. Over the past decade, there are dozens of new and revised introductory and general psychology texts that have been written, and still we find coverage of African psychology and its discipline's Kemetic roots conspicuous by its absence. Nevid (2007), for example, in the several hundred page text, continues to define psychology in ways that not only avoids the soul or spiritual elements, but does not differ appreciably in its definitions from other text books from years past. Ironically, Myers (2010), in his magnificent 717-page introductory psychology text that many consider a standard in the field, defines psychology as "the science of behaviors and mental processes" (p.6). Behaviors in that context are defined as "anything an organism does (as an observable action)," while mental processes are defined as "internal subjective experiences we infer from behaviors (sensations, perceptions, beliefs, feelings)." Despite the fact that he does a wonderful job of desegregating the text with pictures of African-American adults and children, includes pictures and mention several well-known African-American psychologists from history's past, and includes a brand new section of one chapter on the variable of culture, the entire book never discusses the notion of an African-centered psychology or an African cultural reality in the discipline. What makes this omission curious is the timeline of people and events in psychology that frames the beginning of the Myers text. It includes Francis Cecil Sumner (the first African American to receive a Ph.D in psychology in 1920), Kenneth and Mamie Clark (and their groundbreaking work on doll preference and racial self-identification that was used in the Brown 1954 Supreme Court decision), Inez Proser (the first African-American woman to receive her Ph.D in America at the University of Cincinnati in 1933), and the fact that psychology differs across cultures. However, there is no mention of any culturally specific psychology or the plethora of literature on multiculturalism (Ponterotto, Casas, Suzuki, & Alexander, 2001; Sue, Ivey, & Pedersen, 1996; Sue & Sue, 2003), African psychology (Nobles, 1986; Myers, 1988; Kambon, 1992 Asante, 2003; Ani, 1994; Akbar, 2004; Neville, Tynes, & Utsey, 2009; White, 1972, 1984), and cultural competence (Pope-Davis, Coleman, Liu, & Toporek, 2003; Ivey, D'Andrea, Bradford-Ivey, & Simek-Morgan, 2002; Constantine & Sue, 2005) that dominate much of the counseling landscape. Within these realms, you find extensive references to psychology's true origins, yet those students being introduced to the discipline for the first time find no such mention or coverage in their introductory coursework. This is but one of the many reasons this text is so necessary.

As previously noted, psychology has been around for thousands of years and dates back to ancient KEMET (sometimes illustrated as KMT)

(African-Egyptian) civilizations (Nobles, 1986). However, as a discipline, psychology, like history, anthropology, and many other fields of study, has fallen victim to the attempts by many to both: (1) destroy and/or otherwise erase its historical connections to ancient Africa and (2) transplant its roots into European civilization. We are reminded by Nevid (2007) and Myers (2010) that traditional psychology, as we know it in this country, was assumed to extend back only as far as the laboratories of Wilhelm Wundt in Germany around 1879. In its simplest form, traditional psychology was an attempt to explain the behaviors of the Europeans from a European frame of reference. After becoming popularized in America, Euro-American scientists began to engage in the same practice of defining and understanding the behaviors of various Euro-American peoples.

In their attempt to understand the mind and behaviors of their people, many European and Euro-American scholars began to develop theories of human behavior (i.e., Freud, Jung, Rogers). Theories are sets of abstract concepts that people assign to a group of facts or events in order to explain them. Theories of personality and/or psychology, then, are organized systems of belief that help us understand human nature and make sense out of scientific data and other behavioral phenomena. It is important to realize, however, that theories are based on philosophies, customs, mores, and norms of a given culture. This has certainly been true for those theories that emerged out of the Euro-American frame of reference.

In their attempt to explain what they considered to be "universal human phenomena," Euro-American psychologists implicitly and explicitly began to establish a normative standard of behavior against which all other cultural groups would be measured. What emerged as normal or abnormal, sane or insane, relevant or irrelevant, was always in comparison to how closely a particular thought or behavior paralleled that of White Europeans and/or European Americans. For many White social scientists and psychologists, the word *different* (differences among people) became synonymous with deficient, rather than simply different.

The presumptive attempt at establishing a normative standard for human cognition, emotion, and behavior was questionable at best for obvious reasons. The philosophical basis of this body of theory and practice, which claims to explain and understand "human nature," is not authentic or applicable to all human groups (Nobles, 1986). White (1972) in his article "Towards a Black Psychology" speaks to this issue clearly when he contends that "it is difficult if not impossible to understand the lifestyles of Black people using traditional psychological theories, developed by White psychologists to explain White behavior." White further asserts that when these theories are applied to different populations, many weakness-dominated and inferiority-oriented conclusions emerge. The foundation for an authentic Black psychology is an accurate understanding of the Black family, its African roots, historical development and contemporary expressions, and its impact on the psychological development and socialization of its members. One has only to examine the psychological literature as it relates to Black people to appreciate White's point.

Appreciation of White's (1972) perspective is enhanced when one looks first at the so-called science of psychology and then at the resulting conclusions that emerge from these research practices. In commenting on the science of psychology, Boykin (1979) argues that there are inherent biases and subjectivity in the investigation and application of scientific principles despite their claims to the contrary. Thus, he believes that biases inherent in Eurocentric perspectives render research investigations and resulting conclusions invalid at most, or at least, inappropriate.

It is important to note, however, that questions of bias could be dealt with in *less confrontive* ways if one believed the intent of scientists and psychological scholars to be honorable. When one considers that scientific intent was and is supported by racist ideologies (Guthrie, 1976; Hilliard, 1997; Nobles, 1986; Thomas & Sillen, 1972;), then challenging and confronting those biases become even more important. As such, one can now better appreciate the critique of science and psychological (scientific) inquiry provided by Nobles (1986), who argues that research has been used as a tool of oppression and represents a form of "scientific colonialism."

The construct of colonialism harkens back to times of old when many European countries/nations (but not exclusively so) sought to conquer and control the human and natural resources of a certain country or region of the world. In essence, they were acquiring by force the people, land, and both natural and economic resources belonging to a particular nation. The term "scientific colonialism" then represents the political control of knowledge and information, in order to advance a particular group's agenda and/or prevent another group from advancing its own. According to Nobles, scientific colonialism is operationalized in several ways. These include:

> ***Unsophisticated Falsification:*** deliberate attempts to erase and/or otherwise disguise the African origins of an idea or the historical contributions of African people;

> ***Integrated Modificationism:*** assimilation of a known concept into existing ideas such that the result is a distorted version of the original meaning and intent; and

> ***Conceptual Incarceration:*** where all information is viewed from a single perspective to the exclusion of other world views or frameworks.

As a consequence of this biased and inappropriate method of inquiry, much of the research and scholarship written by European Americans about African Americans is severely tainted. Let us now turn our attention to the outcomes and resulting conclusions of that science.

HISTORICAL THEMES IN PSYCHOLOGICAL RESEARCH

Historically, research on minorities in general and Blacks in particular has shifted focus several times. In fact, Thomas and Silen (1972) and Sue (1978) concluded that it is difficult to fully understand and appreciate the status of

TABLE 2.1 Historical Themes in Black Psychological Research

	Inferiority	Deficit-Deficiency	Multi-Cultural
Definition	Blacks are intellectu-ally, physically, and mentally inferior to Whites	Blacks deficient with respect to intelli-gence, cognitive styles, family structure	All culturally dis-tinct groups have strengths and limitations.
Etiology of Problem	Genetics/heredity,	Lack of proper environ-mental stimulation; racism and oppressive conditions, individual	Differences viewed as differ-ent; lack of skills needed to assimilate
Relevant Hypothesis and Theories	Genetic inferiority, Eugenics	Cultural deprivation, Cultural enrichment	
Research Examples	White (2010) Morton (1839) Jensen (1969)	Moynihan (1965) Kardiner and Ovesey (1951)	J. White (1972) Nobles (1972; 1981)

ethnic minority research without reference to several general themes or models. These models include: (1) the inferiority model, (2) the deprivations/deficit model, and (3) the multicultural model. Table 2.1 provides a conceptual outline of these research trends, and a brief review follows.

Inferiority Models

The inferiority model generally contends that Black people are inferior to Whites. Its focus emerges out of the theories of genetics and heredity, which contend that the development of the human species is determined by heredity and views this process of development as "in the blood" or encoded in the genes. This model apparently afforded for some a scientific basis for viewing Blacks as inferior. Examples of these assertions of racial inferiority, as reported by Clark (1972) were heard as early as 1799 when Professor Charles White spoke of the Negro as being "just above the ape in the hierarchy of animal/human development, having a small brain, deformed features, an ape-like odor, and an animal immunity to pain." These inferiority assertions contin-ued into the mid-1800s, when studies on cranial capacities showed that a European skull held more pepper seed than an African skull, and thus con-cluded that Blacks have inferior brains and limited capacity for mental growth (Clark, 1972). These assertions of racial inferiority continued well into the 1900s and were promoted by many leading Euro-American psychologists. In fact, a comprehensive examination of the literature related to the history and systems of psychology would reveal that in every decade encompassing 1900 to 1970, there was a prominent American psychologist (many of whom were presidents of the American Psychological Association [APA]) who was a proponent of the genetic inferiority hypothesis (Guthrie, 1976, 1998). Although such facts may be new information for many students in psychology, certainly most students and laypersons are aware of the well-publicized assertions of racial and intellectual inferiority by Arthur Jensen (1969).

Deficit-Deficiency Model

The deficit-deficiency model began to emerge around the late 1950s to early 1960s, and suggested that Blacks are somehow deficient with respect to intelligence, perceptual skills, cognitive styles, family structure, and other factors. Unlike the inferiority model, the set of hypotheses suggested that environmental rather than hereditary factors were responsible for the presumed deficiencies in Blacks. Dhe deficit model arose in opposition to the inferiority model and was formed by more liberal-minded psychological and educational researchers who sought to place on society the burden for Black people's presumed mental and intellectual deficiencies. For example, it was somehow concluded that the effects of years of racism and discrimination had deprived most Black people of the strengths to develop healthy self-esteems (Kardiner & Ovesey, 1951) and legitimate family structures (Moynihan, 1965). From this deficit model came such hypotheses as "cultural deprivation," which presumed that because of the inadequate exposure to Euro-American values, norms, customs, and lifestyles, Blacks were indeed "culturally deprived" and required cultural enrichment.

Implicit in the concept of cultural deprivation, however, is the notion that the dominant White middle-class culture established that normative standard discussed earlier in these writings. Thus, any behaviors, values, and lifestyles that differed from the Euro-American norm were seen as deficient. By and large, the model of the Black family that has received the most attention has been the deficit-deficiency model. This model begins with the historical assumption that there was no carry over from Africa to America of any sophisticated African based form of family life in communal living. The assumption further indicates that either viable patterns of family life did not exist because Africans were incapable of creating them or they were destroyed beginning with slavery in the separation of biological parents and children, forced breeding, the slave master's sexual exploitation of Black women, and the cumulative effects of three hundred years of economic social discrimination. The deficit-deficiency model assumes that as a result of this background of servitude, deprivation, second-class citizenship, and chronic unemployment, Black adults have not been able to develop marketable skills, self-sufficiency, future orientation, planning and decision-making competencies, and instrumental behaviors thought to be necessary for sustaining a successful two-parent nuclear family while guiding children through the socialization process.

A variation of the deficit-deficiency model was the Black matriarchy model. In a society that placed a premium on decisive male leadership in the family, the Black male was portrayed as lacking the masculine sex role behaviors characterized by logical thinking, willingness to take responsibility for others, assertiveness, managerial skills, achievement orientation, and occupational mastery. In contrast, the Black female was portrayed by this model as a matriarch who initially received her power because society was unwilling to permit the Black male to assume the legal, economic, and social positions necessary to become a dominant force within the family and community life. Having achieved this power by default, the Black female was portrayed as being unwilling to share it. Her unwillingness to share her power was presumed to persist even when the Black male was present and willing to assume responsibility in the family circle, since she was not confident of the male's ability to follow through on his commitments. Confrontation over decision making and family direction was usually not necessary because either the Black male was not present in the household on any ongoing basis or he was regarded as ineffective by the female when he was present.

Multicultural Model

The rise in the multicultural model has been stimulated by the contention that behaviors, lifestyles, languages, and so on can only be judged as appropriate or inappropriate within a specific cultural context (Grier & Cobbs, 1968; White, 1972; Pedersen, 1999; Sue, Ivey, & Pederson, 1996; Ponterotto et al., 2001; Sue & Sue, 2003; White & Henderson, 2008). The multicultural model assumes and recognizes that each culture has strengths and limitations, and rather than being viewed as deficient, differences among ethnic groups are viewed as simply different. More recent contributions to the multicultural literature have followed in these same footsteps and continue to contribute to a more enlightened understanding of culturally different people generally (Hall, 2010), African American (Jones, 2003; Hilliard, 1997; Parham, 2002), Latinos (Santiago-Rivera, Arredondo, & Gallardo-Cooper, 2002), Asian Americans (Loo, 1998), and even persons with disabilities (Stone, 2005). Although the multicultural model is the latest trend in research with respect to minorities in general and African Americans in particular, and is certainly a more positive approach to research with culturally distinct groups, it is by no means immune to conceptual and methodological flaws that have plagued psychological research efforts both past and present.

In some respects, this new emphasis on ethnic pluralism has helped researchers focus on culture-specific models in a multicultural context. African psychology has been the forerunner of an ethnic and cultural awareness in psychology that has worked its way into the literature on child development, self-image, family dynamics, education, communication patterns, counseling and psychotherapy, and mental health delivery systems. The blossoming of African-centered psychology has been followed by the assertion on the part of Asian American (Sue & Wagner, 1973; Sue, 1981), Chicano (Martinez, 1977), and Native American (Richardson, 1981) psychologists that sociocultural differences in the experiential field must be considered as legitimate correlates of behavior. The development of an ethnic dimension in psychology suggested that other non-White Americans wanted to take the lead in defining themselves rather than continuing the process of being defined by the deficit-deficiency models of the majority culture. The evolution of the ethnic and cultural perspective enlarged the scope of psychology. It served as a corrective step that reduced psychology's reliance on obsolete and inaccurate stereotypes in defining culturally distinct people. This movement has now exploded onto the field of counseling psychology as more and more professionals recognize, as Sue, Ivey, and Pederson (1996) so rightly acknowledge, that traditional theories of counseling and psychotherapy inadequately describe, explain, predict, and deal with the richness of a culturally diverse population. Their admonition is echoed by a host of new and exciting research and scholarship that speaks to the necessity of culturally specific and culturally diverse theories, assessments, and therapeutic practices in the areas of Latino(a) psychology (Santiago-Rivera, Arredondo, & Gallardo-Cooper, 2002), Asian psychology (Loo, 1998), traditional healing practices (Moodley & West, 2005; Mc Neill & Cervantes, 2008), and even disability studies (Stone, 2005).

Black Behavioral Norms

Given the negative conceptions of Black people and Black behavior that emerged from the Euro-American frame of reference, it was clear that an alternate frame of reference was not only appropriate, but absolutely necessary. Whether one considers the awarding of Sumner's degree in 1920, the establishment of the Association of Black Psychologists (ABPsi) in 1968, or the era in ancient KMT, as the marker for the establishment of the discipline of Black psychology, is an interesting debate (Nobles, 1986). What is undebatable, however, is the recognition that general psychology had failed to provide a full and accurate understanding of the Black reality. As such, the discipline of Black psychology and the new emergence of an African psychological perspective can be defined as a discipline in science (continuing to evolve) that is attempting to study, analyze, and define appropriate and inappropriate behaviors of Black and African people from an Afrocentric frame of reference.

A second point made by White (1972) in his article that is reinforced by White and Parham (1990) and Parham, White, and Ajamu (1999) is that Black psychology as a discipline should emerge out of the authentic experiences of Blacks in America. On the surface, White's contention seems absolutely logical. However, I believe that this premise requires closer scrutiny. For years, Black psychologists in the discipline of Black psychology have concerned themselves with trying to combat negativistic assumptions made about Black people by White society in general and traditional psychology in particular. In doing so, many of the writings have been reactionary in nature in their attempts to combat the racist and stereotypic assumptions perpetuated by the Euro-American culture. In that regard, Black psychology has served a vital purpose in the evolution of thought about the psychology of African-American people. In their attempt to negate the White middle-class norm and to assert the necessity for analyzing African-American behavior in the context of its own norms, Black psychologists have been attempting to establish this normative base that is uniquely Afrocentric. In developing that norm, however, new questions are now being raised about whether or not the behavior of Black people in

Need for a Worldview That Emerges from an African-Centered Frame of Reference

Problem:
- **Normative Standard**
- **Generalizability of Norm**
- **Difference Equals Deficiency**

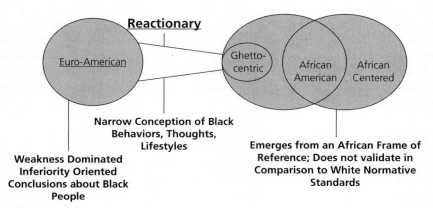

FIGURE 2.1

America constitutes a reasonable normative standard of what appropriate and/or inappropriate behavior should be. In fact, if one examines the research related to Blacks, the normative standard that developed emerged for the most part from the analysis of behaviors and attitudes of Southern-born, working-class, ghetto-dwelling Black people (Akbar, 1981). Although this norm was certainly more valid than the Eurocentric perspective, it introduced biases against large numbers of Blacks who did not fit the newly developed stereotype of what a "real" Black person should be. Figure 2.1 attempts to illustrate how ghetto-centric norms are indeed based on a relatively small sample of Black people, and are influenced by a Eurocentric perspective of what Black normative behavior should be.

One can readily see the problem in adapting this ghetto-centric norm to all Black people in the criticism being shown at "The Cosby Show" in television during the late 1980s and early 90s, and to some extent, shows like "My Wife and Kids," which stared Damon Wayans and Tisha Campbell in the 2000-2005. Much of the negative press about "The Cosby Show," and more recently "My Wife and Kids," that has emerged from the Black community has to do with the assumption that the characters and/or the shows themselves are not "Black enough." Many assume (inappropriately so) that you cannot be Black, middle-class, have two professional parents working, and have a loving family that displays caring concern, strength, and character, all in a single episode. Fast forward twenty years from those 1980s, and with the explosion of cable news shows, you now have networks like CNN developing and airing shows like "Black in America I & II" in spring and summer 2009. These documentary-oriented stories help to chronicle both the challenges that confront African-descent people, as well as the successes that result from stable families, hard work, and perseverance through adversity. However, even despite the premier and re-run episodes of these shows on national and international television, the biases this country and the world continue to harbor toward people of African descent are quite remarkable, even as they seek to create and sustain a "Black Norm" of what the typical African American is like.

Not surprisingly, many Black psychologists continue to recognize, what others have decades before, which is the difficulty that these historic and contemporary shortsighted perspectives have created for Black people. Akbar (1981, 2004) has suggested that this "Black norm" has two major limitations. First, it validates itself in comparison to a White norm. Thus, even as we write this fourth edition in 2009-10, African Americans continue to be compared with their White counterparts on statistical profiles ranging from educational achievement, economic viability, health status, crime and justice, employment status, and relationship/family stability, and mental health, to name a few. Second, the norm assumes that the adaptation to the conditions of America by Blacks constitutes a reasonable normative statement about African-American behavior. Akbar (1981, 2004) had the unique vision to recognize that oppression, discrimination, and racism are unnatural human phenomena; as such, these conditions stimulate unnatural human behavior. Thus, many of the behaviors displayed by Blacks as they attempt to adjust and react to hostile conditions in America may be functional but often prove self-destructive. For example, one who perceives his or her employment options as limited or nonexistent (because of discrimination) may turn to a life of crime in order to provide himself or herself with what are perceived as basic necessities. Such an individual might be seen selling drugs for profit, burglarizing a local establishment, engaging in prostitution or pimping, or other illegitimate endeavors. The problem with the ghetto-centric norm is that it legitimizes such behavior.

Because of these questions, many psychologists are now suggesting that statements about normative behavior should emerge from the values, norms, customs, and philosophies that are African-centered. Truly, this debate about what constitutes normative Black behavior is likely to rage on within the discipline of Black psychology for many years. Readers may ask, however, "What is this African-centered perspective or norm, and how does it manifest itself in the Black community?" In the first edition of *The Psychology of Blacks,* White (1984) offers an excellent synthesis of the African-centered value system; and not surprisingly, that synthesis continues to be one of the best analyses even after more than twenty-five years.

THE AFRICAN WORLDVIEW

White (1984) views the holistic, humanistic ethos described by Nobles (1972) and Mbiti (1970) as the principle feature of African psychology. There appears to be a definite correspondence between the African ethos and the Afro-American worldview in terms of the focus on emotional vitality, interdependence, collective survival, the oral tradition, perception of time, harmonious blending, and the role of the elders. Some have questioned the utility of an African normative base, given the enormous tribal and geographical variability among African people. However, to discount the presence of an African norm because of differences is analogous to missing the forest for the trees. Certainly, these are individual differences, but there are more commonalities than differences, and it is those common themes that provide the foundation for the African worldview.

The African worldview begins with a holistic conception of the human condition. There is no mind-body or affective-cognitive dualism. The human organism is conceived as a totality made up of a series of interlocking systems. This total person is simultaneously a feeling, experiencing, sensualizing, sensing, and knowing human being living in a dynamic, vitalistic world where everything is interrelated and endowed with the supreme force of life. There is a sense of aliveness, intensity, and animation in the music, dance, song, language, and lifestyles of Africans. Emotions are not labeled as bad; therefore, there is no need to repress feelings of compassion, love, joy, or sensuality.

The basic human unit is the tribe, not the individual. The tribe operates under a set of rules geared toward collective survival. Cooperation is therefore valued above competition and individualism. The concept of alienation is nonexistent in African philosophy since the people are closely interconnected with each other in a way of life that involves concern and responsibility toward others. In a framework that values collective survival, where people are psychologically interdependent on each other, active aggression against another person is in reality an act of aggression against oneself (Nobles, 1972). The idea of interrelatedness extends to the whole universe, arranged in a hierarchy that includes God, humans, animals, plants, and inanimate objects in a descending order.

People are linked in a geographical and temporal frame by the oral tradition, with messages being transmitted across time and space by word of mouth or the drums. Each tribe contains a *griot,* an oral historian, who is a living record of the people's heritage. The spoken word is revered. Words take on a quality of life when they are uttered by the speaker. In the act of *Nommo,* the speaker literally breathes life into a word. Nothing exists, including newborn babies, until a name has been uttered with the breath of life. When words are spoken, the listener is expected to acknowledge receiving the message by responding to the speaker. This is known as the call-response. The speaker sends out a message or a call, and the listener makes a response indicating that he or she has heard the message. The speaker and the listener operate within a shared psycholinguistic space affirming each other's presence.

Time is marked off by a series of events that have been shared with others in the past or are occurring in the present. Thus, when an African talks about time in the past tense, reference points are likely to be established by events such as a daughter's marriage or a son's birth, events that were shared with others. When an African is trying to make arrangements about meeting someone in the immediate future, a specific time, such as three o'clock, is avoided. The person is more likely to say, "I will meet you after I finish milking the cows." The primary time frames in African languages are past and present.

There is no word in most African languages for the distant future. The distant future has not yet happened; therefore, it does not exist. In this fluid perception of time, there is no guilt about wasting time. Time is not a monetary commodity but an experience to be shared with others.

Time is also considered to be repetitive. The major events used to designate points in time, such as conception, birth, the naming ceremony, puberty, and marriage, repeat themselves throughout the life cycle. There is a cyclical, rhythmic pattern to the flow of events—the coming and going of the seasons, the rising and the setting of the sun, and the movement through the stages of life. Nature's rhythms are believed to have been put in order by God, who knew what He/She was doing. The essence of life is to be able to move harmoniously with the cyclical rhythms of the universe's internal clock. The goal is not to control or dominate the universe, but to blend creatively into the tempo and pace of the seasons of life. Life is broken down into a series of stages beginning with conception, followed by birth, the naming ceremony, puberty, initiation rites, marriage, adulthood, and old age. Death is seen as a stage of life. The living dead are still members of the tribe, and personal immortality is assured as long as one's memory is continuously passed down to each generation by the tribe's oral historian. Since immortality is guaranteed by the passing of one's memory forward, there is no pervasive fear of old age and death. The tribal elders are valued because they have accumulated the wisdoms of life's teachings. In the hierarchical arrangement of the cosmos, they occupy a position just below that of the Supreme Being and the living dead.

PERSISTENCE OF THE AFRICAN-CENTERED WORLDVIEW

In order to better grasp the worldview that emerges from an African reality, it is first necessary to understand, and in some cases re-examine, the notion of culture. Culture has been inappropriately equated with a number of superficial variables like food, music, clothing, and artifacts. Although each of these items is a representation or a manifestation of culture, they are not culture in and of themselves.

Culture is a complex constellation of mores, values, customs, tradition, and practices that guide and influence a people's cognitive, affective, and behavioral response to life circumstances. In essence, culture provides a general design for living and a pattern for interpreting reality (Nobles, 1986). Thus, in seeking to clarify and understand the African-centered worldview, the relevant question becomes: How do African Americans construct their design for living, and what patterns do they use to interpret reality? Take for example, a July 2009 incident in Cambridge, Massachusetts, where Harvard Professor and African-American intellectual Henry Louis Gates is arrested by that city's police at his home for "disturbing the peace and disorderly conduct." The incident made national headlines and was the subject of intense debate on all major networks for weeks, with opinions being shared on both sides about the significance of race in this circumstance. However, there is more at play here than the fact that Professor Gates is African American and the police officer(s) was White. What is clear is that in that situation each participant's mindset, and ultimate response that never de-escalated until Gates was booked at the local jail, was influenced by his or her design for living and pattern for interpreting reality. Contextually, Gates is returning from a trip abroad and is just arriving home with his driver and bags in toe. Because he experiences some difficulty in opening the door to his house, he motions to his driver to provide him with some assistance. Now, you have two Black males, on a porch in a predominantly White suburb of Boston, attempting to gain entry into a house. A vigilant neighbor observes the two men, and calls police, assuming that Gates and his driver are attempting to break in and gain illegal entry. That's when the police respond. Before they arrive, Gates has entered his home and is putting things down. Once the police have arrived, he is asked to show identification to verify his local address, but perceives that his interrogation is moving way beyond the boundaries of what is acceptable, particularly having just produced the identification the police demanded. Gates reportedly demands to know the name and badge number of the officer in charge, and emotions escalate, tempers flare, and ultimately, Professor Gates is arrested for what can only be imagined as being belligerent to the police.

Professor Gates' worldview is sensitive to issues of race and the hostile and discriminatory practices police routinely use toward African-American males. Thus, his emotional tone is born out of that experience. The police officer is sensitive to the potential for a burglar to be at the Gates residence, and whether influenced by race or not, is not about to tolerate any hostile feelings coming from a citizen who was just a suspect in an alleged break-in. His emotional tone and response is born out of that experience as a law enforcement official who responds to a citizen call for police intervention for what is perceived as a crime. Thus, irrespective of who the public thought was right or wrong in this affair, what is abundantly clear is that neither man was able to look past race to see the cultural perspective of the other, a perspective that might have allowed the situation to resolve itself in a more peaceful manner. But let us continue articulating the notion of culture.

One of the clearest expressions of an African-American cultural manifestation in psychology was provided by White (1984) in the first edition of *The Psychology of Blacks*. White believed that the African ethos helped to create a collective psychological space for African Americans independent of their oppressors where they could generate a sense of worth, dignity, affiliation, and mutual support. Included in the delineation of that ethos, despite the historical context of slavery and oppression, were principles and practices such as self-determination and definition; the intergenerational continuity enhanced by and through the oral tradition; a strong religious faith, including participation in organized worship; immediate and extended family supports; language and expressive patterns; and personal expressions through music and the arts.

African-Centered Psychology Comes of Age

In further delineating the persistence of the African ethos into the life space of African Americans, Parham (1993, 2002) has synthesized the work of Nobles (1972), White (1984), Myers (1988), and others through his comparisons of cultural worldviews. Thus, let's review these again to ensure that you have a firm grasp of the differences in worldviews between certain cultural groups. In contrasting the African-American and European-American worldview across selected primary dimensions, Parham suggests that the "designs for living" be seen in the adherence to particular value systems by each cultural group. He first identifies eight variables that are then used to compare and contrast the two culturally different worldviews. The dimensions are listed as self, feelings, survival, language, time, universe, death, and worth. On one end of the spectrum is a Euro-American worldview; on the opposite end, the African American.

Regarding the sense of *self,* Euro-Americans relate to a fragmented personality in which cognitive, affective, and behavioral dimensions are seen as separate and distinct. Regardless to whether the psychological theories are classical (i.e., Freud's three structures of personality) or contemporary (i.e., Burne's transactional analysis), their analysis and application include an imposition of a "difference equals deficiency" logic to particular segments of the personality structure. The African-American self begins with a holistic integration of its parts rather than fragmentation. At the core of the African self is an understanding of the fundamental nature of the self as spiritual, which permeates the cognitive, affective, and behavioral dimensions.

Regarding *feelings,* the Euro-American tradition values suppression of emotions in favor of rational imperatives. In the African-American tradition, emotions and feelings are intended to be expressed while serving as a check on expressions that are more rationally based.

The *survival* dimension in the Euro-American context embraces an individualistic and competitive relationship to people and the society at large. In contrast, the African worldview promotes a more collective orientation to people, family, and social interactions. This value of collective survival is reflected in the Asante proverb: "I am because we are; and because we are, therefore I am." In essence, this truth explains that an individual is only important to the degree that he or she contributes to the maintenance and the well-being of the tribe or the group.

Regarding *language,* the Euro-American culture gives credence to that which is written, that communicating with a style that appears to be formal and detached. In the African tradition, much more credence is given to the oral tradition with an emphasis on the interconnectedness between the speaker and the listener. With respect to *time and space,* Euro-Americans tend to be very future-oriented and perceive time as a commodity to be invested (i.e., "time is money"). African Americans are more present-centered with a reference to the past. Time is also seen as something to be experienced in the moment, rather than invested with special emphasis or meaning given to circumstances surrounding an event.

In relationship to the *universe,* Euro-Americans relate it with a desire and need for control and manipulation of things and people. In the African-American worldview, the orientation is usually toward harmony and balance, as everything is seen as interrelated.

Regarding the concept of *death,* Euro-Americans see death of the body as the end. Therefore, there is an urgent, almost obsessive, desire to preserve life and avoid the realities of getting old. In the African-American worldview, death is seen as another transition from this life into the next. And because of the belief of spirit as the essence of the human being, one is able to better accept and embrace the spiritual transition of those who have joined the community of ancestors. Finally, *worth* in the Euro-American tradition is determined and measured by material attainment and possession. In the African tradition, one's worth was measured by contribution to community and collective uplifting. Parham's analysis, while allowing for individual variations, nonetheless recognizes how the African-American design for living and pattern for interpreting reality are reflected in the culture of the people.

With the persistence of the African ethos in the historical and contemporary life space of African Americans, more recent scholars have utilized its principles as the foundation for this African-centered psychological perspective. Regardless of whether the topic or analysis is African-American families in therapy (Boyd-Franklin, 1989), African-American male-female relationships (Powell-Hopson & Hopson, 1998), identity development (Cross, 1991), personal biographies (Gates, 1994), or the experiences of being a Black man in America (McCall, 1994; Obama, 2004), these themes discussed above continue to resonate with clarity and consistency.

What we are arguing here is the recognition that the notion of culture is central to a more deep-structured analysis of African psychology that seeks to move beyond the basic level understandings of the discipline. In helping us to embrace this idea more thoroughly, Ani (1994) has provided us with an analysis of culture at the deep structural level. Her work suggests that culture (1) unifies and orders our experience by providing a worldview that orients our experience and interpretation of reality; (2) provides collective group identification built on shared history, symbols, and meanings; and (3) institutionalizes and validates group beliefs, values, behaviors, and attitudes (Ani, 1994). In a similar way, Nobles (1986) helps to inform our thinking about the concept of culture by suggesting that it represents the inner essence and outer envelope of human beingness.

As we seek to engage these constructs of culture, Grills (2002), Parham (2002, 2006), and King, Dixon, and Nobles (1976) before them, provide us with a more formalized structure through which to examine how culture is operationalized across various racial/ethnic groups. Individually and collectively, they suggest that there are five domains of information that represent elements of culture at the deep structure level, and that these domains are central to developing a better working knowledge of the construct. The five domains include: Ontology (nature of reality), Axiology (one's value orientation), Cosmology (relationship to the Divine force in the universe), Epistemology (systems of knowledge and discovering truth), and Praxis (consistency in the context of one system of human interaction).

Ontology	Axiology	Cosmology	Epistemology	Praxis
Nature of Reality	Value System	Relationship to the Divine	System of Knowing and What is Truth	Systems of Human Interaction

ONTOLOGY   An integration of personal and familial lived experiences; religious/spiritual insight and history.

AXIOLOGY   Collectivistic; one's worth is based on one's contribution to the group's well-being and advancement; present and past oriented; group/cultural survival and ownership.

COSMOLOGY   Spiritual/religious connection as integration of family and culture; divinity falls on a spectrum of ancestral hierarchy that dictates a reverence for those that have preceded us; connection, conservation, and protection to mother earth.

EPISTEMOLOGY   Oral history (i.e., ancestral history), direct lived experiences; Western science is limited and not the universal truth of insight and understanding.

PRAXIS   Connectedness to others and congruence with others; religious/spiritual guidance and standard for one's thoughts and behaviors; family guidance and shared wisdom; shared lived experiences influence the integration and acceptance into one's behavioral repertoire.

Examination of these five domains within the context of African-American people's lives allows us to develop a template that is useful in distinguishing areas of convergence and divergence between persons of African descent and other cultural groups, and even Eurocentric psychology Parham (1993) has invited us to consider before. Table 2.2 illustrates our comparison of cultural manifestations.

As a consequence of this discussion, it opens the way for us to explore the extension of these cultural elements into a set of assumptions that guide the work of African-centered psychologists in theory and practice. Thus,

TABLE 2.2 Value Systems

Euro American	Dimensions	African-American
1. Fragmented Dichotomized Dualistic	**SELF**	Holistic Spiritness made evident
2. Suppressed/ Controlled	**FEELINGS**	Legitimate/Expressed/Vitality/Aliveness
3. Individual/ Competitive	**SURVIVAL**	Collective/Group "I am because we are, and because we are, therefore I am."
4. Written/Detached	**LANGUAGE**	Oral/Expressive/Call Response
5. Metric/Linear	**TIME**	Events Cyclical
6. Control	**UNIVERSE**	Harmony-Ontological Principal of Immortality
7. End	**DEATH**	
8. Material Possession	**WORTH**	Contribution to One's Community

African-centered psychology, in using African values, traditions, worldview as the lens through which perceptions of reality are shaped and colored, examines processes that allow for the *illumination* and *liberation* of the *spirit* (one's spiritual essence). Thus, if culture does provide a general design for living and a pattern for interpreting reality, then African-centered psychology, in relying on the principles of harmony within the universe as a natural order of human existence, recognizes:

- The *spiritness* that permeates everything that exists in the universe.
- The notion that everything in the universe is *interconnected.*
- The value that the *collective* is the most salient element of existence.
- And the idea that *self-knowledge* is the key to mental health.

African psychology then is the dynamic manifestation of the unifying African principles, values, and traditions whereby the application of knowledge is used to resolve personal and social problems and promote optimal human functioning.

THE DEVELOPMENT OF BLACK PSYCHOLOGY— THE MODERN ERA

In the opinion of the senior co-author of this text, the modern era of Black psychology begins in 1968 with the formation of the ABPsi. Graduate schools in psychology were still turning out a combined national total of only three or four Black Ph.Ds in psychology per year.

Some major departments of psychology at this late date had not produced a single Black Ph.D psychologist. The grand total of psychologists among the more than ten thousand members of the APA, Psychology's most prestigious organization, was less than one percent. At the annual convention of the APA in San Francisco in August/September of 1968, approximately fifty-eight Black psychologist delegates and their guests came together to give form and substance to the idea of a national organization of Black psychologists.

In the more than forty years since its formal beginning in 1968, the modern era of Black or African psychology has established its presence across several areas of psychology. The impact of the efforts of African-centered psychologists has been felt in the fields of counseling and clinical psychology, community mental health, education, intelligence and ability testing, professional training, forensic psychology, and criminal justice. Black psychologists have presented their findings at professional conferences, legislative hearings, and social policymaking task forces. They have also served as expert witnesses in class action suits designed to make institutional policies more responsive to the needs of African people. In light of the social phenomena and institutional policies that continue to affect the mental health needs of the African- American community, we believe that ABPsi is a vital and necessary resource and will remain so in the future.

In order to better appreciate the ways in which ABPsi responds to more contemporary mental health needs of the African-American community, it is important to understand where we have come from in the forty years since ABPsi's inception. It was the Algerian psychiatrist Frantz Fanon (1967) who remarked that each generation, out of relative obscurity, must reach out and either fulfill its legacy or betray it. Those sentiments speak volumes about the challenge to carve out a place for an African-centered worldview within the discipline of psychology that the ABPsi has taken up. It is important to understand that, in Parham's view, the foundation for the ABPsi, indeed the discipline of African psychology, was more than just a group of frustrated men and women who were unhappy with the APA's posture regarding persons of African descent. Clearly, there were angry sentiments about what many perceive as the incongruence between what APA professed and what the organization and its affiliates practiced. But that doesn't come close to telling the entire story. The context for this initiation of the ABPsi was born out of a social struggle for civil rights, where the themes of "I am somebody," "Black Power," and "self-determination" became the rally cries for most Black Americans at that time. Within that struggle was a challenge confronting Black psychologists about whether an "integrationist" (work within the APA to achieve progress) vs. a "nationalist" (break away from the APA and form an independent organization) philosophy was the best strategy to achieve social and professional progress for Black psychologists. In addition, the bias against persons of African-descent promoted by many prominent White members of the APA demonstrated clear prejudices in intelligence and personality measurement, and helped to usher in a practice where testing and assessment practices were used as tools of oppression. Clearly, the betrayal of objectivity of APA's pseudo-scientific theories and instruments was very pronounced. Consequently, we argue that the struggle for an African-centered psychological prospective was less about a personality clash between African-American and White members of an association; it was essentially about a what Thomas Parham (2009) has termed a "cultural war,"

In reminding ourselves that culture is a complex constellation of mores, values, customs, and traditions that provide a general design for living and a pattern for interpreting reality, it is important to understand the context in which that war was waged. Given that the cultural sterility within traditional psychology was quite pronounced, it was incumbent upon professionals and students alike to engage in a battle that was waged on four fronts. These fronts include: a war of ideology, a war of values, a war of self-determination, and a war of cultural relevance. This, we believe, is what the Association of Black Psychologists has been about for the past four decades.

WAR OF IDEOLOGY   The ideological conflict centered on who and what African people are. Black psychologists were right to argue, as Hilliard (1997) reminds us, that there is something wrong with a psychology and a psychological prospective that leaves any group of people strangers to themselves, aliens to their culture, oblivious to their condition, and inhuman to their oppressors. Furthermore, Carter G. Woodson, in his groundbreaking work on *The Mis-Education of the Negro*, reminds us that if you allow people to control the way you think, you do not have to assign them to an inferior status; if necessary, they will seek it for themselves. Indeed, it has been a war of ideology.

WAR OF VALUES   Consistent with the descriptions referenced previously in this chapter, there is a different set of cultural values that are embraced in an African-centered worldview. These have become the foundation of the African and African-American psychological prospective. These values include the necessity and importance of spirituality, the inner connectedness of all things that exist on the planet and in the universe, that the collective is the most salient element of existence, the idea that self knowledge is the key to mental health, a belief in the transformative possibilities of the human spirit, and the need for self knowledge that was rooted in one's own cultural traditions.

WAR OF SELF-DETERMINATION   The ABPsi had to struggle with the idea of whether to be part of the APA or totally separate from it. In this regard, we are reminded of the words of the Honorable Marcus Garvey, who challenges us to remember that chance has never satisfied the hope of a suffering people. It is only through hard work, persistence, and self-reliance by which the oppressed have ever realized the light of their own freedom. In that regard, the ABPsi up until most recently has been the only autonomous ethnic psychology association in this country. The conflict over self-determination was a quick battle as the ABPsi decided to establish its own headquarters (Washington D.C.); create its own newsletter (Psych Discourse); develop its own scholarly journal (*Journal of Black Psychology*); and host its own convention, which meets annually each August in cities all across this country, and occasionally, internationally.

WAR OF CULTURAL RELEVANCE   The ABPsi, and indeed the discipline of African psychology, has always believed that psychology had to be relevant to a broad array of persons of African descent. Said another way, psychology had to be relevant to the people. African psychology had to be relevant in improving the lives of people it devised theories to describe, and treatment modalities to administer. In addition, it had to be able to shape a future that not only transformed lives, but also instilled hope and possibility for a brighter future. Indeed, if Fanon was right that each generation has an opportunity to fulfill its legacy or betray it, the ABPsi over the past forty-plus years has reached out and seized that opportunity to fulfill their legacy.

In summary, African-centered psychology, and the psychology of Blackness, is an attempt to build conceptual models that organize, explain, and facilitate understanding of the psychosocial behavior of African Americans. Without question, these models are based in the primary dimensions of an African-American/African worldview. Having now been exposed to the basic tenets of African psychology, one should be able to see specific areas of emphasis, which although rooted in an African-centered worldview, provide congruence and continuity with the principles on which the discipline was founded in 1968. The discipline of African-centered psychology continues to define the construct in meaningful ways, render African psychological principles relevant to the contemporary needs of the African-American community, achieve better integration of the concept of spirituality, and help to define and in some cases redefine the task of therapists and healers. In addition, the discipline continues to promote the need for social advocacy and to plan interventions in the larger social arenas where public policy impacts on the mental health of people in the African-American community.

For those interested in the organization, we can report that the ABPsi has grown from a handful of concerned professionals into an independent, autonomous organization of more than 1000 members, who see their collective mission and destiny as the liberation of the African Mind, empowerment of the African Character, and illumination of the African Spirit. ABPsi has been guided for the last forty years by a member-elected board of directors, regional representatives, and national staff. The chronology of ABPsi presidents are as follows, with those who have transitioned to be with the Ancestors denoted with an asterisk*:

CHRONOLOGY OF THE PRESIDENTS OF THE ASSOCIATION OF BLACK PSYCHOLOGISTS

Charles W. Thomas, Ph.D. (1968–1969),* Robert Green, Ph. D. (1968–1969)

Henry Tomes, Ph. D. (1969–1970), Robert L. Williams, Ph.D. (1969–1970)

Stanley Crockett, Ph.D. (1970–1971), Reginald L. Jones, Ph.D. (1971–1972)*

James S. Jackson Ph.D. (1972–1973), Thomas O. Hilliard, Ph.D. (1973–1974)*

George D. Jackson, Ph.D. (1974–1975), William Hayes, Ph.D. (1975–1976)

Ruth E.G. King, Ed.D (1976–1977), Maisha Bennett, Ph.D. (1978–1979)

Joseph Awkard, Ph. D. (1979–1980), Daniel Williams, Ph.D. (1980–1981)

David Terrell, Ph.D. (1981–1982), Joseph A. Baldwin, Ph.D. (1982–1983)

William K. Lyles, Ph.D. (1983–1984),* W. Monty Whitney, Ph.D. (1984–1985)

Melvin Rogers, Ph. D. (1985–1986), Halford H. Fairchild, Ph.D. (1986–1987)

Na'im Akbar, Ph.D. (1987–1988), Dennis E. Chestnut, Ph.D. (1988–1989)

Suzanne Randolph, Ph. D. (1989–1990), Linda James Myers, Ph.D. (1990–1991)

Timothy R. Moragne, Psy.D. (1991–1992), Maisha Hamilton Bennett, Ph.D. (1992–1993)

Anna M. Jackson, Ph.D. (1993–1994), Wade Nobles, Ph.D. (1994–1995)

Thomas A. Parham, Ph.D. (1995–1996), Frederick B. Phillips, Psy.D. (1996–1997)

Kamau Dana Dennard, Ph.D. (1997–1998), Afi Samella B. Abdullah, Ph.D. (1998–1999)

Mawiya Kambon, Ph.D. (1999–2000), Anthony Young, Ph.D.(2000–2001)

Mary Hargrow, Ph.D. (2001–2002), Harvette Gray, Ph.D.(2002–2003)

Willie Williams, Ph.D. (2003–2004, James Savage, Ph.D. (2004–2005)

Robert Atwell, Ph.D. (2005–2007), Dorothy Holmes, Ph.D. (2007–2009)

Benson Cooke (2009–2011), and Cheryl Tawede Grills (2011–13)

Each administration has also committed itself to nurturing ABPsi, an organization whose mission is to advance the discipline as a whole. Thus, although the necessity for the development of an African-centered psychology goes almost without question, the recognition that general psychology had failed and continues to fail to provide African Americans full and accurate understanding of an African reality and that applications of Eurocentric norms result in the dehumanization of African people, were and are major forces that stimulate the growth of the contemporary African psychology movement.

3

■ ■ ■

The Spiritual Core of African-Centered Psychology

Over the past one hundred years, the discipline of psychology has exploded onto the academic and scientific scene, advancing theories of human behavior, theories of normal and abnormal development, and theories of the personal and situational variables that contribute to one's personality makeup. In fact, there are entire schools of thought that have been developed as a way to synthesize the vast array of ideas proposed by various theorists who are convinced that their theory is the most compelling in the understanding of the human psyche. There are Euro-American schools of thought that are labeled psychodynamic, neo-analytic, behaviorism, humanistic, cognitive-behavioral, and existential (Myers, 2010).

MISSING ELEMENTS

In illustrating this point, many psychoanalytic theories are anchored in the works of Sigmund Freud, who viewed human nature as a dynamic interplay between the unconscious, preconscious, and conscious mind. Each domain is believed to be responsible for navigating perspectives that influence how each individual responds to internal instinctual drives (unconscious), repressed or stored memories (preconscious), or to the demand of the external environment (the conscious). Freud's approach advanced the notion that the personality comprised three interrelated parts labeled the ID (basic instincts that operate according to what is pleasurable and satisfaction seeking), EGO (conscious choices that are anchored in perceptions of reality), and the SUPER EGO (a mental conscience influenced by parental values and principles of morality). Psychoanalytic theory also proposed five stages (oral, anal, phallic, latency, and genital) of development in a person's life, each focusing on a region of the body that aligned with the instinctual and pleasure seeking tendencies that were believed to be the most salient at that point in time. The goals of a psychodynamic clinician include: helping clients/patients recognize how unresolved issues in childhood continue to exert an influence in their lives and helping clients gain insights into the roots of dysfunctional or maladaptive coping or lifestyle choices.

A contemporary of Freud who advanced a theory of his own was Alfred Adler. His Adlerian approach, which is also referred to as individual psychology, believed that human nature was primarily influenced and motivated by social interests. If the development of those social interests proceeded in an orderly fashion, he believed that individuals would help to connect to society as a social whole, develop an interest in and empathy for other members of the community and society, and contribute to the general social good, while taking a high degree of responsibility for their own actions that aligned with those outcomes. Unlike Freud, however, Adler believed that the conscious rather than unconscious aspects of an individual's personality exerted the most salient influence, in helping them to strive for perfection in navigating social interactions. In recognizing that people possessed a strong desire for social validation, Adlerian clinicians also recognize that unsuccessful resolution of that desire and need would lead to complexes of inferiority, or superiority, each of which might influence a person in negative or unproductive ways. The goal of Adlerian therapy then is to assist individuals in developing productive, wholesome, and healthy lifestyles, free from the self-centered tendencies that erode social networks; and to help people gain insights into how maladaptive or inaccurate feelings developed in childhood will continue to exert a negative influence in their lives unless they can be successfully revisited and resolved in therapy.

A third school of thought that emerged from traditional psychology is the Behavioral school. Owing its origins to theorist like B.F. Skinner, John Watson, Albert Bandura, and others, Behaviorists believe that all behavior, whether adaptive or maladaptive, is learned and reinforced in some way within one's environment. They focus on the present and here and now, rather than one's developmental past, and believe that with insight and specific behavioral analysis, new schedules of learning and reinforcement can assist individuals in developing and sustaining good and healthy adaptations and adjustments to life circumstances. Thus, their therapeutic focus is on helping clients modify or eliminate less constructive behaviors from their lives, while helping them develop and learn more healthy and useful ways of being in the world. In a related way, the Cognitive-Behavioral school of thought was developed and influenced by individuals such as Albert Ellis. He believed that people learned to conceptualize their world in ways that gave too much attribution to events and situations and not enough to their own ability to think rationally or irrationally. Cognitive-Behavioral clinicians understand that it is not situations or circumstances that cause people to feel certain emotions or behave in particular ways. Rather, they believe that it is their belief system about those events that has the most influence. Therapy then becomes a process of discrimination and analysis where internal dialogues about oneself, other people, or situations are examined as a way of identifying what is both rational and irrational. Clients then gain insight into how they contribute to the emotional distress or unsatisfactory behavioral outcomes in their lives, while learning to replace irrational unproductive thinking with thoughts that are more healthy and rational.

Interestingly, each of these differing schools of thought is grounded in a set of assumptions about the nature of reality, the development of one's personality, how and why people develop distress in their lives, and what role the counselor or clinician should play in helping to alleviate their discomfort. Yet, while each of these theoretical schools of thought in Eurocentric psychology diverges on many of these variables, they do converge on a common belief that the individual personality is composed of intellectual (cognitive), affective (emotional), and response (behavioral) dimensions. Admittedly, they do differ on which dimension of one's personality they believe is the most salient in managing the dynamics of one's life and lifestyle choices, and which dimension should be targeted for therapeutic intervention.

Fortunately, the complex nature of the human psyche does not easily lend itself to tight or even concise explanations. Therefore, most presentations of personality development present these schools of thought as a broad lens through which to seek understanding of the human condition. Interestingly, our concern in this chapter is less about which school one considers adopting as his/her best explanation of the individual psyche, and more about a specific element of the psyche that to us, appears conspicuous by its absence. In psychology's traditional realms of understanding, analysis of the individual personality has been constrained by an assumption that the most salient aspects of the personality are the id, ego, or super ego (e.g., theories of Freud, Jung, Adler), or composed of the cognitive (the way people think, e.g., theories of Ellis), affective (the way people feel, e.g., theories of Rogers), and behavioral domains (the way people respond to their reality, e.g., theories of Skinner, Bandura, or Watson). Thus, when teaching students about the structures of the psyche, or conceptualizing a client's degree of debilitation who presents themselves for mental health treatment, the analysis is typically limited to these three domains, irrespective of which school of thought plays the most prominent role in a professor's or clinician's thinking. This practice does a tremendous disservice to people of African descent and other members of the human family, because it ignores what is arguably the most important element of a person's beingness, their *spirit* (Parham, 2002; Nobles, 2008). Imagine you are a client of African descent who in presenting yourself to a clinician for some counseling and therapy is greeted with clinical eyes that appear to look through you. They look to your left, to your right, and even over your head, seeing aspects of your self but never really connecting with the authentic you. That is illustrative of what happens in many therapeutic encounters when the core of who you are is ignored or not otherwise acknowledged.

The failure of traditional psychology to embrace the notion of genuine and authentic spirit has occurred for several reasons. These include: rigid adherence to an outdated belief that psychological constructs and variables must be measured; failure to embrace the full spectrum of psychological health and wholeness in deference to an obsession to weakness and pathology; and a tendency to cloud discussions of "spirit" with discussions of religious and spiritual beliefs. The first point about rigid adherence to outdated beliefs that all psychological constructs must be measured to rate relevance is a curious one in that there is so much discussion about the affective and intuitive nature of the individual psyche. Psychological and counselor educators spend countless hours training students to rely on clinical instincts when attempting to empathize with clients whom they are treating. Yet, attempting to measure the instincts or intuitions that often inform decisions about which questions to query clients about or which directions to pursue in therapy would prove a difficult task, even for the most seasoned clinicians. The failure to embrace the full spectrum of psychological health and wholeness is a tendency many psychologists and counselors are beginning to question, partly because of the movement of "positive psychology." This movement is beginning to gain some traction within the discipline but has yet to be fully embraced in a way that the majority of those counselors and clinicians doing therapeutic work incorporate such perspectives into their client conceptualizations. In part, the conceptualization issue is fueled by the reliance on psychological instruments that continue to be pathology-oriented, even in their revised forms (e.g., MMPI-II). The tendency to cloud discussions of "spirit" with discussions on religious and spiritual beliefs is problematic as well. The fact that people chose to align their lifestyles with a particular religion simply implies that they are believers in GOD, and support the doctrines of that denomination. In recognizing that people's faith is a strong anchor in one's life and can be a major support system in times of trouble and adversity, many psychological service providers do ask about religious affiliation as a standard part of an intake interview. They also refer to a client's religious affiliation and adherence to doctrines of theology as a way of gaining insights into past behaviors, as well as perspectives into how an individual client might rely on that body of ideas as a support in navigating their way through certain life challenges.

This latter point is significant in its impact because it anchors spirituality in a cognitive activity of belief systems analysis, rather than an experiential base that aligns one's energy and life force with that, which already exists in the world, in connections with other members of the human family, and with the DIVINE. This tendency to look at spirituality within the context of religious affiliation and belief system analysis can be seen in the work of Armstrong and Crowther (2002), who talk about the importance of client spiritual and religious beliefs in helping them navigate challenges in their life. Spirituality and religiosity are also seen as a prime coping mechanism in helping people cope with the challenges of academic life (Herndon, 2003), health concerns (King, Burgess, Akinyela, Counts-Spriggs, & Parker, 2005; Holt, Lewellyn, & Rathwell, 2005), and even racism and oppression (Manning, Cornelius, & Oklindaye, 2004). Similarly, Constantine, Lewis, Connor, and Sanchez (2000) argued for the necessity for clinicians to be "aware" of client's spiritual and religious beliefs in any therapeutic recommendations, and that such perspectives should be incorporated into graduate training. It is no wonder then why clinicians and academicians alike are becoming more in tune with spiritual and religious beliefs, given that graduate training programs and counseling/clinical training sites report the incorporation of religion and spirituality in curriculum modules (Brawer, Handall, Fabricatore, Roberts, & Wajda-Johnston, 2002). Despite this fact, trainees and students have occasionally reported discomfort with such discussions (Souza, 2002). Thus, while the recognition and importance of spirituality are more universally accepted in this new millennium, it is our belief that the profession continues to suffer from both the absence of spirituality in the core or revised theories of personality, and a failure to adequately distinguish spirituality from religion and religiosity (Schulte, Skinner, & Claiborn, 2002; Souza, 2002; Serlin, 2005; and Wendell, 2003). Nevid's (2007) second edition of *Psychology: Concepts and Applications,* for example, mentions spirituality only once in the entire text, and even then, associates the concept with the positive psychology movement. Despite the fact that Nevid attributes the origins of positive psychology to the work of Seligman (2003), rather than with African-centered psychologists like Myers (1988); White (1972, 1984); Nobles (1986); White, Parham, and Parham (1980); and others who were talking about strength-based psychology decades before, he gives no coverage to the construct of spirituality in any depth. Similarly, Myers (2010) introduction to psychology text mentions spirituality very briefly, and only then in the context of a factor correlated with faith, health, and healing in helping individuals managing their stress.

Thankfully, there are those scholars who have sought to distinguish between the two constructs (Mattis & Jeager, 2001; Berkel, Armstrong, & Cokley, 2004), and their work has provided some clarifying perspectives. Two decades ago, Burkhardt (1989) sought to explore the concept of spirituality by suggesting that it was a process involving the unfolding mystery through harmonious inner-connectedness that springs from inner strength. In suggesting that life's experiences provide challenges that allow us to confront the purpose and meaning of life, individuals are believed to discover that purpose in relation to a higher being (God) and others in their lives. Meraviglia (1999) also weighed in on the discussion by asserting that spirituality is the experience and expressions of one's spirit in a unique and dynamic process reflecting faith in God or a supreme being; connectedness with oneself, others, nature, or God; and an integration of the dimensions of mind, body, and spirit. Also contributing to the discourse on spirituality is the work of Mattis (2000); and while her perspectives were anchored in the opinions of a primarily female sample, she captures a potent definition from the narratives provided by her women participants. Mattis concludes that spirituality was a belief in and connectedness to a higher internal and external power; consciousness and meta-physicality; understanding and acceptance of self; guidance and life instructions; peace, calm, and centeredness; positively influencing relationships with others; life purpose and meaning; and facilitation of efforts to manage adversity through support, strength, ability, and willingness to cope.

In extending the discussion, Mattis and Jager (2001) argue for a relational framework in studying religiosity and spirituality among African Americans. They advance the assumptions that religion and spirituality are relational phenomena and the very act of faith and belief in a higher power (God) places each of us in relationship with that divine force, as well as others in our lives. They define "religion" as a shared system of beliefs, mythology, and rituals associated with a God, and religiosity as an individual's adherence to those practices, beliefs, and doctrines. Spirituality on the other hand refers to an acknowledgement of a non-material force that permeates all affairs, human and non-human. Cervantes and Parham (2005) also discuss both the importance of spirituality in a counseling framework, and the necessity to distinguish between true spirituality and religiosity. In supporting the work of Nobles (1998), they argue that "spirit" is the core, animating principle and energy, and is the essence and substance of all matter. Spirit is described as the basis of all existence, including what we see and do not see. Spirit, they believe, likes Nobles and others before them, is the energy and life force in each human being, which acting like a Divine spark, gives humans their beingness.

In extending the discussion on spirituality, other authors have moved beyond mere definition to outline a multidimensional perspective on the construct (Jones, Wainwright, & Yarnold, 1986; Saint-Laurent, 2000). These dimensions, when taken individually, are represented in many definitions of spirituality. They include heightened awareness, connectedness to all living things, enlightenment, self-transcendence, compassionate wisdom, loving kindness, increased appreciation of how sacred life is and can be, and the capacity to serve others. Not only do these dimensions of spirituality distance themselves from religion and religiosity, but they also provide a way to view how spirituality is manifested in the life of each individual. These multidimensional aspects of spirituality represent an evolution of sorts, as some describe the construct as a process, rather than a product. Here, Brussat and Brussat (1996) inform our thinking by suggesting that embracing spirituality is really about embracing life's journey toward wholeness, where awareness is expanded, one's internal center is strengthened, one's purpose achieves clarity, inner demons are transformed, conscious intention is directive, and movement toward a deeper connection to one's spiritual self evolves.

In examining the various concepts of spirituality, one begins to see a parallel between these definitions and the conceptual template used for centuries by African people to describe their experience. While time and book length do not allow for an exhaustive review of differing African tribes, customs, and traditions, we focus here on the ancient Kemetic people of North Africa, the Yoruba people, the Bantu-Congo tradition, and the Akan people of Ghana, and their concept of spirituality, as articulated by Anthony Ephirim-Donkor in his 1997 text on *African Spirituality*. In doing so, we acknowledge that over the last three decades there has been a gradual but steady reengagement with indigenous African spiritual traditions in the United States brought about largely by influx of Cubans and Haitians into the United States and by African American traveling to and from the African continent. As result, there has been a steady increase in the African-American adherents to traditions like Vodun (by way of Haiti), Palo Mayombe (Bantu-Congo system), Santeria (by way of Cuba/West Africa), Ifa (by way of Nigeria) and the Akan tradition (by way of Ghana). Not surprisingly, a number of African-American psychologists have also become initiates into these traditions. Some have even begun to explore the psycho-spiritual modalities of these traditions and their potential heuristic and healing value in the psycho-therapeutic process (Grills and Rowe, 1998; Rowe & Msemaji, 2004; Nobles, 2008).

Within the African worldview, the basis of all knowledge is self-knowledge, and the self when distilled to its essence is spirit. Thus, within the African conception the basis of all knowledge is spiritual knowledge because all that exists is first and foremost spirit. Right away, it becomes apparent that we are dealing with a very different epistemology—a different order of knowledge—one that supplants the Western materialist mode of knowing and replaces it with an affective epistemology. Cheryl Grills (2004), along with Piper-Mandy and Rowe (2010), asserts that this epistemic shift is fundamental to the African-centered perspective, while Nobles (2008) notion of Sakhu positions African-centered psychology outside of the Western epistemological frame and recenters it within a Kemetic vis-a-vis indigenous African order of knowledge, thus suggesting a rethinking of relationships between the knowing, the knower, and the known.

THE CORE OF SPIRITUALITY

In exploring the core of spirituality in its African manifestation, it is important to travel back in time and engage the construct where civilizations first began. In doing so, perhaps no place better represents the concept of spirituality than ancient Kemet (Egypt), for it is there along the Nile Valley that early manifestations are evident. Concepts such as GOD, spirit and spirituality, systems of human interaction, and spirit energy existing in several domains are very evident. Kemetic people believed in supreme beings or deities who were thought to be responsible for creation, ruling the world, and controlling the universe. They also believe that rulers or pharaohs were the human manifestation of divine energy endowed by the CREATOR to rule over particular kingdoms or dynasties. Thus, as early as recorded time, you see a connection between GOD as a supreme being and those charged with managing the affairs of the people. The connection to the CREATOR was not simply a belief manifested in the titles given to or offices held by particular rulers, but rather was articulated in the expectation that those in high office should rule in ways that were pleasing to GOD. In essence, leadership in ancient times involved a social contract where one's position was intended to uplift the people and community, and address the needs of the collective before ministering to oneself. This is evident as one explores the concept of Ma'at (Karenga, 1990; Parham, 2002). Dr. Karenga (1990) explains that Ma'at was a code of conduct and a standard of aspiration for all of the ancient Kemetic people. It was characterized by seven cardinal virtues: truth, justice, righteousness, harmony, order, balance, and propriety. Thus, each citizen of a kingdom, whether pharaoh or servant, was expected to adhere to these behavioral aspirations. In doing so, one operationalizes the connection to the divine CREATOR by ruling and behaving in ways that would prove most aligned with the spiritual system of the time. Thus, there was no domain of daily life, including education, social, economic, political, religious, or family where Ma'at was not the attitudinal or behavioral aspiration. Beyond the aspirational nature of human conduct, it is also important to understand why such systems of human interaction carried such a high degree of salience for both ruler and citizen alike. The ancient Africans believed that at the end of one's life, people could achieve a oneness with the CREATOR by having their heart weighed against the feather of truth (Ma'at). If their heart was found to be as light as a feather, then they were judged by the assessors to have lived a good life, and were then presented before GOD's throne by the Son of GOD (no one comes to the Father except through the Son). That feat was achieved by living one's life in harmony with what was known as the forty-two sacred truths (or declarations of innocence), which included such admonitions as: "honor thy father and mother, thou shall not kill, steal or lie, and thou shall not bare false witness against thy neighbor or covet thy neighbor's material possessions." Indeed, this was a very elaborate and complex spiritual system.

Parallels can also be found in the Yoruba system and philosophy of spirituality, who like their Kemetic and Nubian Brothers and Sisters, believed in a SUPREME BEING, a heaven and earth, divine spirits or deities, and the existence of ancestral spirits beyond their earthly human forms. The Yoruba believe in a SUPREME BEING called OLDUMARE, who is the CREATOR and ruler of all things. They also believe in the existence of Orishas, who while serving as emissaries of OLDUMARE, earned their divine status through their great deeds. Thus, we see common elements of the concept of CREATOR, spirit beings, and the necessity of proper conduct in this African belief system. For the Yoruba, there is a belief in a power or energy that permeates the entire universe of human beings, plants, animals, and even inanimate objects. This energy emanates from the CREATOR and connects everything to the divine force in the universe, while various deities serve as the intermediaries between God and man. There is also an invisible and visible world, the latter of which has a physical and spiritual dimension. Physical disease in the Yoruba conception is a function and structure of body organs, but mental disorders are believed to be a result of several domains: natural sources, supernatural sources, preternatural sources, and inherited sources. Believing also in the relationship between people and the social environment in which they live and conduct their affairs, mental illness does have a social significance for interpersonal relationships. Thus, the Yoruba believe that irregularities in the physical/biological or social realm, which might be caused by deficiencies at birth, as a function of heredity, or resulting from certain social afflictions, can be the basis of mental illness. However, despite the techniques of traditional psychology and even medicine to diagnose and treat problems in individual domains, the Yoruba believe that assessments and interventions must be conducted in the biological, spiritual, psychological, and social. Those intervening are typically healers, who often specialize in being a herbalist, rainmaker, or diviner. Often, it is the diviners who are the most popular and inspire the most faith among the people, for they have the power to see beyond the physical to explore the spiritual, and it is in that realm where healing must take place. The Yoruba also believe that individuals acquire and choose their destiny prior to the transformation into a corporal being, but they are induced to forget the contents of that destiny prior to birth. Thus, the only way for a human being to access that destiny is through the power of divination; where in accessing the spiritual aspects of the visible and invisible world, aspects of their destiny are revealed to them by what are referred to as "witnesses to destiny." Mention should also be made here that the Yoruba believe that every aspect of mental illness cannot be cured, nor can it be cured permanently. They do however understand and believe that mental illness in people is often controlled by spirits and, because it may represent a spiritual attack, can only be addressed spiritually.

The Akan spiritual system also merits discussion here. Within the context of metaphysics, the Akan believe that each person has a nature that is both physical and spiritual. For the Akan, the interchange between the soul that originates from the CREATOR (kra); the physical body that serves as a container for the vital organs (nipadua); and the spirit or energy (sunsum) that, while immaterial in its power and nature, accounts for one's intellect, personality disposition, character, and individuality is the essence of African people's lived experiences. Ephirim-Donkor (1997) helps us understand that in the formation of an individual's life, the spirit (ntoro) of the male mingles with the blood (mogya) of the female to form the physical component of the personality. Thus, human beings were believed to have two components: one biological that was derived from the mother and one spiritual that was derived from the father. The father's sunsum is transmitted to his children during sexual intercourse and procreation, so that the "ntoro-sunsum" molds the child's personality and disposition during a child's formative years. So important was a father's influence on a child that children who do not come under that aegis may experience unhealthy lives, psychological maladies, or even death. Thus, in dealing with a psychological ailment later in life, one could not simply address the physical symptom consistent with the way Western medicines deal with illness and disease. Rather, one must address the spiritual core of the problem. In that regard, the Akan system would simply ask how one who struggles with a particular ailment could be properly treated without dealing with the spiritual elements of an individual's personality.

The Bantu-Congo system of cosmology also provides some fascinating insight into the concept of spirituality, that intangible energy and life force we have been speaking about. This system, as articulated by Fu-Kiau (1991, 2001) in his writings, argues that individuals are sacred at birth; and as human beings (muntu), we have the capacity for self-healing power. Humans are believed to be a "rising and living sun" who at the moment of their birth enter into a living community with a radiating potential for health and healing. That potential, or divine spark that constitutes their electrical energy, is bolstered or weakened by the circumstances surrounding their conception. Life then is about a process of perpetual and mutual communication of radiating waves of energy that are given off and received by individual human beings. Those waves, or oceans of energy as Fu-Kiau (2001) describes them, can be both positive and negative, and individuals can either be sensitive to or immune to the energy, in reacting to life circumstances in adaptive or maladaptive ways.

There are several factors believed to impact one's self-healing power; one of these is conception. Fu-Kiau explains that parents are the first and most important variable involving the functioning capacity of an individual's self-healing power. Collectively, they are believed to be responsible for children who are weak or strong or healthy or not. The Bantu-Congo believe that parents can be deliberate or unwitting players in the development of their children by what they do when selecting each other as mates and how they come to engage in the act of procreation. By selecting each other as partners, they seal the biogenetic rope that determines the composition of that seed of possibility that will become their children. The circumstances surrounding the act of lovemaking (both the mental state of mind and the physical state of being) then contribute to that energy that bonds the two parents together, influencing the character and overall mental and physical health of that child whose being is a result of that act between the mother and the father. Because both biogenetic and situational factors influence outcome in this case, adults attempt to avoid any circumstance during the act of love making or procreation that potentially depletes or contaminates the energy flow between those individuals, including angry or hostile spirits, alcohol or drug use, etc.

Another factor is gestation, or the physical environment in which the fetal child is carried and nurtured in the womb. The womb becomes the first physical environment that the child grows up in, and this environment influences both their eventual physical health and their self-healing power. Thus, nutrients or contaminants/toxins that a mother takes into her body can have the effect of either reinforcing a healthy first environment or contributing to the deterioration of one, making a child more vulnerable to illness once he or she is born. This latter circumstance is what is believed to contribute to health challenges a person experiences later in life, and a depletion of their self-healing power's potential.

That self-healing power and potential is central to an individual's well-being, according to the Bantu-Congo philosophy. Illness, both physical and mental, is believed to be related to a state of "body electron regression." In this regard, the body's and mind's loss of functioning efficiency and power is believed to be caused by a loss of the body's balance of energy, rather than by bacteria or virus. Thus, mental disorder and life dissatisfaction are related to a person's self-healing power being able to produce and regulate sufficient spiritual energy to manage daily stresses, life adversities, occasional depression, and situational anxiety. Thus, with this system of beliefs, much like that of the Ancient Kemetic, Akan, or others, one questions how any intervention by a mental health professional who does not address the fundamental nature of spirit, energy, and life force in a person could be effective.

THE ASSUMPTIONS OF SPIRITUALITY

The exploration of these belief systems still begs the question of what we mean by spirituality and how spirituality is manifested within African psychology principles and practices. Perhaps it makes sense to continue this segment of our discussion by delineating the assumptions that guide our thinking here. It is our position that the ultimate nature of reality is spirit, and that everything on this earth and in the universe that lives is spirit. We also believe that human beings are divine spirit energy manifested in human forms, and to be human is to be spirit energy in motion. We also assume that consciousness represents the ability of the human being to be aware of oneself in relationship to others, and all material things; and that the connection to the human condition is experienced through a review of one's history, one's experiences in the present, and one's anticipation of the future. As such, we also assume that our humanity is affirmed by recognizing the humanity in others, where reciprocal human relations and proper conduct are the experiential anchors of our beingness. What we are saying here, as Nobles (1986) and Ani (1994) have before us, is that spirit in its most elementary form is an energy or life force that is the inner essence and outer envelop of human beingness. Human beings emit energy that is both given and received by self and others across the spheres of time, place, person, and space. The modes of expression that serve as conduits to those spiritual connections to others are consciousness, emotions (joy, laughter, love, affirmation, belonging, pain, anger, and even hurt), and behaviors (both verbal and nonverbal). It is also our belief that life experiences provide opportunities to manifest spirit in relation to other people and the world around us. We also believe that humans are on a trajectory in life, seeking to align their consciousness with their destiny (this is the essence of the principle "Ori-Ire"). Consequently, there are forces in the universe that will both facilitate and/or inhibit that journey, and one's culture then helps to insulate the modes of expression from those forces that would negatively alter one's trajectory toward their own divine destiny.

THE MANIFESTATION OF SPIRITUAL ENERGY

In understanding that the core of our humanity is spiritual energy and life force, it seems appropriate to understand how that energy is manifested in the lives of African-descent people, and other members of the human family. In viewing the different systems and philosophies of various African traditions, the spiritual essence of human being is said to exist in the spirit of the ancestors, the biogenetic makeup of their parents, the intrauterine environment of the womb, the world of the mundane after birth, and back to the spirit world in which status as an ancestor is the goal. However, once arrived in the world where the spiritual and material join, the goal is to both search out and embrace one's destiny, while also leading a life that is ethically and morally proper. For the Akan, Ephirim-Donkor (1997) reminds us that they believe that prior to consciousness, children are endowed with a clairvoyance that enables them to maintain close rapport with the spirit counterparts in the ancestral world. Thus, children are both highly valued and cared for safely because of their telepathic ability and the possibility that they could be the ancestors arriving from the spirit world. Once growing in consciousness and with the cessation of their paranormal activity, children enter a phase of deliberate indoctrination

and education with the cultural mores, values, and ethos of African people designed to help them become good citizens. The goal here is to prepare young
children, and subsequently adolescents for the adult world, complete with the
obligations and responsibilities that accompany it. As a result of this deliberate
socialization, young people begin to exhibit the characteristics that allow them
to function effectively within the social, economic, political, spiritual, and
psychological domains of life, managing their affairs with standards of ethics
and morality.

In sum then, spirit energy reigns in various realms of reality (the past,
present, and future; the yet to be born, living, and deceased), and we contend
that the energy is then mobilized to meet the needs of the human organism, be
they physical, emotional, psychological, behavioral, or spiritual. Within the
African psychological tradition, that energy is often expressed across a number
of domains, and that can include relationship to the DIVINE force in the
universe, self-awareness of one's being and becoming, personal growth and
development, relationship and inner connectedness to others, alignment with
fundamental principles or truths (i.e. Ma'at), religiosity, and even the capacity
for resilience when life's hardships intervene to throw major challenges and
obstacles in the path of each man and woman. What are we saying with this
latter point? We are saying that there is a duality to our spirituality. And so, we
understand that anytime you have spirituality, particularly as it relates to African
descent and oppressed people, you will always find, as West (1999) reminds us,
instances of unjustified suffering, unmerited pain, and undeserved harm. The
question is not why does oppression or adversity occur, but rather, how do we
cope with it? The question, as we see it, in using our African-centered cultural
competencies in building for eternity is: How do we learn to transform the pain;
transcend the harm; and improvise on the suffering to achieve some level of intellectual, emotional, behavioral, and spiritual liberation for ourselves and the
clients we work with? And the recognition of this duality further requires that
we understand that where there is pain, there is healing; where there is despair,
there is hope; where there is suffering, there is comfort; and where there is a
mistake, there is redemption. That is the promise that our African-centered psychological theories should make to us; not that life will be trouble free or that
we are labeled with a diagnosis each time we show human vulnerability, but
that principled strength will be that rock to cling to in the storms of life.
Furthermore, once we find ourselves and the psychological spaces our clients
occupy taxed in ways that instigate excessive feelings of anxiety, depression,
fear, guilt, anger, and hurt, we should help ourselves and our clients understand
that there is a self-healing power within each of us that resides at the spiritual
core of our being.

Given this review, it now seems appropriate to ask ourselves several
questions and examine the tenets of the spiritual nature of one's personality
in an African-centered context: what are the assumptions that should guide a
clinician's discussions of spirituality; what does spirituality do for clients as
well as each of us; and what can it offer to our clients, students, community
folks, and indeed to the discipline of African psychology as a whole? By way

of assumptions, we have argued that there is a spiritual essence that permeates everything that exists in the universe. It is also assumed that spirit is DIVINE, as each individual's energy and life force is connected to that DIVINE force in the universe. We also assume that since spirit is energy, which can neither be created nor destroyed, it existed before, during, after, and beyond material existence. Finally, we are clear in assuming that the spirituality and religion are not the same. Within the context of these assumptions, we now ask ourselves: What can spirituality do for each of us as members of the human family, and why is it important for African people?

- First, spirituality becomes connected to authentic personhood, by providing an attachment to the Divine Force in the universe.
- Second, spirituality allows us to think more holistically about the personal nature of our being and one of the sources of our personal debilitations.
- Third, spirituality provides for and affirms our sense of power, by acknowledging the healing potential in all of us, and each person's ability to transform and transcend situational circumstances in ways that are beneficial.
- Fourth, spirituality helps demonstrate our connectedness to other members of the human family, as well as our relationship to all other things in GOD's universe that have life.
- Fifth, spirituality provides an assured sense of purpose, by instigating and alignment between one's consciousness and one's destiny (consistent with the Yoruba concept of Ori-Ire).
- Sixth, spirituality as an energy and life force becomes an aspiration in life such that it assists in our striving for a more ethically and morally centered way of being in the world. In that way, as children grow into adolescents, adolescents into adults, and then adults move into being eldership, being deemed an elder is less a function of arriving at a certain age plateau commiserate with retirement, but rather a title one earns by achieving some level of existential perfection in managing one's affairs with integrity and righteous character.

These are among the primary benefits that spirituality offers to each of us who constitute a healing presence in the lives of the students we teach, the clients we treat, and the people we touch. And it seems to us that our mission is to incorporate the notion and concept of spirituality into our instruction in the classroom, the counseling and clinical work we provide in therapy offices, and in the community centers we all find time to touch and interact with.

CLOSING

In closing this chapter, we would leave you with an important note of caution. We have deliberately introduced this notion of spirituality in this fourth edition because it is too important of the concept to be ignored in our work as psychologists and healers. We want you to see, much like the Bantu-Congo tradition articulated by Fu-Kiau (1991), or more recently the concept of spirituality addressed by Wade Nobles (2008) that makes plain the tri-fold unfolding nature of human beingness. They believe that to be human is to be an unfolding radiating spirit existing in the realms of the yet-to-be born, the living, and the afterlife (see tri-fold) that expresses itself as an ongoing process of being, belonging, and becoming through the complex experiences of culture and tradition (Nobles, 2008). That spiritual energy, as in interacts with our consciousness, continues to evolve in ways that allow for insights into who we are at the core of our being, who we belong to in the context of synthesizing cultural space and time, what power we possess in interacting with one's environment, and what possibilities we have to become a fuller manifestation of our divine potential. In essence, to be human is to be spirit in motion.

SPIRITUAL ILLNESS

While the understanding and articulation of the composition of spirit is important for our comprehension, we cannot close this chapter, however, without some mention of how one's spirit becomes ill or otherwise contaminated. Recall that whether one's spirit is nurtured in the womb or impacted after birth, there is a constant interaction with the environment. If that environment is healthy, nurturing, and otherwise supportive, then the flow of good energy is unabated, there is a conscious recognition of oneself and one's relationship to the DIVINE, there is a community connectedness to other members of one's cultural group as well as other members of the human family, there is an alignment of one's behaviors in support of a healthy and affirming lifestyle, and there is a social order guided by a respect for interpersonal contact and intimate relationships that are grounded in the tenets of Ma'at. However, if that environment becomes contaminated by chronic exposure to environmental toxins of the material or psychological variety, or agents of aggression that impose hostile and aggressive acts of malice, brutality, and hatred, then the being, belonging, and becoming motions of that spiritual energy are likely to be infected. And, given the spiritual connection to one's ancestral lines, it is highly possible that the infection, impurity, or contamination can be manifested in intergenerational ways, being passed down from adults to children, and beyond. Parenthetically, it should also be noted that much like an infected person can become a carrier of disease and illness, so to do people, once sufficiently infected by the virus of dehumanization and negative spiritual energy, begin to infect others in ways that are analogous to self-imposed destruction. In essence, if the "host" culture of brutality and racial denigration is racism and White supremacy perpetuated by particular racial groups (i.e., White people), and that chronic mental, spiritual, and physical brutality is imposed on African-American people over space and time, then it is possible that African-American people, once infected and unable to resist the spread of that mental disease, will no longer depend on White people and racism to contribute to their dehumanization: They adapt that mantle themselves. Remember, it was Carter G. Woodson (1933) who reminded us that if you allow people to control the way you think, then you do not have to assign them an inferior status; if necessary, they will seek it for themselves. Thus, when one looks at the condition of African-descent people in America and globally, one can see the vestiges of that contaminated spiritual energy that manifests itself in the ideas of reference African Americans ascribe to themselves (derogatory labels like nigger, nigga); the negative attitudes and feelings we project onto other Black people (Black people are less than human, so I ascribe no value to their life or existence [see the out of control homicide statistics for young Black males nationally]); the deteriorating relations we have with other people of African descent who represent our children, family, and our community (increasing incidence of child and elder abuse, sexual assault, family disintegration, unhealthy male-female relationships, and gang participation); and the patterns of behavior we display in response to life situations and circumstances (use and abuse of alcohol, drugs, and tobacco; consumption of unhealthy foods that contribute to obesity, diabetes, cardiovascular disease; and other illnesses).

Thus, if you are a clinician or counselor committed to treating an individual who may be depressed about a situation, anxious about certain aspects of their life, unsatisfied with the quality of their familial or intimate relationships, concerned about their relationship with their children or parents, troubled by their lack of productivity, confused about their identity, unhappy with their self-image, or angry about instances of unfairness and inequality in their life, you cannot assume that the target of your therapeutic intervention is relegated to their thoughts, feelings, or behaviors. For in reality, there is some degree of spiritual contamination that is negatively impacting their lives, and it is the spiritual nature of their existence and humanity that must be addressed if healing is going to occur.

Finally, it is our belief that people can never learn to love, appreciate, and respect things in other people that they first do not understand, love, and appreciate in themselves. Professionals and students alike cannot expect to align their spirit and the energy and life force it represents, with another member of the human family (particularly African-American clients), if they themselves are out of touch with their own energy, and disconnected from the source of their ultimate power, which is their spirituality. For it is in spirit and spirituality that human authenticity lies, and it is there that African-centered psychology differs from Freud, Adler, Rogers, Ellis, Perls, and the other personality theorists who are caught in the throws of conceptual incarceration that only sees their Eurocentrically oriented theories focused on cognition, affect, and behavior as the gateway to our psyche. And even in cases where the importance of spirituality is mentioned or recognized, much like in the works of Corey (2005), it continues to be anchored in an acknowledgment of a counselor's need to recognize the client's religious preferences and what importance they play in the client's life. This is essentially belief system analysis. In this current space and time, that simply will no longer do. African psychology has embraced a different reality than the one we have all been trained and indoctrinated with. For in reality, we are not human beings having occasionally spiritual experiences; but rather, we are spiritual beings having occasional human ones (Yogi Yogananda, 1946).

4

■ ■ ■

The African-American Family

Analysis and portrayals of the African-American family have been among the most talked about and studied aspects of Black life in America for many decades. But perhaps we should begin this discussion with a look back to some of the earliest conversations and debates of the Black family, so that we can provide a proper context. In the 1940s, an important debate centering on the African-American family was begun, and it would indelibly shape the way African-American life and culture would be studied, researched, taught, discussed, and understood in universities, federal agencies, and think tanks around the country for decades. And in the process, it would not only shape public perceptions about the African Americans and African-American families but also play a pivotal role in shaping public policy on the African-American family as well.

The "debates" were carried out in a series of articles, lectures, and books by two scholars operating at the height of their scholarly powers. These scholarly exchanges were notable in a number of regards: for the topic under discussion, African-American cultural identity and humanity; for the high quality of scholarly rigor and trenchant analysis brought to bear on the debate; for the respective ethnicities of the two men involved in the debate; for the disciplinary and sociopolitical spaces from which those arguments were advanced; and for the ways in which the ensuing discourse and scholarship would shape public policy around the African-American family. The echoes of which can be still heard in contemporary discussions and policies devoted to addressing the current challenges confronting African-American families.

The respective position that each scholar advanced was as divergent as the two men advancing them—one an African-American scholar (or in the parlance of the day, a Negro) and the other a Jewish-American scholar. And while the ethnicity of the scholars was not central to the debate, it was not insignificant. This was after all the 1940s and racial apartheid with all of its pernicious cultural logic was still enshrined in the law—the Civil Rights Act was not passed until 1964, followed by the Voting Rights Act in 1965—as was an American brand of xenophobia that had been unleashed in the advent of World War II with Roosevelt's Executive Order 9066, which interned Japanese Americans in concentration camps. It was against the backdrop of these historic events and the general mood of the country that the race/ethnicity of the scholars took on a significantly larger sociopolitical dimension.

One scholar was a sociologist by training; the other an anthropologist—both had received exemplary training from top-tier programs, from pioneers in their respective fields. The sociologist had taken his doctorate in sociology from the University of Chicago, at the time the preeminent program in the country, under the direction of Robert E. Parks, who had pioneered a method of urban sociology rooted in a theory of social disorganization that would become highly influential.

The anthropologist had taken his doctorate from Columbia University, the first doctorate anthropology program in America, under the venerable Franz Boas, who himself had practically pioneered the field of cultural anthropology in the United States. Both scholars had done fieldwork with African populations outside of the United States. The sociologist had conducted a study on the black family in Brazil, while the anthropologist had done fieldwork in Dahomey (now Benin). Each had produced controversial works on African Americans that challenged the orthodoxy, radically altered the prevailing logic, and enhanced a particular understanding African-American life and culture. And each would go on to pioneer critical areas of study within their respective fields.

That one scholar would be a sociologist and the other an anthropologist was not unusual and very much in keeping with the prevailing cultural logic of the times, at least as it extended to discussions on African Americans. In the 1940s and 1950s, in most centers of power and learning African-American inferiority was not merely an assumption—it was accepted prima facie, as fact. In this intellectual climate of the 1940s and 1950s, the question was not *if* African Americans were inferior, but rather *what* were the causes of their inferiority. For many sociologists working in this area, the disciplinary emphasis was on understanding which of the assumed pathological forms of African-American social disorganization was most responsible for African-American inferiority.

In anthropology, the question upon which most anthropologists occupied with the question of race focused their gaze was on African-American acculturation to European American culture or the lack thereof (i.e., the pathological cultural orientation of African Americans). Although both disciplines employed different methods, they shared the same epistemological assumption: That middle-class European Americans were the normative, thus appropriate, evaluative standard. It was against this canvass of racial apartheid, ethnocentric bias, and pseudo-scientific racism with all of its incarcerating logic that these two scholars attempt to paint two contrasting pictures of African-American cultural realities. It is not overstatement to say that there is no discussion about or scholarship produced on the African-American family that falls outside of the terms of the debate as these two scholars were able to define them six decades ago. The debates came to be known as the *Herskovits-Frazier Debate*.

THE HERSKOVITS-FRAZIER DEBATE

In the 1940s E. Franklin Frazier, an African-American sociologist, was perhaps the most influential African-American scholar in the country, second only to the polymathic W.E. B. Dubois (whom he considered a mentor) whose considerable influence was waning. Frazier was an impressive figure who managed to balance two seemingly disparate worlds. An ardent and vigorous champion of civil rights, who spent most of his scholarly career at historically Black Universities (he was at Howard University for the last twenty years of his career), but who nonetheless was so well respected by his European-American peers that he became the first African American chosen as the head of a national professional association in the United States. In 1948 E. Franklin Frazier was chosen as the thirty-eighth president of the American Sociological Association (then the American Sociological Society). It is worth noting that it was not until 1970 that the American Psychological Association elected a person of color, Kenneth Clarke,[1] as its president.

In 1950, Frazier was among a select group of scholars and researchers from around the world who helped craft the UNESCO statement *The Race Question*, which had challenged the reification of scientific theories such as eugenics. And from 1951 to 1953, Frazier also served as the chief of the division of Applied Social Sciences of UNESCO. Over the course of an illustrious career, Frazier produced a series of seminal books on the African-American life and culture, among them the infamous *Black Bourgeoisie* (1957) and *The Negro Church* (1963)—as well as more than one hundred scholarly articles and book chapters.[2]

However one book above all others established his reputation as a major thinker on race issues. *The Negro Family in the United States* (1939) was/is considered a classic work of sociology by many scholars. In 1939, it received the Anisfield-Wolf Award, which is given for the most important work in the area of race relations. Even W.E.B Dubois, the most important intellectual African America had/has produced and among the most influential thinkers of the twentieth century, thought Frazier's book to be a classic work of sociology. In a book review in the 1940 volume 9 edition of the *Journal of Negro Education*, Dubois wrote that "the book is not only a great and significant contribution to the science of sociology it is also a piece of English literature which one can take joy in reading." (p. 212–213)

In *The Negro Family in the United States*, Frazier asserted, among other things, that African cultures had not survived their violent contact with Western cultures, that the centuries long aftermath of that violent collision with the lethal combination of Western avarice, commerce, and human indifference that spawned the American system of slavery had stripped Africans of all vestiges of African culture. He further argued that the African American was a unique, singular American creation forged in the crucible of the enslavement experience. And that the African-American family's social disorganization was a byproduct of its unsuccessful attempt to adapt to the various socio-ecological pressures produced as a result of slavery and oppression. That in fact, African Americans suffered from what the Harvard sociologist Orlando Patterson following Frazier's lead would later term as *Natal Alienation*. And as we will see momentarily, in many regards, Frazier's work would inadvertently lend support to the foundation subtending the cultural deprivation school of the thought that informed so many of the policies developed around *rescuing* the African-American family.

The Jewish anthropologist Melville Herskovits's experience, training, and field study had brought him to a different conclusion, one that challenged and directly contradicted the thesis put forward by Frazier. Herskovits in his path-breaking book *The Myth of the Negro Past* (1941) asserted that there were indeed West African cultural retentions and cultural patterns that had not only survived slavery but could also be directly linked to West African cultures, and that many of these Africanisms were still a vital and vibrant part of African-American culture. In many regards, Herskovits book was written as a rejoinder to Frazier's *The Negro Family in the United States* (1939).

Herskovits was an impressive figure in his own right, widely credited with introducing the notion of cultural relativism into anthropology. In 1948 (incidentally, the same year that Frazier was elected president of American Sociological Association) Herskovits founded the first major interdisciplinary African studies at Northwestern University. A long-time defender of African human rights, he was among a small chorus of voices after World War II that advocated strongly for African Independence. Herskovits is considered by many to be the doyen of Africana studies in the United States.[3]

In discussing the Herskovits-Frazier Debate, it is important to note that all through the 1940s and 1950s American Apartheid was not only deeply embedded in the social mores and cultural fabric of American life, it was still the law of the land, ensconced in the Constitution. Thus the debate, whatever its intellectual merits, can neither be sufficiently understood simply by an examination of the contending points of the debate. For subtending the debate was a complex miasma of racial and cultural complexities fused to an equally complex sociopolitical context, all of which not only informed and shaped the debate. Aside from the intriguing irony of a European-American scholar (Herskovits) arguing that African Americans had African cultural traditions that had not only survived in some forms but also informed contemporary African-American cultural life,[4] and an African-American scholar (Frazier) arguing that slavery had destroyed all vestiges of African culture, there was a larger sociopolitical context hovering ominously over the debate: Civil Rights—the African-American quest for human rights and equal opportunity. For while Herskovits had advanced a provocative thesis that highlighted the distinctive Africanity of African Americans in the form of African cultural retentions, it was also equally true in the pre-civil rights social and political climate of the1940s and 1950s, and as a European American, he was free to argue for an African-American cultural distinctiveness in a way that was not true for Frazier. For Frazier, as an African American, a staunch civil rights activist and a pragmatist, there was much more at stake than a scholarly debate. That is, the pragmatic strategy for Frazier as an African-American scholar was to focus on a narrative of cultural assimilation rather than one of cultural differentiation—to emphasize the prosaic Americaness of African Americans. Thus, Frazier's focus on the Americaness of African Americans fits well into the prevailing civil rights narrative on racial acceptance, assimilation, and equality.

In this regard, it could be argued that both arguments were shaped by the social, cultural, and political context of the 1940s and 1950s. Both perspectives had some inherent limitations that also carried with them socio-political implications. Herskovits' position, which advanced a notion of cultural complexity, attempted to situate African Americans within the broader dimensions of an African context. However, in so doing he risked potentially giving rise to an argument that placed them further outside of the American one. Frazier, who sought to situate African Americans within the mainstream American sociocultural context, had placed them culturally outside of the African context. The debate would span two decades. Both the Frazier's and Herskovits' positions continued to reverberate in many academic discussions and public policy debates on African-American life and culture throughout the 1960s and into the 1970s. The essential tensions of the Herskovits-Frazier debate have never been fully resolved and can be found in nearly every policy debate on African-American life and culture from education to IQ, from theories poverty to theories identity, from social sciences to the humanities.

As we have seen, one of the central elements of the Frazier school of thought was its insistence that the American system of slavery was nearly ubiquitous in its oppressive force and control over every aspect of African life on the plantation, and that the effect was the total eradication of whatever African culture had been carried in the cargo holds of the slavers' ships. And while the Herskovits' perspective was compelling, it was the Frazier perspective that was the dominant one until the 1970s. A straight line can be drawn from Frazier's work[5] to later works by Kenneth M. Stampp's *The Peculiar Institution: Slavery in the Ante-bellum South* (1956), Stanley M. Elkins' *Slavery: A Problem in American Institutional and Intellectual Life* (1969), and Eugene D. Genovese, *Roll, Jordan, Roll; the World the Slaves Made* (1974). And most notably in Daniel Patrick Moynihan's *The Negro Family: A case for National Action* (1965) in which both Frazier and Elkins were cited.

Even as we write this fourth edition of this text, now some 70 years removed from those earliest discussions, the psychological, sociological, and even educational literature are bursting with study after study that seek to render judgment about the family's viability in maintaining a cohesive unit of intergenerational continuity (Sudarkasa, 1981), rearing their children properly (Fields, 2003), stimulating intellectual growth and creativity (Desimone, 2001), providing for economic support of it's members (James, 1998), indoctrinating and socializing children in culturally congruent values and ways of behaving (Mc Adoo, 2006), and serving as a source of protection for nuclear and extended family members (Hill, 1971; Taylor, Jackson, & Chatters, 1997). In some respects, we are delighted to see the continued focus on the African-American family for much of what exists in the literature today stands in sharp contrast to 1940s portraits illustrated earlier, the distorted and racist paradigms of decades ago (Moynihan, 1965; Rainwater, 1970), and even more recent television documentaries whose insights into Black family life and culture were too contaminated by the mindsets of old (Moyers, 1986).

In the former regard, we are reminded about the notion of a tale of two conversations that not only helps us frame a historical context for research on African-American families, but also sets the stage for understanding the debates and implementation of public policy as well. On February 21, 1965, at the Audubon Ballroom in Manhattan, a tall, handsome, angular man with a warm smile and a piercing, intelligent gaze stepped to the microphone to address a rapt audience of about 400 people, most of whom had assembled at the Sunday afternoon meeting of the Organization of Afro-American Unity (OAAU) eager to hear the electrifying speaker share his solutions to the African-American dilemma. As the speaker began to deliver his remarks, there was a coordinated disturbance, followed by a maelstrom of fire and lead. When the shooting subsided, screams, confusion, and gun smoke hung in the air like cumulus clouds, and the speaker, Malcolm X, lay bleeding to death on the stage of the Audubon Ballroom, felled by assassins' bullets. Malcolm X would be pronounced dead on arrival at Columbia Presbyterian Hospital. He was 39.

Prior to his death, Malcolm X had been calling for a reassessment of African-American realities, an assessment rooted in collective self-definition, self-defense, and self-determination incorporated in a form of Pan African unity. His call for African-American unity and self-development rooted in African-American culture would reverberate in the Black Power/Black Arts movements of the late 1960s and early 1970s. (The reverberation of those ideas would resonate within a small coterie of thinkers within psychology and eventually give birth to the Black Psychology Movement).

Malcolm X's call for a sort of African-American unity rooted in the reclamation of what was both best and beautiful about African-American culture was not new or even original. Malcolm was standing firmly within an intellectual and cultural tradition, an unbroken circle that traced its roots from the Haitian revolution through the enslaved African revolts through the abolitionist movements, extended from the nineteenth century through the twentieth century in the form of African-American discourse, debate, disputation, and scholarship. It expressed itself most palpably in the works and words of the nineteenth-century thinkers like David Walker, Edward Wilmot Blyden, Alexander Crummell, Frederick Douglass, and Martin Delaney. And its vitality continued into to the twentieth century with thinkers like Anna Julia Cooper, Hubert Harrison, Marcus Garvey, Carter G. Woodson, and the inimitable WEB Dubois among others, thinkers, and activists who attempted to wrestle with the "Negro problem" by focusing on African-American cultural integrity. Malcolm X in calling for African-American cultural unity was tapping into deep reservoir of African-American cultural integrity and resiliency.

In the same universe but in a different world, Daniel Patrick Moynihan, a relatively young sociologist, serving first within the John F. Kennedy, and then the Lyndon B. Johnson Administration as the Assistant Secretary of Labor for Policy Planning and Research, was constructing a different narrative on

African-American life and culture, one that would offer his own solution to the "Negro Problem." In March of 1965, a month after the assassination of Malcolm X and less than a year after the passage of the Civil Rights Act of 1964, it would be advanced as part of the Johnson Administration's Great Society, which Johnson had outlined in his State of the Union in January of that year, as part of larger vision to address poverty, racial injustice, education, medical care, and urban problems. Moynihan's discussion of the challenges facing the African-American family and the possible solutions would be laid out in *The Negro Family: The Case for National Action* or as it later became known *The Moynihan Report*. In cautioning that the Civil Rights Act of 1964 was only the beginning—and not the end—of African-Americans struggle for equality, Moynihan (1965) wrote in his report that:

> The racist virus in the American blood stream still afflicts us: Negroes will encounter serious personal prejudice for at least another generation. Second, three centuries of sometimes unimaginable mistreatment have taken their toll on the Negro people. The harsh fact is that as a group, at the present time, in terms of ability to win out in the competitions of American life, they are not equal to most of those groups with which they will be competing. Individually, Negro Americans reach the highest peaks of achievement. But collectively, in the spectrum of American ethnic and religious and regional groups, where some get plenty and some get none, where some send eighty percent of their children to college and others pull them out of school at the 8th grade, Negroes are among the weakest.

He went on further, noting that the "most difficult fact for White Americans to understand is that in these terms the circumstances of the Negro American community in recent years has probably been getting *worse, not better.*" The Moynihan report identified a "new kind of national goal: the establishment of a stable Negro family structure." For Moynihan, then, the major impediment to African-American progress was the gradual erosion of the African-American family, the root causes of which were slavery, racial injustice, and their structural corollaries unemployment and poverty—with the matriarchal structure of the African-American family serving as both a behavioral cause and effect. Thus, before 1965 was three months old, the public policies that would inform how African-American family life and culture would be understood, as well as how those policies would inform and transform African-American life for the next four decades, had already been firmly established.

The Moynihan Report, however well-intentioned, fused European-American cultural norms with a particular brand of European-American ethnocentrism, which was informed by a belief in the cultural and intellectual inferiority of African Americans. The result was public a cultural deprivation model—one which denied African Americans the very attributes that are characteristic of all human groups—cultural variation, adaptation, innovation, and complexity—which then became reified as public policy. The Moynihan

Report assumed African Americans to be a monolith. As the cultural critic, Greg Tate put it:

> Perhaps the supreme irony of Black American existence is how broadly black people debate the question of cultural identity among themselves while getting branded as a cultural monolith by those who would deny us the complexity and complexion of a community, let alone a nation. If Afro Americans have never settled for the racist reductions imposed upon them—from chattel slaves to cinematic stereotype to sociological myth—it's because the black collective conscious not only knew better but also knew more than enough ethnic diversity to subsume those fictions.

However, the belief in cultural and intellectual inferiority of African Americans was not new in America, it was/is as fundamental to the development of the United States as the constitution, which was enshrined in that very document until the thirteenth and fourteenth amendments. It can be found in the seminal ideas of the European Enlightenment in the works of such thinkers as David Hume and John Locke and in the nineteenth-century works of de Gobineau and Francis Galton, among many others. It should be said that every scholar is a prisoner of her/his time, and the freedom of insight comes from recognizing the limitations imposed by ones temporal-spatial incarceration. The Moynihan Report was, in many regards, emblematic of the scholarly zeitgeist of the 1960s in which the knowledge produced about African-American life and culture was often produced by European-American scholars who were positioned, either by virtue of culture or by virtue of perspective, on the periphery of the African-American experience.

Perhaps the most salient flaw in the Moynihan Report was its prima facie assumption that African Americans had no culture worthy of consideration, thus no internal cultural resources to resuscitate itself, and that whatever African culture they possessed after enduring the middle passage was ineradicably destroyed upon contact with the American system of slaveocracy. This fundamental assumption allowed the Moynihan Report to accept as truth that African Americans were merely dark-skinned European Americans and thus to view any deviations from the European-American cultural norm as a form of deprivation. Because this conceptual incarceration presented itself as fact, it appears that Moynihan never consulted a long unbroken stream of African-American scholarship, debate and discourse on African American-cultural integrity that began in the seventeenth century and crystallized in the twentieth century.

For there in the social science literature exists an uninterrupted conversation between African-American thinkers about African-American life and culture—its strengths, aspirations, and limitations—as well as numerous forward thinking agendas for African-American progress[6] This unbroken intergenerational conversation began with the arrival of the first Africans to American shores in the seventeenth century. It continued through the eighteenth century to reaching a crescendo with the nineteenth-century nationalist and abolitionist thinkers like David Walker (1829), Bishop Henry McNeal Turner, Henry

Highland Garnett, Edward Wilmot Blyden (1908), Alexander Crummell and Martin Delaney (1852), who were animated and inspired by the Haitian Revolution. And it continued right into the twentieth century in the ideas and actions of thinkers as varied as Alain Leroy Locke, Zora Neale Hurston, Langston Hughes, Anna Julia Cooper, Charles Johnson, Carter G. Woodson, and WEB Dubois, among many others.

This long intergenerational conversation, however, seemed to have escaped Moynihan's attention and research. Moynihan did not create the cultural deprivation/cultural deficit thesis; he merely appropriated it from a different much older narrative: cultural inferiority. In order to understand how the themes of cultural inferiority and cultural deprivation came to inform much of the research on the African-American family that Moynihan and other social scientists of the 1960s and 1970s came to lean on, it is important to provide some additional historical context. For much of the research and scholarship on the African-American family that has shaped the public policies that have their crystallization in a much older debate, one which profoundly influenced Daniel Patrick Moynihan research and his ensuing report.

In this latter regard, we fast-forward over twenty years into the mid-1980s, when the award winning journalist Bill Moyers, who was then with CBS, was recognized for his work entitled: "CBS Reports: The Vanishing Family—Crisis in Black America." According to the New York Times, it was described by the panel of judges as "an unflinching account that tries to understand why this disintegration started and why it continues." It was recognized with a "gold baton," which was annually awarded to the program "judged to have made the greatest contribution to the public's understanding of important issues or news events." While the larger mainstream media may have viewed that piece of journalism as award winning and insightful, the airing of that program contributed mightily to the perpetual stereotypes authored in the 1960s and 1970s, which described the Black family as headed mainly by women single head of households, who were plagued by generations of poverty, low education, teenage pregnancy, a welfare mentality, oversexed and irresponsible male figures, and a mindset that saw no way out of the impoverished conditions that so dominated their inner city lifestyles.

There is no arguing that there is a segment of African America that resembles the cast of characters and the conditions endured in that documentary of more than 20 years ago. However, what is disturbing are the slices of Black life curiously omitted in Moyers' (1986) piece, and the way those distorted depictions continue to resonate with the national psyche where poverty, unemployment, teenage pregnancy, female-headed households, and violent surroundings are the templates used to characterize the modern-day life in African America. There are a host of other realities in Black family life that deserve equal coverage, and numerous stories of survival, commitment, and determination that not only more accurately reflect contemporary life among America's citizens of African descent, but also point to a people's resolve that is more "strength based" (Hill, 1971) as opposed to pathology driven. What about those families that have two parents? What about those whose children grew up without getting pregnant, being arrested, dropping out of school, or meeting an untimely death at the hands of street crime or gang violence. How about those families who are solidly middle class, have well-educated parents, own rather than rent their own home, attend church regularly, send their children to weekend and summer camps, give generously of their personal resources in philanthropic ways, take care of aging and elderly parents, and send their children to colleges and universities all across this nation. If we are going to understand the psychology of African Americans, we must have a more genuine and authentic feel for the people, their history, culture, and social conditions. This chapter seeks to do just that.

SNAP SHOTS VS. VIDEOTAPES

Every picture captures within its frame a fragmentary moment of reality—an element of truth. However, we must also be clear when we look at the photo, more reality escapes the lens than is captured within it, and the viewer relies on context real or imagined to interpret the meaning of the picture. So too there is no arguing that Moyer's snapshot captured some realities for a segment of African America. However, what is disturbing is that Moyers' (1986) piece assumed that the snapshot *was* the entire picture, and thus the whole segments of African-American life were curiously omitted in a way that distorted larger realities, distortions that continue to resonate with the national psyche. Poverty, unemployment, teenage pregnancy, female-headed households, and violent surroundings realities in African-American life are to be sure but they are not African-American life. They are snapshots of segment of African-American life and culture. This important distinction escaped Moyer's lens—his apperceptive field—and thus he failed to capture fully the larger realties of modern-day life in African America. In effect, when Moyers was taking pictures of the trees, he mistakenly assumed he was taking pictures of the whole forest. His documentary piece, however award winning it was, never bothered to make an entire "videotape" of the realities of Black life in America.

There are a host of other realities in African-American family life that deserve equal attention if one seeks to develop a more accurate picture of the African-American family. However when the lens is positioned to capture only those realities that are pathology driven rather "strength based" (Hill, 1972), the larger reality escapes the frame. There are, after all, numerous individual and collective stories of success and survival, courage and perseverance, resilience and determination in the face of seemingly insuperable odds that more accurately reflect contemporary life among America's citizens of African ancestry.

THE INDICTMENT AND RESPONSE TO BLACK FAMILY LIFE: WHITE VS. BLACK PORTRAYALS

Portraits of the historic Black family from a more culturally specific perspective have been provided by such notable scholars as Billingsley (1968), Staples (1994), Johnson and Staples (2004), Mc Adoo (2006), and Myers (1982).

Collectively, they paint a very comprehensive picture of Black family life and culture that stands in sharp contrast to those proposed by researchers in the Eurocentric-oriented perspective. Gates (1994), for example, in his memoire entitled "Colored People," discusses the range of biological and social supports that formed his family network. In arguing for the importance of the extended family network, despite the two parent intact family he grew up in, he ably articulates how the extended family contributed to a wholesome upbringing where attributes of mutual support, caring, loving, discipline, accountability, achievement with a standard of excellence, determination, and a sense of real community were all part of that experience for African-American families, even in a small West Virginia town. He also reminds us that the "colored world" was less about a neighborhood and more about a condition of existence. The profile of Harvard University's Du Bois Professor of African-American studies paints an interesting picture of Black family life in rural America. Beyond the interesting portrait however is a revelation that in spite of family composition, the successful family unit does find a way to continue meeting the needs of its youngest and most elderly members. This point is reinforced in the writings of Barack Obama (2004, 2006), arguably one of the most important and influential figures to be thrust onto the American political and media landscape. Obama's story is typical of a slice of life in African-American families where some Black children are products of inter-racial unions, experience some separation from one or the other parent, struggle with economic hardship, and then grow up in a family system where extended family members assist the single-parent mother or father in supporting childrearing efforts. In Obama's case, you see a strong influence by his grandmother and grandfather, who at some point in his early life, assumed the primary role for care giving. But again, more important than the family composition was that family unit's ability to provide for his basic necessities, and instill in him a proper socialization, complete with family lessons and values that were forged out of the experiences that collided with their life's journey. Among these included: love and respect of parents and elders, the importance of education, a multicultural understanding and acceptance of the human condition, difficulties of being different and how that makes adjustments difficult, the value of work, and the importance of service to one's community and country. Indeed, these have served him well as he has ascended to the highest office in the country, being the first African American in the history of the United States to do so. All of this has occurred against a backdrop of a challenging childhood, where adolescent rebelliousness, negative peer influence, some drug use, and less than total focus in school characterized earlier parts of his life. And yet, with the help of family, he found a way to persevere through adversity, graduate from high school, receive an Ivy League education, graduate at the top of his class at Harvard Law School, serve terms in the Illinois State and United States Senate, and then become the president of the United States.

While the Obama story is a fascinating study in character development of a young African-American male who grew up without his father, caution must be exercised in looking at his story, for it echoes a too familiar but concerning tone about the unavailability of Black Fathers in the lives of their children. Our concern for the way Obama's experience is likely to be portrayed in the larger media reinforces what Connor and White (2006) discuss in the text on Black fathers. In their book, they discuss the important roles that African-American fathers play in the lives of their children and families. Connor and White underscore the realities of social fathering and generative fathering, where despite media portrayals to the contrary, African-American men do engage their children in meaningful ways, love and care for them, and desire interaction with them as well.

CONTEMPORARY DEMOGRAPHIC PROFILES

Understanding the African-American family of today does require some reliance on statistical data derived from sources like the U.S. Census data (2000), and national studies on Black family life (Taylor, Jackson, & Chatters, 1997; Johnson & Staples, 2004; Jones & Jackson, 2005; Mc Adoo, 2006). These scholars paint a much more comprehensive and informative portrait of the Black family, and it is their perspectives we rely on for our profile. To begin with, we note a significant population shift in demographic percentages where African Americans are no longer the only racial ethnic group of significant size in America. Clearly, Latinos and Asians are now commanding their share of the demographic proportions, and African-descent people are but one of many groups collectively referred to as "people of color." In the 1970s, there were 22.6 million African Americans, constituting some 11 percent of the population. In 2003, that number had grown to 36.4 million, making 13 percent of the population. Data also suggest that population centers are also changing in urban versus rural preferences, while geographical locations seem to have remained constant. In the 1970s, 60 percent of Blacks lived in urban cores of U.S. cities, compared to just 53 percent in 2005. This represents a shift away from the central cities of America. However, 54 percent of all African Americans continue to reside in the South, with 19 percent in both the Midwest and Northeast regions, and 8 percent in the West.

There were some 8.7 million African-American families according to the 2000 U.S. census (the last year in which a full census was taken), compared to only 4.9 million in 1970. The growth in the number of families has indeed increased, but the percentage of married couple families has declined over the past thirty-five years from 68 percent in the 1970s to a mere 48 percent in the early 2000s. While the decline in intact nuclear families is of significant concern, the profile illustrates that nearly half of all Black families do enjoy a two-parent lifestyle. This data stands in sharp contrast to that presented in the documentaries previously discussed where 100 percent of the characters profiled came from single-parent unions.

The family's ability to meet many of its needs, in some respects, is contingent upon labor force participation. Data reveal that overall 66 percent of African Americans participate in the labor force with Black men participating at a rate of 68 percent and Black women at 64 percent. Whites on the other hand participate at rates of 74 percent and 61 percent for men and women respectively, according to the 2000 census. Interestingly, some scholars and authors continue to argue that persons of African descent suffer the most persistent forms of racism and discrimination, and there are some data that seem to reinforce that sentiment. In 1970, the unemployment rate for Blacks was a staggering 10 percent compared with just 5 percent among White workers. In the early 2000s, the unemployment data still reveal that Black unemployment is still twice that of their White counterparts. Within the labor force, Whites are twice as likely to be in white-collar jobs compared with Blacks, and 54 percent of Blacks are employed in blue-collar positions. Pay equity for African descent people continues to be an issue as well as Blacks continue to earn just sixty-one dollars for every one hundred dollars earned by White men and women. In the 1970s, African Americans earned on average $22,000 per year compared with $37,000 for Whites. In the early 2000s, African American's average income had risen to $27,900 per year, while the income of their White counterparts averaged $44,400. Consequently, poverty continues to be an issue many, but not all families confront, but the effects are more keenly felt among those single-parent households.

CHALLENGES CONFRONTING TODAY'S FAMILIES OF AFRICAN DESCENT

In thinking through the challenges confronting today's African-American family, it is important not to romanticize the family structure too much. That posture sets a dangerous precedent for it invites those who research and study this element of Black life in America to rationalize away defects in the way families function, and attribute any peculiarities to "something cultural" that must have its origins in the recesses of African history and culture. If the truth be told, even with its strengths, there are aspects of Black family life that still do not function well. And perhaps, that remains one of the central challenges of an African psychology movement and perspective: to help the family extricate itself from the quagmire of social pathologies that conspire to destroy the functioning efficiency of the family unit.

Among the biggest issues families must address is poverty, and the grip that this social disease has on our community. Ironically, there is no specific definition of poverty that experts agree on. Some might argue for a strict definition based on specific income levels. Others might choose a more qualitative definition where insufficient access to material means necessary to meet an individual's or family's basic needs is what defines the construct. In this latter case, it is also important to understand that the qualitative dimension of the discussion also invites one to consider that there are psychological and not just economic factors that create an air of deprivation. In this regard, it is important to be mindful of the poverty of spirit, a poverty of affirmation, a poverty of opportunity, and a poverty of hope and optimism about one's future.

Poverty of Spirit

The poverty of spirit exists when conditions in a person's life help to instigate decreases in both psychic and behavioral energy, where it becomes difficult to muster the initiative, drive, and determination necessary to address family issues.

Poverty of Affirmation

A poverty of affirmation exists when life circumstances and personal interactions with people provide no validation, support, or encouragement an individual or their family members need to carry on life's daily functions, or to navigate their way through life's challenges.

Poverty of Opportunity

The poverty of opportunity occurs when individuals and their family members see the doors to legitimate opportunities to achieve personal and collective goals closed and/or otherwise non-existent.

Poverty of Hope and Optimism

The poverty of hope and optimism occurs when one's perspective on the present and future is clouded by seeds of doubt that things in one's life can and will get better, or that one has the ability to effect the changes they would like to see happen for themselves or their family members.

   Thus, while it is important to acknowledge that definitions of poverty vary considerably depending on whom the author is and the index being used, it is not difficult to see that poverty has both a quantitative as well as a qualitative dimension. However, what does tend to forge agreement among many experts is the degree to which standards of poverty are measured against the economic norms for a particular country, society, or segment of society. Across the United States, Americans enjoy an economic standard of living where the average median household income is approximately $50,233 (U.S. Census Bureau, Housing and Household Economic Statistics Division, 2007). For African Americans, the median income rates for single-race Blacks is $34,000 for males and $31,000 for women. In measuring the median income rates against this profile, we find that some 12.5 percent of Americans generally live at or below the poverty line, accounting for an astounding 37.3 million people. More astounding than that is the dramatic way in which poverty specifically impacts the African-American community. Here, data reveal that more than 24 percent of African-American families live in poverty, a rate more than twice the national average.

   What is challenging about these data is not simply the lower income levels of African-American families, but the attributions families make about their circumstance in particular and why poverty exists in general. Arguably, many persons might contend that the lack of income and employment opportunities, combined with a rising consumer price index, creates and fuels the conditions for poverty to reign. Others with a more socially oriented conscience might attribute poverty to racism and oppression, particularly given the way it disproportionately impacts persons of African descent. Still others might argue for a public policy analysis where social policies and legislative mandates conspire to maintain the status quo in keeping African Americans locked at the bottom of the economic ladder. In reality, it would be hard to argue against any of these perspective and we suspect that all have a great deal of merit. However, to attribute poverty to factors solely outside of individuals and families is to reconcile a reality that not only says that lives are totally controlled by external factors alone, but also that people are powerless to change their condition. Despite how easy it would be to embrace such a perspective, it is our contention as African-American psychologists that African-American families must challenge themselves to address those economic factors and variables that they can control.

Another issue that must be addressed is the female-headed family unit, and the degree to which men are involved in the lives of their children. This remains a critical issue for today's African-American family because a sizeable percentage (48 percent) of families are single-parent, with only about 5 percent being single-father headed (Fields, 2003). Adding to this dynamic is the fact that while other cultural groups see divorce as a major contributor to this phenomenon, single parenthood in African-American families is a circumstance driven primarily by couples and/or individuals having children who have never been married. Thus, the need to negotiate one's relationship with children who are the product of non-marital unions is challenging to say the least. There are dynamics connected to the mother's parents (if the child is born to a teenage mother), the male's parents, and the degree to which the male is seen as an important part of the child's life and expanding family unit. Conversely, there are issues of responsibility and the degree to which the male is willing and able to step up to his responsibilities as a father. Needless to say, this becomes a delicate balancing act, but there are men who successfully negotiate this relationship terrain, and thus stand in sharp contrast to the stereotypic images promoted by the majority culture, who portray African-American males as irresponsible, lazy, unreliable, and uninvolved. Successfully negotiating the relationship terrain does not mean that there will be no hurdles to navigate. Belgrave and Allison (2006, 2010) remind us about issues of "residential status" and the fact that many African-American males make their homes in residential accommodations that are different than their biological children. Thus, being present in a child's life requires more effort and energy to balance both the instrumental and expressive roles for that child and their mother, regardless of whether the male and female are in a committed or noncommitted relationship.

Another issue that must be addressed is the relationship dynamics that influence the marriage, separation, and divorce rates among African Americans. We focus here on relationship dynamics because much of what has been offered in the literature over the last two decades seems to focus on economic factors as a primary contributor to marriage rates (James, 1998; Belgrave & Allison 2006) among African Americans. In this regard, discussions center around the economic viability of the Black man, the economic independence of the Black woman, or the differential ratios of males to females and how that impact availability of potential mates. However, it is our position that family stability does not begin with the institution of marriage, but rather, begins with the mindset of both males and females that is forged in the formative years of adolescence and young adulthood. In previous editions (Parham et al., 1999), we have argued that building healthy families must begin with our youth and the socialization/childrearing process. Among those lessons that must be taught are helping our children learn to love themselves with a specific focus on understanding and appreciating their divine nature and interrelationship to the Creator. This lesson is paramount. Another lesson centers around the need to develop an identity and vision of manhood and womanhood that is culturally congruent and is centered in the affirmation of humanity of both males and females. Here, both males and females learn to explore their instincts and feelings, learn to develop social networks of friends and acquaintances, identify the types of relationships that exist and how they apply those to different persons in their life, and learn to manage the dynamics of intimacy that allows relationships to reach higher plateaus of personal engagements between partners, based on issues of sharing and commitment. Assuming that the primary caregivers can teach them (youth) to love themselves, develop and crystallize their identities, and expose them to healthy functional models of parenting and family life, the next step in building healthy families is to teach them to successfully navigate the dynamics of male-female relationships. In this regard, there are several challenges that must be worked through. The first of these is learning to relate to potential partners out of a sense of respect, genuine caring, friendship, love, and true intimacy. Too often, young men and women seek to meet their own personal needs by manipulating others. This style of relating to others becomes so habitual that it becomes difficult to access and utilize more genuine styles of relating.

The second challenge involves learning to sustain relationships through tough times. When relationships with others are surrounded by a climate where everything is going well, it is easy to focus on the pleasantries of socializing. However, when the frustration and anxiety of negative circumstances exert an influence on the attitude of either person in a relationship, it becomes difficult to muster the level of understanding and tolerance necessary to endure through the unpleasant event or circumstance. A third challenge requires that each person be taught to develop greater levels of personal insight and awareness into themselves and their background experiences. Generally, events from our past, especially ones that are negative and inflict deep pain and hurt, color and shape the way we respond to present circumstances. In a similar way, males and females must come to understand how their past experiences with pleasure and with pain exert an influence upon the contemporary realities of their relationships. A fourth challenge or lesson relates to teaching our youth to recognize and emulate healthy, functional models of family development. Too often our youth are exposed to dysfunctional images that cloud their vision of what is healthy in relationships and in strong African-American families.

A fourth issue that must be addressed is the impact of **teenage pregnancy** on the lives of African-American youth. And while the data have seen slight increases and decreases over the years, recent data from the National Vital Statistics Report (Martin et al., 2009) paint an interesting and distressing picture for Black youth. Nationally, there were 435,436 births to teen mothers in 2006, up significantly from the previous years of 1990-2005. Among African-American youth, data reveal that teen births were 62 per 1000, compared to 16 per 100 for Asian-Pacific Islanders, 38 per 1000 for Whites, and 82 per 1000 for

Hispanic/Latino youth. Data from 2007, which is now available, show a 1 to 2 percent increase in the teen birth rate nationally, with youth aged 15 to 19 accounting for that trend. Rates for their younger aged counterparts (aged 10–14) declined slightly and remained at that level. While these statistical profiles do paint an interesting picture, they say little about the impact that teen pregnancy will have on the lifestyles of these youth when they mature and grow into adulthood. Teen births are known to bring medical complications from low birth weight, and have higher rates of infant mortality. In addition, teen mothers are more likely to drop out of school and/or discontinue their education, and are less likely to marry in adulthood. The offspring of teen mothers are also more likely to have chronic medical problems, display cognitive and intellectual deficits, and develop behavior problems while in school that lead to juvenile delinquency (Mather & Adams, 2006). Clearly, the necessity for intervention by African-American psychologist in this domain is a point of serious concern for Black youth, and also for the long-term viability of the African-American family.

A fifth issue centers around the parenting styles of both men and women and how these struggle with ways to balance children's needs for love, approval, validation, and indulgence, with needs for structure, critical feedback, discipline, and deprivation. In this regard, we are mindful from our own observations that parent interactions with children are characterized by a higher frequency of critique vs. praise. Parents have learned to operationalize the critical nature of their roles, but underutilize the nurturing parts. This is a key factor in helping youth to develop a positive sense of self in relation to the world, and a more prominent sense of efficacy in managing the challenges of growing up Black in America.

Lastly, we wish to comment on the challenge of African-American affluence and the necessity to balance needs to work and struggle to maintain one's lifestyle, with those needs of younger family members whose developmental spaces require more "lap time," as opposed to money to purchase the latest technological device or gadget. In these times of economic challenge and deprivation, many parents are working hard at one, two, and sometimes three jobs to make ends meet, and to help their families survive. Jobs are demanding more of American workforce generally, and managing the duties and responsibilities of a job or career requires long hours. However, despite the demands of the job, African-American children need the support of their parents and primary care givers in order to successfully navigate the challenges of childhood and adolescence in America. With the advances of new technology and innovations like cell phones, computers, and personal data assistants, our youth seem to spend more time with "things" rather than people. While gadgets improve our communications access and increase our entertainment options, it is our opinion that they are not a substitute for the personal interactions, face-time, and quality conversations that young people need to have with the older adults in their lives.

In considering the African-American family of present day, we are reminded of some old elder wisdom that says, "The more things seem to change, the more they stay the same." Clearly, the African-American family in 2010 and beyond must make some fundamental changes in the structural elements illustrated in the statistical profile just cited. However, if we embrace those aspects that need to remain constant, it would be those cultural values and traditions that have helped the African-American family persevere through hundreds of years of trying times. Fundamentally, the *family* rather than the *individual* is at the center of one's universe, and the point around which all else revolves. The African ethos of a holistic self in which one's individual self is perceived only in relation to the tribe or group is paramount. The family is held together by a set of common values involving interdependence, mutual aid, resilience, communalism, and collective responsibilities (Nobles, 1978, 1985); thus, the individual is connected to other persons in the extended family network. These values transcend gender roles and allow both men and women to participate in and contribute to the management of economic resources, childrearing, community activism, and other issues of family life without being categorically restricted on the basis of gender. The fluid distinction between social sex roles offers both men and women in the Black family network the opportunity to emerge as decision makers, influence molders, and household managers.

It could be argued that the Black extended family exists and persists primarily because Black people faced the common fate of oppressive economic and social conditions, and that it exists out of necessity as a way of surviving an oppressive class system. It would follow from this argument that the Black-extended family would disappear as Black people moved up the socioeconomic ladder. Yet the extended family does not seem to be disappearing with rising economic fortunes. Mc Adoo's (1979, 2006) work with upwardly mobile and upper-middle-class Black families suggests that not only does the extended family model persist when Blacks move up the socioeconomic ladder, but the Afro-American values of mutual aid, interdependence, and interconnectedness also remain as the guiding ethos of family existence.

Ultimately, we believe the measure of a family's stability is its resourcefulness and its ability to adapt to environmental realities and challenges in ways that help the family unit meet its needs. And as we write this fourth edition and move from 2010 and beyond, our attitudes on the African-American family are consistent with the position taken by Hill (1971) almost forty years ago, and more recently by Boyd-Franklin (1989), who suggested that Black families utilize specific strengths in attempting to meet the needs of its members. Among other African-American researchers of the Black family, there is virtually unanimous agreement that the characteristics that help Black families to develop, survive, and enhance are consistent with Hill's (1971) analysis of Black family strengths. These include strong kinship bonds, strong work orientation, strong achievement orientation, adaptability of family roles, and a strong religious orientation.

Despite our belief in the continuity of African-centered traditions, an objective appraisal of Black family life in contemporary America reveals some inconsistency between core values of African-American families and modern practices. Staples (1994) echoes this point by suggesting that structural conditions help to create extreme dissonance between African-American family ideology and actual family arrangements. Thus, how a family wishes to function versus how it actually functions is oftentimes incongruent.

In an effort to suggest how families might achieve a greater level of congruence between ideology and common practices, we again close this chapter with some perspective from Wade Nobles (1998, 1985). First, Nobles suggests that families must understand their common historical experience (i.e., racial oppression) and their common cultural ancestry (African spiritual essence). Doing so, then, allows the family, regardless of composition, to focus on specific tasks or performance expectations in understanding its mission and purpose. African-American families consist of several individual households with the family definition and lines of authority transcending any one household unit. Although role definitions are flexible and interchangeable, families exist to provide support, nurturance, guidance, protection, and security. Although child-rearing is a primary function in most families, more common tasks involve the legitimization of "beingness" (one's humanity), establishing codes of conduct, delineating boundaries, establishing provisions for the acquisition of knowledge and the exchange of information, and mediating concrete conditions.

Endnotes

1. Kenneth Clark had conducted a series of doll studies that proved to be instrumental in Brown V Board of Education decision which struck down Plessy V. Ferguson 1898?
2. See inter alia. . . . Frazier books.
3. The Melville J. Herskovits Library of African Studies housed at Northwestern University, established in 1954, remains to this day the largest separate collection of Africana in the world.
4. Herskovits was not the first scholar to make the argument about cultural retentions. David Walker in David Walkers Appeal (1829), Martin Delany African life and Customs (1908) and WEB Dubois had all anticipated Herskovits arguments.
5. Talk here about DuBois's pioneering studies on the Black Family and the Philadelphia Negro and about how Dubois was a mentor to Frazier.
6. The Condition, Elevation, Emigration and Destiny of the Colored People of the United States, Politically Considered, (1852); Black Classic Press, reprint (1993); The Voice of Anna Julia Cooper: Including A Voice From the South and Other Important Essays, Papers, and Letters (Rowman & Littlefield, 1998). See also Moses, Wilson Jeremiah. Alexander Crummell: A Study of Civilization and Discontent. New York: Oxford University Press, 1989. For a more in-depth discussion of the nineteenth-century Black nationalism, see Wilson Jeremiah Moses' *The Golden Age of Black Nationalism*, 1850–1925.

5

■■■

Coping with Racism and Oppression: Social Disparities That Impact Black Lives

With the dawn of the twenty-first century, individuals and groups alike are pondering the notion of how to secure their futures in the best possible way. Clearly, African-American people are similarly questioning what their futures will bring and what the critical issues of that time will be. Although it is tempting to project our focus into the future, African-American folks cannot lose sight of our historical past, for doing so leaves us potentially vulnerable to situations and circumstances that constrict opportunities, and expose people to physical and psychological danger. This is true, even in an age when America has seen fit to elect its first African-American president, and the perceptions that we as a country have made significant social progress are being echoed more and more.

REMEMBERING A RACIST PAST

If you don't understand White supremacy (Racism), what it *is,* and how it functions, everything else you think you understand, will only confuse you. (Fuller, 1969)

We claim for ourselves every single right that belongs to a free-born American, political, civil and social; and until we get these rights we will never cease to protest and assail the ears of America. The battle we wage is not for ourselves alone but for all true Americans. It is a fight for ideals, lest this, our common fatherland, false to its founding, become in truth, the land of the thief and the home of the Slave. . . (W. E. B. Du Bois, 1906)

On August 28, 1963, a crowd of 250,000 had assembled on the National Mall under an oppressive canopy of heat and stifling humidity—the kind of heat typical of DC in August. They had come in the peaceful spirit of social protest, political provocation, and human progress. They had traveled from all over the United States by planes, trains, buses, and automobiles—from Atlanta and Albany, from Birmingham and Brooklyn, from Chicago and Chattanooga, from DC and the Mississippi Delta, from New Orleans and New Haven, from Jamestown and Alexandria—to cash a promissory note for human dignity and equality that had been written with the blood of their ancestors. They had been summoned there on this hot and humid day by the "Big Six": A. Philip Randolph (the president of the Brotherhood of Sleeping Car Porters), James Farmer (president of the Congress of Racial Equality), John Lewis (president of the Student Nonviolent Coordinating Committee), Martin Luther King Jr. (president of the Southern Christian Leadership Conference), Roy Wilkins (president of the NAACP), Whitney Young (president of the National Urban League), and Bayard Rustin, a journalist, civil rights veteran and one of the organizers of the first Freedom Rides.

When Roy Wilkins stepped to the podium to address the congregation that had answered the clarion call for the *March on Washington for Jobs and Freedom*, the thermometer needle rested lazily at 82 degrees. It had already been a long day; they had been serenaded by Joan Baez and Marian Anderson, and taken to church by Mahalia Jackson's rendition of "I've been buked and I've been scorned." And, a number of speakers had already attempted to varying degrees to move the crowd, among them were the young, passionate SNCC activist John Lewis (now the Distinguished Gentleman from Georgia) whose original fiery speech had been toned down, Floyd McKissick of CORE, and Whitney Young Jr. of the National Urban League. And, Dr Martin Luther King Jr. had yet to share his visionary view from the metaphorical mountaintop.

This day would be noteworthy in another synergistic regard. On the eve of this momentous event, which would help propel the Civil Rights Act of 1964 and Voting Rights Act of 1965 in to law, the person who perhaps had done more to advance the cause of civil rights than any other single individual in the twentieth century would not live to enter the proverbial Promised Land. Before Roy Wilkins began his prepared remarks, he confirmed the sad news that had already been moving through the crowd: Dr. W. E. B. Dubois had transitioned to the community of ancestors the day before. That morning someone had overhead Sidney Portier, James Baldwin, and John Killens acknowledging solemnly that the "Old Man Died." Roy Wilkins's words on that day captured the precise importance of Du Bois to this moment when he acknowledged that "it is incontrovertible that at the dawn of the twentieth century his was the voice calling you to gather here today to this cause." With that felicitous pronouncement Roy Wilkins called the audience to a moment of silence in honor of Dr. William Edward Burghardt Du Bois.

W. E. B. DU BOIS AND THE SOULS OF BLACK FOLK: RACISM AND OPPRESSION—THEN AND NOW

David Levering Lewis, Dubois's superlative biographer, in his biography illustrates so effectively the many ways W. E. B. Dubois's life and mission personified the modern civil rights movement and its quest to end racism, oppression in the pursuit human rights and equality. Du Bois was a founder of the NAACP, America's oldest civil rights organization, one of the chief architects (along with Sylvester Williams and George Padmore) of the Pan Africanism, a pioneering sociologist and historian, a novelist, an essayist, and an editor.

In a life that began five years after the Emancipation Proclamation and spanned nearly a century, he would bear witness Tilden-Hayes Compromise of 1877, which effectively ended Reconstruction and began the systematic disenfranchisement of African Americans in the American South and spurred the rise of Jim Crow; he would witness both the ascendancy of Booker T Washington as the most powerful African American in the United States and the concomitant rise of Washington's accommodationist philosophy as well help to precipitate its fall; he would be a major intellectual and activist force in two major twentieth-century movements—Civil Rights and Pan Africanism—that would lead to independence on two continents; see the enactment in to law of Plessy versus Ferguson in 1898, which made de jure segregation law, and he would see Brown versus Board of Education in 1954, which ended Jim Crow and paved the way for the Civil Rights. By the sheer force of his intellect, activism, and pen, he would help to dismantle American apartheid. As Lewis eloquently observes, "In the course of his long, turbulent career, W. E. B. Du Bois attempted virtually every possible solution to the problem of twentieth-century racism—scholarship, propaganda, integration, national self-determination, human rights, cultural and economic separatism, politics, international communism, expatriation, third world solidarity."

As a writer, he would produce significant works in nearly every genre of writing, non-fiction, and fiction, from scholarly monographs and novels, to biography and autobiography, to essays and journalism, to pamphlets and editorials. And as a scholar, a veritable library on African-American life and longing accumulated under his pen. He would produce at the time a definitive history of the trace in enslaved Africans (1898), pioneering works in urban sociology (1899), on the African-American family, *on Reconstruction* (1935), on the African role in world history (1939). His books and ideas would influence numerous disciplines and profoundly shape the way that African Americans, their life, their culture, and their history were understood, and simultaneously change the terms of the debate on "The Negro Question." And thus we think it only appropriate that any discussion about coping with racism and oppression should start with Du Bois, because he more than any other scholar by examining the deleterious effects of racism and oppression on the psyche of African Americans placed them at the forefront of American cultural and political life, and in so doing helped advance the quest for civil rights and sojourn to end of racism and oppression.

THE SOULS OF BLACK FOLK: THEN-RACISM AND OPPRESSION AT THE DAWN OF THE TWENTIETH CENTURY

When Du Bois stepped onto the world stage in 1903 at age 35, he already had accumulated an impressive portfolio of achievements that would have satisfied many a career—first African American to take a Ph.D from Harvard (1895); nearly another in economics from the University of Berlin, which he would have taken had not the pernicious forces of white supremacy blocked him; a pioneering study of the trade in enslaved Africans (1898); groundbreaking research in urban sociology while at the University of Pennsylvania (1899); several studies at Atlanta University that profoundly changed the way African Americans populations were studied and understood. But the effort that would catapult him to the center stage of race relations, pit him against Jim Crow, Booker T. Washington, and Tuskegee Machine, and the wealthy and powerful patrons of privilege and white supremacy would be a small collection of essays perfectly titled *The Souls of Black Folks*.

The Souls of Black Folks (1903) was more than just a call to arms for all those who were prepared for civil rights—it was a manifesto against White supremacy and its progenies Jim Crow, racism, and racial oppression. It was simultaneously an existential treatise on the psychological impact of racism and oppression on African Americans, a demand for justice and equality and a literary masterpiece. The use of the spirituals as an exploration of African-American culture and well as the use of song lyrics as epigraphs antedated the trendy use of Hip Hop lyrics that have now become vogue in scholarly circles. The fourteen essays were crafted with skill of pyramidal stonecutter, revolutionary in its tone, and written with the clarity and prescience of a clairvoyant. His pronouncement that the problem of the twentieth century would be the color line sadly remains true in the twenty-first century. To understand just how revolutionary the *Souls of Black Folks* was one has to understand the historical context in which it was written.

THE ATLANTA COMPROMISE AND THE RISE OF BOOKER T WASHINGTON

At the end of the Civil War, a period of reconciliation between the North and the South was begun. As part of that reconciliation, the North would help rebuild and rehabilitate the South. That period of reconciliation and rehabilitation became known as the Reconstruction Era. With President Abraham Lincoln setting the pace as the major policymaker (until his assassination in April 1865) combined with the occupation of southern states created the formation of new, racially integrated state governments. In southern states where Democrats previously had a stronghold, Republicans now controlled of all Southern state governorships and state legislatures, with the exception of Virginia. Prior to the reconstruction era, there had been about 137 African-American officeholders; most of whom resided outside the South. During the newly emergent Reconstruction era, the Republican coalition elected numerous African Americans to local state and national offices: During the period from 1870 to 1876, there were 633 African-American state legislators, 15 African-American congressmen, and 2 African-American senators. The election of 1876 and the resulting *Hayes-Tilden Compromise of 1877* would place a hold on America's democratic promise for nearly a century. It would be no overstatement to suggest that from 1877 to 1964, every aspect of African-American life across all nine dimensions of people activity—economics, education, entertainment, labor, law, sex, politics, religion, and war—would be controlled, either directly or indirectly, by European Americans and dictated by their interests.

The Hayes-Tilden Compromise of 1877 was an informal, unwritten deal that settled the disputed U.S. Presidential election of 1876. As a result of the compromise, Republican Rutherford B. Hayes was awarded the White House over Democrat Samuel J. Tilden under the provision that Hayes would withdraw the federal troops that were propping up Republican state governments in South Carolina, Florida, and Louisiana. It in effect ended reconstruction and introduced Jim Crow—American Apartheid—to the South, disenfranchised African Americans and gave succor and support to American terrorism in the form of the Ku Klux Klan. However, African-Americans response to this reign of terror was to organize and continue their fight for equal rights, which only exacerbated racial tensions in the South.

In 1895 at the Atlanta Exhibition, Booker T Washington would give a speech that would offer a compromise, one which would profoundly shape race relations in the South and in many ways set race relations back. His compromise was that in exchange for African-Americans' willingness to sacrifice enfranchisement, that is, political power, civil rights, and higher education, the South would cede to them the right of an industrial education and self-contained economic development. In short, African Americans would cede civil rights and voting rights for economic opportunity. Washington believed that in time that African Americans would become so economically indispensible to the South that they would be able to eventually leverage hat economic power into political power. To the racists in the South, the tacit admission of inferiority was agreeable; to the racists in the North, it struck a patriarchal cord of divine order. And Washington's philosophy garnered motive force in the support of powerful and monied interests. Washington and the Tuskegee Machine counted among its supporters some of the richest and most powerful businessmen and politicians of the era.

Among his patrons were such diverse captains of industry and politicians as Andrew Carnegie, John D. Rockefeller, Julius Rosenwald, Robert Ogden, William Baldwin, and William Howard Taft, many of who donated large sums of money to agencies such as the Jeanes and Slater Funds, the General Education Board (GEB), and the Southern Education Board (SEB), which largely controlled the financing of education for African Americans in the South. He was seen as a spokesperson for African Americans and became a conduit for funding educational programs. And slowly, he gained the support of a majority of African Americans in the North and the South; even Du Bois himself supported Booker T Washington. The widespread support by powerful and wealthy businessmen and politicians combined with the support of many African Americans in the South made Booker T Washington arguably the most powerful and influential African American in the American history. And his Tuskegee Machine, a formidable force to reckoned with. Nearly ever African appointment, large and small, was vetted through him, President Theodore Roosevelt sought his counsel on nearly every aspect of African-American life, and he singlehandedly wielded the power to make or break careers, which he did not hesitate to use against anyone who opposed the Tuskegee philosophy. As a result, Booker T Washington and the Tuskegee Machine were virtually unassailable. Du Bois initially supported Booker T Washington's strategy of accommodationism as a form of gradualism; however, he began to increasingly see it not so much as a strategy but as an overt admission of the inferiority of African Americans, and his concern grew that tacit admission that was becoming hardened logic in the minds of European Americans. And that African Americans were not moving gradually to equal rights but instead moving steadily backward.

It was in this context that Du Bois wrote the Souls of Black Folks asserting African-Americans rights to full enfranchisement, to equal education and civil rights. His essay in the Souls entitled *Of Booker T. Washington and Others* was tantamount to a declaration of war with Booker T Washington, the Tuskegee Machine, and its financially and politically powerful European-American patrons. And with that collection of fourteen essays, the modern quest civil rights and human dignity was born; and though he would die in Ghana on the eve of the March on Washington for jobs and freedom, having lost faith in America's ability to live up to its constitutional ideas, he renounced his American citizenship. It was out of this profound appreciation and debt of gratitude for a singular, courageous voice that had refused to accept the Faustian bargain, whose sheer determination and intellect had kept the train of civil rights from being derailed that Roy Wilkins, president of the NAACP—which Du Bois had helped found and guide it its early days—spoke those words that possessed a quality of truth that perhaps second only to the words that King would share on that humid, historic day in 1963. Dr. W.E.B Du Bois more than any single person ". . . at the dawn of the twentieth century was the voice calling [them] to gather . . . to this cause."

THE SOULS OF BLACK FOLK: NOW-RACISM AND OPPRESSION AT THE DAWN OF THE TWENTY-FIRST CENTURY

In his text *The Souls of Black Folks,* W. E. B. Du Bois prophetically announced that the color line would be the problem of the twentieth century. Now as we have entered the twenty-first century and are opening its second decade, many of us wonder whether real and substantial progress has been made in the area of race relations. There are many who would point to the historical markers of social justice as indicative of progress. Certainly, we may hesitate to argue against achievements like school desegregation, civil rights, voting rights, and affirmative action as reasonable measures. One might also point to the purported declines in overt racism by Whites toward Blacks as evidence of progress in dealing with the color line issue Du Bois raised more than a century ago. Even the election of Barack Obama as the first African-American president would seem to signal that the nation is ready to develop a strategic plan for addressing the problem. And yet, there is restlessness in the spirit and psyche of the people of African descent that reacts with skepticism to this notion of progress because they know that there are some roads to progress we as a society have not traveled extensively enough. Whether progress is illusory or not will undoubtedly be the subject of continued debate. In this regard, evidence of African-American progress in areas such as education, politics, employment, and economics will be contrasted with arguments citing, for example, Blacks being disproportionately represented in hate crime statistics throughout the counties and cities of this country.

SALTWATER FISH IN A FRESH WATER WORLD: RACISM AND ACCULTURATION—REFRAMING THE DISCOURSE

Most of what we think of when we think of racism falls along the lines of racial instantiations that is single instances of overt or inadvertent racism. And in that regard, while such an instance might be quite traumatic it in and of itself, it does not suggest that there is a structural, i.e., systemic element to racism. But what if racism is not just reduced to instantiations but is instead imbricate, or layered throughout the culture? Then, we would be talking not just about a single instance here and there of individual racism, but rather about the cumulative effects of racism and oppression over the course of one's life span in America, and the impact that it would have on one's economic opportunities, educational opportunities, health outcomes and disparities, employment opportunities, residential and geographic opportunities, inequities in the dispensation of justice, and most important for this text—one's psyche. In short, what we would in fact be exploring is the presence and impact of racism and oppression in all aspects of African-American life across all nine dimensions of people activity—economics, education, entertainment, labor, law, politics, religion, sex, and war. And that as Frances Cress-Welsing (1991) argues, it (racism) may be both conscious and unconscious.

In many regards, understanding the impact of racism and oppression on African Americans is analogous to what renowned psychologist Wade Nobles has often referred to as saltwater fish placed in polluted fresh water. Our contemporary discourses on racism and oppression all tend to focus on the saltwater fish (peoples of color) determining their fitness based on their abilities to mimic fresh water fish (European Americans) and not the polluted fresh water (the cultural scripts and mores that support and affirm racism, implicitly and explicitly). In this regard, Brofenbrenner's Ecological Systems Theory (1979) may be some explicative import. According Ecological Systems Theory, there are five interlocking systems with each system containing roles, norms, and rules that may inform and transform psychological development. The five systems are:

- Microsystem: Immediate environments (family, school, peer group, neighborhood, and childcare environments)

- Mesosystem: A system comprising connections between immediate environments (i.e., a child's home and school)
- Exosystem: External environmental settings that only indirectly affect development (such as parent's workplace)
- Macrosystem: The larger cultural context (European-American culture vs. African-American culture, national economy, political culture, subculture)
- Chronosystem: The patterning of environmental events and transitions over the course of life

While Brofenbrenner's developmental theory is primarily meant as a development tool, it does raise an interesting question: What if racism and oppression are built into all five levels of the developmental experience of African Americans? What if social and structural processes such as racism, socio-economic status, and acculturation conspire to produce inequities in health? It would mean that racism and oppression not only add additional psychological stressors, but that it is in fact harmful to African-Americans health. Recently, a number of researchers have begun to explore this very premise. Wilson (1997; 2009) has explored ways in which structural forces and behavioral patterns in urban centers can have a profound influence on inequities in SES. Collins and Williams's (1999) research has shown a strong correlation between racism, segregation, and mortality. While Williams and Collins (1995) looked at socioeconomic status and racial differences in health, exploring the "ways in which major social structures and processes such as racism, acculturation, work, migration and childhood SES produce inequities in health." Karoly (1993) found that in terms of some economic indicators, there has been a decline in African-Americans economic status. These researchers and others have noted at least three ways in which racism can affect health, (1) it can transform SES indicators, (2) it can restrict access to quality health-related services, and (3) racial discrimination may create various forms of psychological that may have deleterious effects on mental and physical health.

Williams and Collins (1995) further note that there are other mechanisms underlying SES and racial differences in health such as the quantity and quality of medical care, health behavior, working conditions, environmental exposure, and power differential between European Americans and African Americans. Moreover, Williams and Collins (1995) have demonstrated an inverse relationship between racial residential segregation and racial disparities in health. In short, a mounting body of research may indicate that the overall systemic impact of racism may have negative influence across a wide range of social and structural processes that have a negative relationship to not only African-American morbidity and mortality, but also overall health outcomes for African Americans. Understanding the psychology of oppression and how one copes with it requires a special recognition of all of these factors.

A CONTEMPORARY LOOK AT OPPRESSION

Despite this historical review, and those perceptions that with the election of Barack Obama, all is well in America, it is, however, important to make a distinction between the concepts of desegregation and integration, for not doing so contributes to an illusion of social progress that lulls folks into a false sense of security that things really are better than they appear, and that physically and psychologically, the struggle for civil and human rights is no longer necessary. Desegregation as a construct brings back memories of the old civil rights movement of the 1950s and 1960s, where members of the African-American community were engaged in protest that sought the right to attend schools, ride buses in any seat or section of the vehicle, drink out of public water fountains restricted by racial codes, stay in public accommodations, vote for elected officials, and enjoy a broader array of civil and human rights than were otherwise not accorded to citizens of African descent. In essence, people were seeking the right to occupy the same geographical space without threat of reprisal or personal injury. This was the goal and outcome of desegregation. The goal of integration was intended to allow persons of any color to see themselves reflected within the fabric of society's institutions and agencies. Full integration meant being a full participant in American society, with all of the rights and privileges given to any citizen. Integration, it seems to us, was not simply about the outcomes produced, but also the process dynamics that helped to produce them. It was about decision-making ability and being able to share in proposing and evaluating alternatives that led to particular outcomes. Integration was also about choices, and feeling free to exercise choice in where one lived, attended school, shopped for clothes or food, ate a meal, where and how one travelled, participated in recreational and leisure pursuits, and pursued one's dreams. But more than that, choices and opportunities should theoretically lead to a better lifestyle, such that the conditions the masses of African-American people find themselves in would substantially improve. Not only that, integration implies that perspectives should change where individuals believe and have faith, that life is full of promise and potential, that this nation is prepared to live out the full meaning of its creed, and that issues of interest to members of the African-American community would somehow make it to the forefront of the discourse on how this country needed to grow and change toward "a more perfect union." Doing so, of course, would require this nation to make a commitment to have a more honest and authentic conversation with itself about its historical past, its inappropriate treatment of African descent people, and proposals for remedies that address the continuing legacy of racism and White supremacy. Otherwise, the psyche of African-American people is likely to remain suspicious about America's true intent with respect to her citizens of color, and foster a much more defensive and guarded posture by African descent people, when they engage the realities of education, employment, health care, criminal justice, and so on that represent real challenges and opportunities. But do African Americans enjoy the full benefits of an integrated society, or do they merely exist in a desegregated one? In responding to that query, we are reminded that just because we have desegregated the White House does not mean that all social barriers will come down magically because President Obama is in office, and the first family of African descent is now residing in the White House. In addition, Black people in this country are not likely to believe that real and substantial change has occurred regarding issues of racism and social oppression, just because pronouncements are made by conservative and even liberal commentators in the media who blanket the network and cable talk shows with their surface structure analysis of Black life in America. African-American people are more likely to put their faith in a belief that White (1984) labeled the value of direct experience. In essence, they put what Parham calls 5 percent emphasis on and belief in what people say, and 95 percent emphasis on what people do. So, what is it that America has done in its most recent past that provides African Americans with the confident reassurance to know that coping with racism and oppression is a pursuit that needs to occupy less of their time?

AFRICAN-AMERICAN LOYALTY TO A NATION THAT GIVES LESS THAN EQUAL RETURN ON INVESTMENT

Asante's (2003) analysis provides some important insights to this question, as he articulately captures the essence of one slice of life in Black America. That is what we will refer to as the *contract for reciprocal exchange*. This concept represents an ideal that people will invest in a society where they believe that there are legitimate opportunities to participate in society's institutions without restriction, access opportunities without end, and pursue their dreams without being negatively impacted by social barriers. It really represents a question of how loyal (intellectually and emotionally) have African Americans been and should they be to this country in light of the fact that America has given less than an equal return on the investment Black folks have made? African Americans have built this country from the ground up, often from a posture of slaves and servants contributing to the economic and social uplift of America's White citizenry and institutions. They have even built the structures this nation now recognizes as its most cherished symbols of freedom and liberty, including the capitol of the United States (Robinson, 2000). They have fought in every war in which this country has been engaged, from the Revolutionary War, Civil War, both World Wars, the Korean War, Vietnam, the Operation Desert Storm Gulf War, and the current wars in Iraq and Afghanistan. African Americans have even battled social forces for the right to fight and die for a country that denied them full citizenship. African Americans have taken to the streets in the midst of social protest for greater civil and human rights. While some more militant factions of the Black community advocated the overthrow of what was perceived as a corrupt American government during certain periods of the civil rights and Black power era struggles, by and large, the majority of Black people and organizations promoting civil rights have rallied, marched, sat in, protested, and died for the opportunity to more fully participate in the American dream, and help America more fully realize its promise. And yet, in exchange for their loyalty, African Americans have born witness to the vicious legacy of racism and White supremacy that saw men and women lynched; children killed; houses burned; churches bombed; lands stolen; and rights to learn in equal schools, eat at equal lunch counters, ride equally on buses, stay equally in hotels, find equal justice in the courts, and vote equally for political candidates denied. They have witnessed their political and civic leadership being assassinated, those who stayed in office undermined, being denied access to the polling places in this nation because of the color of their skin, and community-based organizations perceived as doing some good in their community being infiltrated by the FBI and intelligence agencies, all while spreading negative press about that organization's intentions (i.e., COINTELPRO program of the FBI under the J. Edgar Hoover administration). Clearly, as Langston Hughes writes so eloquently in his poem entitled "Mother to Son": Life for [them] ain't been no crystal stair!

Perhaps our focus on the historic past is too painful a reminder, for Black people certainly have a present-day social climate that is substantially different than the one just described. Or is it? To muster the strength and courage to arm oneself with the intellectual, emotional, behavioral, psychological, and spiritual weaponry necessary to successfully confront social forces of evil and oppression requires a belief that life continues to be dangerous for African-American citizens, and that we are still living in what the brilliant public intellectual Cornel West (1993, 1999) describes as a "chamber of horrors" and a "twilight civilization." One has only to review America's recent history to get a glimpse of the veracity of this statement. Since the turn of the millennium, in the year 2000, African Americans have both witnessed and been treated to a host of shocking and revealing incidents that without question would challenge their sensibilities about the fairness of America. In 2000, they witnessed what many in the Black community believe is one of the biggest displays of voter disenfranchisement since the historic civil rights era, which helped, in part, George Bush and the Republican Party, claim the White House. Chronicling incidents in Florida and Ohio, two key battleground states in that Presidential race, African-American citizens were robbed of their right to vote for their preferred candidate. Polling place irregularities, names of African-American citizens being dropped from the rolls of eligible voters through a purging process orchestrated by those state's Secretary of State, highway patrol checkpoints that re-routed traffic away from more convenient roads leading to rural polling places, and "hanging chad" ballots were just a few of the questionable, inappropriate, and illegal tactics allegedly employed by the members of the Republican Party and their allies. In the aftermath, African Americans were saddened not only by the loss (some say theft) of the election, but also at the awarding of the election to the candidate whose Father (President George H.W. Bush) had helped put in place Supreme Court Justices that now were adjudicating this case involving Al Gore versus George W. Bush. The Supreme Court decision that led to the awarding of the election to George Bush was a significant one, because here you have the highest court in the land being perceived by many in the Black Community as losing its impartiality in favor of partisan politics, and themselves being the last instrument in an arsenal of many, that was used to validate that the political disenfranchisement of one segment of society's citizens was somehow acceptable practice in a war for the control of the White House and America's political future. To his credit, President George W. Bush did appoint several high-profile African Americans to his cabinet, and to other sub-cabinet posts. These appointments perhaps lent some credence to the idea that he was somehow pro-civil rights, at least in the minds of conservative Republicans. But what did those actions and appointments instigate in the minds of many in Black communities all across the country? Unfortunately, the Bush Administration, and even the political commentators who evaluate the legacy of his eight-year Presidency (2000-2008), failed to understand the simple truth that Parham (2002) has argued many times that there is a difference between skin color and consciousness. Just because persons of African descent are appointed to certain positions does not mean that they bring the mindset and cultural value system to that space that help them color and shape the way each would perform their job. Thus, even with Black people in prominent roles in that administration (e.g., Colin Powell and Condoleezza Rice), there was a creation and implementation of policies and practices (e.g., No child Left Behind, assaults of affirmation and other equity programs, refusal to send a U.S. delegation to the World Conference on Racism, and sanitizing the Department of Justice's Civil Rights Division with individuals who have little sensitivity to people of color an civil rights issues) that either signaled an anti-Black sentiment from the Bush administration, or substantially contributed to crushing the hopes of working class and poor people, who were and are disproportionately African American.

Lessons people in the African-American community have learned in this new millennium do not just occur around election irregularities or official government policies, but also in the areas of responses to natural disasters. In August of 2005, Hurricane Katrina rolled ashore in the Gulf Coast region of the country, leaving behind a record level of devastation and destruction that was previously unimaginable. The force of Mother Nature's fury exceeded all predictions of how bad the storm would be. Unfortunately, the storm took many lives, left whole cities and many communities in ruin, decimated many families, and created an atmosphere of uncertainty and ambiguity that was quite pronounced. Beyond the devastation of the storm, what was more shocking to the victims of the hurricane, and the millions around the country who watch the devastation on daily and nightly news, was the utter contempt and neglect with which a predominantly African-American population in New Orleans was treated. Many were abandoned in the flooded streets and communities of that city, left to fend for themselves with no rescue support from local, state, and especially federal agencies. Victims clung to trees and street lamp poles, stationed themselves on rooftops, and even swam and waded through neck-high water levels, trying to survive. Some relief came, but not nearly enough to accommodate the number of victims. Those lucky enough to make it to shelters were herded into the New Orleans Superdome arena and left there for days without sufficient supplies to manage needs for food, daily hygiene, bedding, medical, or psychological support. Those unlucky in their quest for shelter had to rely on their own instincts and improvisational skills to make it. And yet, even as people struggled to accommodate basic necessities like food, the print and electronic media found a way to characterize their struggles in vastly different ways that appear to be substantially influenced by race. For example, when two White citizens were photographed wading through water taking groceries from a flooded out store, they were characterized as "forging for supplies" necessary to survive in the midst of a tragedy. Conversely, when an African-American couple was photographed doing exactly the same thing, in attempting to survive in the wake of this tragedy, their actions were characterized as "looting." What message did that characterization, and the slow response of the government to this tragedy, send to African Americans?

In the intervening years since the Hurricane Katrina tragedy, this country has seen a local trial with national implications involving the Jenna Six in Louisiana, high-profile police shootings of Black men all across the country, disparate sentencing laws convicting more Blacks for crimes equal to those of Whites, a Department of Justice's Civil Rights Division accused of firing government attorneys in favor of "real Americans," and a brand new case of affirmative action in 2009 where the Supreme Court ruled in favor of White firefighters who sought to declare local remedies in affirmative action promotions and hiring in Connecticut unconstitutional. These circumstances and situations do occur with some frequency in America, despite the evidence of social progress that has been made in other corners of the nation.

THE CHALLENGES OF MICRO- AND MACRO-AGGRESSIONS

On the surface, this country has made legitimate and significant progress in its ability to desegregate institutions that were long holdouts as bastions of White privilege and authority. There are even Internet messages that cycle and recycle through the personal e-mails touting the contemporary successes of African Americans in all walks of life. They include the president of the United States (Barack Obama), the top neurosurgeon (Ben Carson), the current world number one and arguably best golfer of all times (Tiger Woods), the top women's tennis players (Venus and Serena Williams), the highest paid actor in Hollywood (Will Smith), Michael Vick did have the largest contract in NFL history, one of the wealthiest women who also happens to have the number one-rated daytime talk show (Oprah Winfrey), one of the highest paid academicians (Professor Henry Louis Gates at Harvard University), and more. Indeed, the list of names and accomplishments is very impressive. And yet, even for all of the success these individuals have enjoyed, African-American people must still question whether we are better off now than we were decades ago? Has racism been dealt a fatal blow from which it will never recover? Can African-American people relieve themselves of the psychological and emotional armor that for too long has had to protect their psyches from the contamination of racism and oppression? When Barack Obama was elected the president, there was a reported spike in racial incidents and hate crimes across the country. Tiger Woods reportedly received death threats for daring to challenge and surpass the records of past White golfing champions. Serena and Venus Williams were treated to a chorus of boos for Venus's inability to compete in a match due to injury, while their White counterparts received empathy and consoling applause for similar situations at other tournaments. Michael Vick was arrested and jailed for his participation in financing a dog fighting ring, and then reportedly lying to federal authorities. What is ironic about his fall from grace is that he was vilified for his treatment of a DOG, while those who hunt squirrels and moose ("Rocky & Bullwinkle"), ducks ("Daffy"), deer ("Bambi"), and other animals and casts of cartoon characters are celebrated for their trophies and wall mounts. Worst yet, we cry foul for the inhumane treatment of DOGS, while society prances around with its moral indignation, being careful not to step on the homeless people citizens pass everyday, the wounded soldiers our government still fails to provide proper medical care for, the bodies we bring home from what many in the Black community consider an unjust and illegal war, the social decay and pathology that characterizes our inner cities we continue to ignore, and the epidemic of violence in the urban cores of our nation that takes too many lives. All of this occurs while radio disk jockeys refer to African-American women basketball players as "nappy-headed hoe's" (e.g., Don Imus), African-American executives continue to face difficulty in hailing taxicabs in major cities like New York, and even his status as a Harvard Professor did not insulate Dr. Henry Louis Gates from the brutality of police over-reaction when he was arrested in his own home for what was reported as disorderly conduct for demanding to know the name of the police officer sent to his house to investigate a supposed break in.

If the truth be told, the answer to the question about whether African Americans can lay down their psychological armor would be an emphatic no, for even as Black people in this country celebrate the successes of its heroes and heroines, there are social forces that continue to rear their ugly heads. In contemporary form, these social forces are characterized less by the out-and-out racism of days past (even though it is still very prevalent). Instead, African-American people are more chronically subjected to incidents we now know as micro-aggressions and micro-assaults (Pierce, 1995; Franklin, 1999; Sue, 2003; Sue et al, 2007). In documenting the transformation from overt to more covert forms of racial hostility, Pierce introduced the literature to the term "micro-aggression." He defined it as subtle, innocuous, preconscious, or unconscious degradations and putdowns that were capable of being verbal or kenetic (p.281). These putdowns or verbal assaults have the effect of invalidating a person's existence, demeaning and insulting a person's character, and allowing others involved to diminish the self-worth of the individual being engaged principally due to their racial background. Allow us to share an example of a situation that occurred to Dr. Thomas Parham (the lead author) not long ago. While catching a flight from a Southern California airport, Parham arrived at curbside for an early morning flight, and joined the line of those waiting to have their bags checked by a skycap. He was dressed in business attire, with an overcoat that lay open in the front, revealing his suit and tie. As the line moved slowly while each passenger checked their bags and received their boarding passes, Parham is now about five people away from the skycap. He is the only African-American passenger in that line of what has now grown to 15 to 20 people. Suddenly, a White woman exiting a vehicle dropped her bags in front of Parham, directing him to check her items. The assumption here is that Parham, despite his suit and tie, despite him wearing no skycap uniform or hat, must be a skycap, as no other possibility occurred to this woman.

What Parham experienced was not physically threatening in the least, especially since the woman was not his physical equal, nor was she hostile in her tone or temperament. What he did experience was a situation where an individual (perhaps unintentionally) engaged in insulting behavior by first stereotyping his role and function (presumably because of his race) as a person there to lend assistance with her luggage, and then demanding in a fairly condescending tone that he meet her request for service. No where in her request for service was a pleasant tone that should be accorded any individual, irrespective of their social status or position in America, nor was there any recognition that an African-American male, even a highly acclaimed psychologist, author, and speaker in professional dress, could be anything other than a servant to her status as a White woman of privilege.

Incidents like the ones described above occur with frequency to African-American men and women, elderly and adult, adolescents and children, on a daily basis. And yet, in an age where some segments of society are convinced that we have come so far in terms of racial progress, they leave us with the sad reality that for all of the desegregation that has occurred over the last fifty years, the American human family has not seen fit to integrate greater levels of sensitivity into their attitudes and behaviors. It also may be a bit misleading to believe that hardcore racism is extinct, and that such has been replaced by these small circumstantial micro-assaults that only inflict pain on the mind, heart, and spirit of individual people. Rather, it may be more accurate to assume that the social pathology of racism and oppression can be classified along a continuum of micro- and macro-assaults, and traverse the landscape between internal and external dimensions of engagement.

	Internal	External
Micro-aggressions		
Macro-Aggressions		

Macro-assaults are those situational phenomenons that rise above the level of individual insult or degradation to meet a threshold of collective assault on the people's rights, humanity, or even their life. Over the past decade, African Americans have witnessed:

- An election perceived to be stolen by one party over another while their voting rights were denied and abused.
- A hurricane of major proportion where persons of African descent were abandoned and left to die on rooftops, or wallow in the squalor of a filthy sporting arena with no services for food, shelter, clothing, or bathrooms
- Six high school youth were arrested and held in jail in Jenna Louisiana
- Police shootings in countless cities in this nation
- Assaults on affirmative action

These social incidents or macro-aggressions say nothing about the disparities that exist in African America, especially when comparisons are made to other racial/ethnic groups.

CLOSING THOUGHTS

Given this litany of micro- and macro-aggressions, and the disparities that continue to create nightmare realities for Black people, it is safe to say that one should hesitate to lay down his or her psychological armor even in a post Obama era. Still, while it is important to examine the challenges of social pathology that exist in the country, we would be remiss if mention was not made to the ways the contamination from a climate of oppression leaves a residue that impacts the attitudes and behaviors African Americans engage in themselves.

In acknowledging that there are social forces and environmental circumstances (i.e., White supremacy, racism, sexism, discrimination, poverty, unemployment, violence, and drugs) that jeopardize and threaten our futures in significant ways, many of our communities have used, exhausted, and will continue to marshal resources to address these social ills. Yet, to confine the focus as well as selected intervention strategies to external and systemic forces alone implies that African people in America have no part to play in their own rehabilitation and recovery. The myriad of social ills are formidable obstacles that haunt their contemporary reality. But we would argue, as others have before us (Akbar, 1984; Hilliard, 1997), that the biggest challenge is not racism or other social ills. Rather, Parham (2002; 2007) believes that our most daunting challenge as African Americans is the need for mental liberation. Although the notion of mental enslavement is not a new concept, it is nonetheless one that the masses of African-American people have not yet embraced. As African-centered psychologists, it is our opinion that we as African Americans simply are not receptive enough to any construct or principle that forces us to take a critical look at self. But self-exploration and reflection is precisely where we must go, and the so-called educated and socially conscious among us must be charged with that task of helping to liberate the minds, bodies, and spirits of people of African descent. Indeed, Carter G. Woodson (1933) was prophetic when he asserted that yielding control of your (our) mind to alien sources will have you seeking inferior status even before you can be assigned one. And yet it is difficult to argue against this characterization of African-American people's condition when one examines how they respond to their contemporary reality. Whether the yardstick is economic empowerment, political power, health-related concerns, educational achievement, violence in our streets and families, crime, and so on, we as African descent people are substantial contributors to our plight.

Clearly, the principle of self-determination advocated by many of our historical and contemporary leaders demands that adults, adolescents, and children take a critical look at self and explore ways in which internally oriented examination and intervention strategies might prove more beneficial. This must also be the challenge of the discipline of African psychology. This is the critical work that must be done in our struggles to understand identity, in our quest to manage the psychological impacts of racism and oppression, and in our queries about whether to lay down our psychological armor in the name of legitimate social progress.

6

■ ■ ■

The Struggle for
Identity Congruence
in African Americans

One of the more complex tasks of human development is to cultivate a knowledge of who one is at the core of our being. There is nothing more fundamental to one's existence than our identity, both personal and collective. By some accounts, identity is defined as one component of an individual's overall self-concept. It involves the adoption of certain personal attitudes, feelings, characteristics, and behaviors (personal identity) and the identification with a larger group of people who share those characteristics (reference group orientation). Identity can also be described as a search for self-understanding and awareness where individuals begin to adopt certain characteristics that conform or align with self-perceptions of who they are and want to be. Cross, Parham, and Helms (1998) further delineate the identity concept by asserting that for African Americans, identity serves three functions: (1) It provides a social anchor and meaning to one's existence; (2) it serves as a connection to the broader African community across the globe; and (3) it serves as a protection or buffer against the social forces that continually bombard the psyche with non-affirming and, in some cases, dehumanizing messages. In an attempt to better crystallize the identity question, we believe that the real challenge that individuals must confront is how to operationalize one's identity into everyday life. This process of discovery is initiated by asking several fundamental questions. Although human beings find it necessary to locate themselves in time, in place (geography), and in space (Hilliard, 1997), the self-discovery process must also answer questions of how to describe personal character and qualities, how to achieve congruence with one's self-description, and whether there is sufficient room for growth and actualizing of one's potential. It is also important not to ignore the "environmental identity" for irrespective of how one manages the resolution of the personal identity and reference group orientation into some sort of personal synthesis, how the environment treats each person will still have a profound effect on personality development and one's identity.

In support of these fundamental precepts, the work of Fanon (1967) is particularly relevant in delineating three essential questions that each African American should both consider and be able to answer. The issues involve each person understanding: (1) Who am I? (2) Am I who I say I am? and (3) Am I all I ought to be? "Who am I?" is the question of identity, where it is important to understand the nature of one's humanness. "Am I who I say I am?" is a question of achieving congruence in assessing how our spiritual, cognitive, affective, and behavioral dimensions align with our self-definition. "Am I all I ought to be?" is a question of self-actualization of potential where one seeks to achieve the fullest expression of all one is supposed to become.

It is our belief that the personality, consciousness, and the core identity of Black people are African in nature. Whether conscious or unconscious, the personality manifests itself in the attitudes, feelings, behaviors, and spiritual essence of African Americans. Baldwin (1985), and now Kambon and Bowen-Reid (2009), in referencing Kambon's work, provides a clear articulation of the African-American personality in his theory of "African self-consciousness." He writes, "The core component of the Black personality represents the conscious level expression of the 'oneness of being' communal phenomenology which characterizes the fundamental self-extension orientation of African people." Kambon argues that the core of Black personality, or African Self-Consciousness (ASC) is composed of the following four elements: collective African identity, prioritization on African racial-cultural survival, advocacy for and active participation in the perpetuation of African-centered institutions and practices, and a resolute posture of defense against anti-African forces in one's thoughts, attitudes, and behaviors. He sees the basic striving of the African-American personality as being toward the affirmation of the "African Survival Thrust."

According to Kambon, although the African self-consciousness system is partly biogenetically determined, it is also subject to social and environmental influences. When this core system of the Black personality is nurtured developmentally as well as situationally through indigenous personal and institutional support systems, it achieves vigorous and full expression in terms of a congruent pattern of basic traits (beliefs, attitudes, and behaviors) that affirm African-American life in the authenticity of its African cultural heritage (Baldwin, 1985). Despite Baldwin's assertion that normal Black behavior and consciousness is not merely a reaction to adverse environmental elements, his theory clearly recognizes the interaction between individual personality characteristics and social and environmental influences that help to form and shape the individual personality. Assuming that an African-American male or female is surrounded by positive (Black-oriented) institutional and social support systems throughout his or her formative years, then the expected consequence would be the development of a normal, healthy Black personality. Such would be characterized by a strong awareness of and identification with African cultural heritage, strong sense of motivation directed at ensuring collective survival of African people and related institutions, and the active resistance of any force (i.e., racism) that threatens the survival and maintenance of one's people and oneself.

Nobles (1986) has also outlined the prerequisites for normal human functioning based on a culturally centered identity. The parameters include:

1. A sense of self that is collective or extended.
2. An attitude wherein one understands and respects the sameness in oneself and others.
3. A clear sense of one's spiritual connection to the universe.
4. A sense of mutual responsibility (for other African people).
5. A conscious understanding that human abnormality or deviance is any act that is in opposition to oneself (p. 96).

Other writers of the Black experience are quick to remind us, however, that African-American people are not always afforded the luxury of totally surrounding themselves with social and institutional support systems that enhance, promote, and affirm our humanity as African Americans.

In fact, James Baldwin (1963), a noted Black author, writes in his classic text some forty-plus years ago that "to be Black and relatively conscious is to be in a constant state of rage almost all the time." His writings imply that Black people face constant exposure to racist and oppressive conditions in America from a society that neither validates nor cultivates our existence. If Baldwin's analysis is correct (and we suspect it is), then it is entirely likely that the forces that influence the identity development of many African Americans are mitigated by oppression and racism. That being said, it is also important not to get caught in a stereotypical notion of what identity development in African-American folks looks like; for much like Cross (1991, 2001) reminds us, diversity and texture are the core of Black identity development, and not oversimplification. Not all persons of African descent engage or engaged in self-hatred, and not all embraced the dynamics of Black pride and core Black Nationalism that was and is so prevalent in certain corners of the African-American community. However, given the dynamics of oppression that continue to manifest within the context of Black life in America (even within a post-Obama being elected president of the United States era), Cross (1991, 2001) is profound in his insight that the heart of the identity struggle was less about the adoption of self-hatred attitudes and beliefs that emanate from racism and oppression, but rather the transformation of an identity and worldview that became less centered in a Eurocentric reality and more centered in an African-centered one.

And yet, even as we compose this fourth edition, this challenge of identity development remains a difficult task for too many in society, principally because their lives seem to be missing many of the central ingredients that help individuals successfully navigate the pathways through this developmental milestone. The tragedy is further compounded when one considers that the factors that create the voids many of our children seem to be missing are not emerging from the mouths of "red-neck" racists who denigrate everything Black, but rather they emerge from within our own communities and families, who remain oblivious to how their own perspectives and worldviews have been contaminated by systems of racism and White supremacy. For that reason, we begin this chapter with a brief case study of one of the most well-known musical artists and entertainers the world has ever known. His untimely death shocked not just the nation, but the world, and instigated several weeks of memorials and tributes held all over the globe. But more than the long and impressive list of accomplishments and accolades this entertainer has garnered over his all too short life, his story and struggle with what appeared to be issues of identity have much to teach us about raising African-American children in a race-conscious society. Now, no one anecdote can ever capture the complexity of an issue or illustrate all of the challenges associated with the developmental landscape we call childhood and adolescence. But, this figure is so easily recognizable the world over, perhaps the example of what we know of elements of his life will serve as the illustration for our conversations on identity congruence. And while we seek to tread cautiously, in not wanting to jump on a bandwagon of public ridicule for the ways he fell short in his life, we do want to demonstrate the human side of his life that was so full of joy and pain. With that, let us review the life of Michael Jackson.

By all accounts, Michael (born in 1958) and his siblings were raised in a working-class family of humble means, in the Midwest town of Gary, Indiana. After he and his siblings toured the "chittlin circuit" and drew attention from several well-known Motown and Stax Recording artists, they were referred to executives at the famed Motown Records Company. So impressed were they that the Jackson Five, under the direction and management of their father, were signed by Motown Records shortly thereafter. During their childhood years, Michael Jackson and his family were relocated to Southern California, and he was launched on a trajectory that would change the course of his life forever. Auditions turned into record deals; those deals turned into recorded albums; those albums and later music videos turned into number one hits and best sellers toping the music charts; and Michael's status as an entertainment and recording icon was soon solidified. Michael Jackson helped to break down color barriers in the Pop Music world, forcing it, as Gilmore (2009) writes in Rolling Stone Magazine, to acknowledge that the rightful "king" could indeed be a young African-American male. During his life, Michael Jackson also set records of a different sort, that of giving. He appears to have had a very giving heart and generous spirit, setting a Guinness Book record for the most charitable giving and charities supported by a pop star. From the United Negro College Fund (UNCF), the Sickle Cell Foundation, and neighborhood YMCA's, his eyes were never far from the challenges that confronted members of the African-American community. And, his support for those causes was unwavering. And yet, with all of that fame and huge fortune he amassed over the course of his life and 40-plus years entertainment career, it appeared to us that Michael Jackson, who many consider the "King Of Pop," constantly wrestled with finding a comfort zone that would allow him to both know, appreciate, and love who he was as a young male of African descent, complete with the phenotypical features that are unique to our racial heritage, and shared with millions of peoples around the world. Upon his death, he appeared to leave this world as a troubled soul, with a personality that reflected the complexities he wrestled with on a constant basis. From those he entertained, he drew praise for his showmanship, while evoking shame for the ways he could never seem to navigate the societal boundaries of a grown man traversing the slippery slopes of childhood friends and acquaintances. He received love from adoring fans and celebrity friends all across the world, and expressions of pride in his connection to the cultural legacy of Black stars and civil rights icons in whose shoes he followed. He received empathy for the pain he felt throughout his childhood and adult years, and respect for the way he practiced and delivered his craft with a standard of excellence that was unparalleled. Indeed, he was a complex man.

The life of Michael Jackson helps to underscore the central challenge in the struggle for identity scholars have written about in their research. That is: "how one maintains a sense of cultural integrity in a world that does not support nor affirm one's humanity as a person of African descent" (Parham, 1999, 2002). His life can also be understood within the context of theories of childhood development, specifically Phenomenological Variant of Ecological Systems Theory (PVEST) advanced by Spenser (1995, 2006). This approach, in attempting to link context of a child's developmental space and culture, takes into account the structural and contextual barriers to identity formation in children. The components of this model include: ***net vulnerability***—where risk contributors are balanced against protective factors in a child's environment; ***net stress engagement***—referring to the experiences that either challenge or support children in negotiating the risks encountered in their life (during childhood, this factor has been most directly linked to parental socialization); ***reactive coping strategies***—where based on vulnerability and cumulative stress, children develop either adaptive or maladaptive coping strategies in response to the challenges they confront. In this factor is the recognition that if a child is challenged with adversity (see negative parental socialization) more than he/she is showered with support, then maladaptive coping may be a likely result (see attempts to alter one's phenotypical features including nose, lips, and skin tone); ***emergent identities***—where the self-appraisal process in prior stages impacts the perceptions of who one is (see a compromised racial identity); and ***coping outcomes***—where children develop productive or unproductive behaviors and attitudes as a result of their identity, stress, and vulnerability experienced in life (see the unproductive outcomes of drug use, withdrawal from relations with peers).

Essentially, within the course of developing a sense of our identity, our physical organism and individual personality attributes interact with the sociocultural environment to help form a context that ultimately shapes the person we become. In a normal developmental situation, individuals receive love and approval from significant others in their life that ultimately allows them to develop impressions of who they are, and how they feel about who they are. In essence, there is a contingent self that develops in each of us, based on the validation and valuation we receive. This, in turn, leads to the adoption of appropriate coping strategies and productive coping outcomes in a child's life. In developmental situations that are less than wholesome and healthy, questions arise about both who we are and how we feel about our identity that, if not resolved successfully, will continue to manifest themselves in adolescence all the way into adulthood, which can be characterized by maladaptive coping strategies and unproductive coping outcomes. It is also important to recognize that the "world" we all seek validation from is not simply the social-cultural environment (i.e. schools, neighborhood acquaintances, community agencies, the media, etc.) we interact with, but more importantly, it starts with our parents and primary care givers. Each of us learns to feel good about ourselves to the degree that we receive love and approval from significant others in our life, who from the time we arrive on this earth, we are dependent on for sustenance and survival. That "contingent self" is a powerful force, for we only learn to love and value ourselves to the degree that we believe the significant others in our life first love and value us.

Many adult parents of African descent must also wrestle with a circumstance that compounds their struggle, for much like the internal world of a child's home, there is also an external world outside of the home and family that also gives out messages about who one is and how the world feels about your existence. When that world, and the messages we incorporate as a result of our exposure to schools, the broader community, and the media are affirming and supportive, there is a high degree of congruence between one's home life and the world we interact with. When the external environment is less than supportive, and perceived as hostile to one's person and identity, the dissonance created then instigates a continue struggle for clarity and closure regarding who one ultimately decided to be and how one decides to live their lives, particularly with respect to race. It also sets up a battle inside of people, who then must decide whether validation from internal or external sources is most salient in their lives. When acknowledging that systems of racism and White supremacy are very potent forces in the external world, one can see how challenging this dilemma can be, and how yielding too much importance to negative external sources with racist intent can subject people to a level of psychological slavery, and also have them imparting those lessons onto their children.

Unfortunately, many primary care givers are themselves contaminated by the vestiges of psychological slavery, and their search for validation and approval from White society has them engaging in behaviors that diminish and/or otherwise negate their Blackness. Such behaviors include restrictions of Black peer groups, avoiding residential neighborhoods that are racial diverse or predominantly Black, color and feature consciousness in their mates that must resemble those of their Anglo counterparts, adoption of certain attitudes and opinions that are anti-African, imposing negative messages about African-American people and culture to children and other young people, and even the denigration of their own phenotypical features such that individuals believe they are less beautiful and worthy of love to the degree that they differ from standards of beauty most closely associated with White men and women.

Such is the case, we believe, with Michael Jackson. Michael reportedly spent his adult years enduring cosmetic change after change, all with the apparent intention of erasing the facial features that defined his Africanness. However, despite the visible changes people could see, Michael Jackson only admitted to some cosmetic surgery on his nose. Hillburn (2009) offers an analysis of Michael's struggles with his appearance. In recalling an occasion where he and Jackson were mulling over some old photos, Michael came across one that elicited a verbal "oh that's horrible," while he physically recoiled while seated. One element of the reaction related to the adolescent acne on Jackson's face. But the most embarrassing part was his perception that "his nose was too big," such that people and fans might no longer consider him "cute little Michael." What this reporter and earlier interviews with other news correspondents (Bashir, 2003) reveal is that Michael also received specific ridicule from his father for his acne problem and his "pug nose." Ironically, while the world loved him in all of his beautiful Blackness (last seen in the cover of his "OFF THE WALL" album), he somehow never believed that he had the validation of the people he needed it from most, which are probably his parents, and most notably his father. Admittedly, Michael Jackson's father must be acknowledged for the tireless energy he put into raising his family, working a blue-collar job to support them before they achieved fame and fortune, and managing the instrumental roles of his parental responsibilities. However, what a shame that, according to Gilmore (2009), Hillburn (2009), and even Bashir (2003), and Michael Jackson's own account in "Moonwalk," he was never able to connect with his father in ways that a son ordinarily would. That relationship, and the reported physical and psychological toll it took on Michael, would never recover. A father driven to help his children climb that ladder of success created rehearsals that moved beyond practice, to rituals where mistakes became less about opportunities to improve song and dance techniques, and more about occasions where harsh words, ridicule, whippings, beatings, and physical abuse masqueraded as discipline from his father. Michael reportedly fought back, but encounters in individual daily battles ultimately yielded to losing a war within himself. Apparently, the contamination to Michael Jackson's spirit was a life long endeavor aided in part by his parent from whom he should have received that unconditional love. Also, it appears he could never reconcile that discrepancy between who he was at the core of his being (a beautiful and talented African-American male), and who he tried to be in an effort to please others he thought that he needed validation from. Ironically, his connectedness to the Black community was solid (even as he became a broader humanitarian), and the congruence between the targets of his philanthropy, and community consciousness he never lost sight of, was impressive. And still, the inner demons, while apparently allowing reconciliation with his reference group orientation (i.e., identification with the African-American and African world community), would allow no such closure with his personal identity. And so, his daily rituals of looking in the mirror reflected an individual apparently unhappy with what he saw. But was it just his physical features he was reported to loath? We suspect not. Indeed, if the man in the mirror loathed anything, if published reports cited earlier are to be believed, it was the absence of non-contingent love and approval he should have received at home in his formative years. So, what does this short analysis of Michael Jackson's developmental circumstances teach us, and people raising African-American children, about the importance of this struggle for identity congruence? Racism and social oppression are alive and well, and the pressure to conform to Eurocentrically oriented social norms is extreme. It is important to not simply love your children silently, but to let them know that they are loved and valued outwardly, and parental critique should be careful to focus on specific behaviors a child can change, and not the physical attributes a child was born with.

Experience has taught us that there is a cycle and a rhythm to life. Just as the seasons of the year move with rhythmic order, so to does the life of a professional entertainer and every young child in Black communities everywhere. Accordingly, while this segment has briefly highlighted the triumphs and tragedy of Michael Jackson's life and legacy in contemporary America, his struggles with his own personality dynamics, and those of countless African-American men and women, were instigated decades before, in a climate where questions of identity, purpose, mission, and the like were the fabric of a social movement for civil and human rights. Consequently, the essence of Michael Jackson's development as a singer and dancer extraordinaire, or for that matter any young Black child, does not begin with his aspirations to be the world's best entertainer, nor in dreams of a father committed to raising the family's standard of living and marketing the product known as the Jackson family children. Rather, it begins decades before when writers and activists like W.E.B. DuBois, Carter G. Woodson, Malcolm X, Martin Luther King Jr., James Baldwin, Maya Angelou, and others stirred the passions of a nation with their precise characterizations of African-descent people's dilemma in America. The individual and collective writings of these individuals framed the discourse on personal and collective identity development as a struggle to embrace the cultural aspects of oneself within the context of a socially oppressive society that neither supported nor affirmed your humanity as a person of African descent. Du Bois's (1903) classic text entitled *The Souls of Black Folks* spoke to the dilemma of balancing two competing worldviews. Woodson's (1933) work on *The Miseducation of the Negro* highlighted the consequences of yielding one's mind to alien (i.e., oppressor) control. Malcolm X and Martin Luther King, through their works and service, underscored the need for social action and cultural pride, while the stylistic works of James Baldwin (1963) and even Maya Angelou talked about the intense emotional pain associated with struggle, and the potential of the human spirit to regenerate itself.

SOCIAL PATHOLOGY OF AMERICAN LIFE

Another factor that has challenged African-American men's and women's sensibilities on the road to identity foreclosure is the prevalence of a social pathology that reeks havoc in the lives of African-descent people. Again, we want to reinforce, as Woodson (1933) has before us, that while some of the idiocy in life is instigated by factors external to people themselves, much of the psychological distress they experience can be attributed to internal forces within the minds of each individual. Thus if people allow others to control the way one thinks, the outcome can be the adoption of an inferior status mentality, even before one can be assigned by whatever force or person people perceive as the oppressor. Famed public intellectual, Dr. Cornel West, also weighs in on this discussion, as he provides the essence of a portrait of Black social misery that characterizes these historic and contemporary times. In "Black Strivings in a Twilight Civilization" (1999), he articulates a very precise analysis of how Black people have adapted to, and in some cases transcended, the misery and pain that characterize their lives. Like Du Bois (1903), Wright (1937, 1964), Ellison (1952), Baldwin (1963), Staples (1972), Majors and Billson (1992), and more recently Dyson (2004), West conveys the conditions of Black suffering, where he even characterized the American experience for Black people as a "chamber of Horrors." The horrors he describes speak directly to the very deliberate assaults and brutal attacks on Black people's minds, bodies, and spirits that have been perpetrated by various elements in American society from the citizenry to the very government to which they pledge their allegiance.

Parham (2009) comments on why he believes Dr. West's work is so profound. With the skill of a lay psychologist, he believes that West is able to capture the essence of the psychological adaptation and emotional tone of African-descent people who engage in profound struggles with the opposing forces of good and evil, while attempting to navigate the pathways to productivity and success. In essence, African-American people construct for themselves spiritual, cognitive, affective, and even behavioral spaces from which to pull on the reservoir of energy used to help them cope with life's circumstances and absurdities. "Black Strivings," as he calls them, are creative and complex structures of meaning, purpose, and feeling that allowed African-descent people to both maintain their sanity in the context of insane conditions and carve out for themselves strategies to sustain their needs for growth, regeneration, and self-preservation. These strategies were born out of African psychological and cultural traditions that help them improvise on, transcend, and sometimes transform their social circumstance using songs from the traditions of blues and gospel music as a way of keeping the faith and keeping hope alive, humor as a way to laugh to keep from crying, and poetry as a way to express insight and outrage, even if only in the abstract. The utilization of these art forms, Parham (2009) and West (2009) before him believe, help to create a cathartic effect similar to that which Black people experience in their therapy sessions with mental health professionals. The strength and resolve of the African psyche to cope and adapt, to seek truth in the midst of falsehood and deceit, to find hope in the midst of despair, to maintain one's sense of African consciousness in the face of hostile threat, and to "keep on pushin" (as the R&B group the Impressions would say) despite life's hardships is the essence of a Black strivings, where ideas of self, recognitions of where and who one is in the world, and strategies to help sustain some movement and momentum in the face of adversity are all part of normal and ordered behavior for the people whose interactions with the American experience has been so hostile.

BALANCING TWO COMPETING WORLDVIEWS

The study of the "psyche" in African descent people is, in fact, a study in adaptation, and not just an exploration of the psyche's composition. Cross (1991, 2001) articulates this point as he argues that the individual psyche and one's the environment collide in ways that mold people's character, and ingrain in them (sometimes rigid) strategies for traversing the landscape of life's interactions with people, organizations, and systems. If people are exposed to and nurtured by a wholesome upbringing that allows for a nurturing and supportive experience, then a healthy sense of self should be the developmental outcome. In that context, individual personalities grow into a full expression of each person's God given possibility and potential. Unfortunately, we recognize, as Cross (1991), Du Bois (1903), Ani (1994), and Parham (2009) do, that the disruptions in this process of normal healthy development, which is often instigated by racism and White supremacy, retard and/or otherwise disturb the cycle of normal growth and development for African-descent people. When such occurs, individuals react in ways that are ultimately functional, but sometimes maladaptive. The clearest evidence of this psychic adjustment and sometimes maladjustment referred to here is reflected in the racial designations that become self-referents (colored, negro, Black, Afro-American, African American), the sometimes self-destructive behaviors we engage in which prove detrimental to individuals specifically and communities generally, and the identity states or "duality" that people experience in their struggle to balance two competing worldviews.

With respect to racial designation labels, it is clear that persons of African descent have struggled with the notion of self-referents and whether to align certain racial designations (i.e., Colored, Negro, Black, Afro-American, African American) with what is popular in mainstream America, or what is more culturally congruent in their own minds and spirits. The choice some people adopt, interesting enough, has often depended on personal comfort, and their willingness to tolerate the potential scrutiny from the larger White society about what White culture finds as an acceptable label. Thus, over the last 300 years or more, persons of African descent have transitioned from self-referents like African, to referents like Colored, Negro, Black, Afro-American, and lately African American.

In other respects, adopting a name became a function of a sort of democratic sanity, where persons labeled themselves with terms the majority of Black folks were using at the time, without much critical thought about historical accuracy, or cultural consciousness and congruence. To a larger extent, however, the adoption of certain racial designations became a function of the political mood of the nation, the level of social unrest that African-descent people marshaled against the larger White society's power structure, and the cultural consciousness people found that enlightened their sensibilities. Stuckey (1987) makes this point very clear in his discussions involving "identity and ideology." He argues in fact that the popularity of certain racial labels was embraced or abandoned based upon both perceived political climate in the country and the Black community's sense of consciousness that was connected to periodic social movements. Regardless of which label has been used or which term enjoyed transient popularity, African psychology has been concerned with the process dynamics surrounding the relationship between racial designation labels, and the reflections these labels cast regarding the identity attitudes of the people who choose to adopt them. This is certainly true for those persons who experience some level of anxiety in attempting to cope with the duality of navigating at least two culturally different worldviews.

With regard to identity states, we have mentioned before and want to reinforce again that Du Bois (1903) is perhaps best known for labeling this duality, where life becomes an intricate dance of maneuvering in two worlds: one White and American, and the other Black, and African centered. His classic text entitled *The Souls of Black Folks* ably articulates the challenges of being a person of African descent in an American experience that has proven to be harsh, destructively discriminatory, brutally oppressive, and anything but supportive for most Black people. Consequently, there should be no surprise that Du Bois's work has been so influential in the articulation of this struggle for identity congruence in persons of African descent. In some respects, Du Bois's work underscores the dilemma of what it means to be Black in America. What is interesting about Du Bois's work, however, is not simply the intellectual constructs he advances (e.g., "double consciousness"), or his belief in a "talented tenth" notion scholars are fond to quoting. For us, Du Bois's life is a mirror in which is reflected the deep pain, psychic scars, and behavioral blisters of trying himself to successfully confront the most fundamental question of that day and this: "to be African or not to be"? In that struggle are the dueling sentiments of courage and fear, and despair and optimism. On one hand, as West (1993) reminds us, that Du Bois courageously argues for that the problems of all Black people needed to be directly attended to. However, Du Bois's work also signals a bias and question about the capability of the masses of Black people to participate in their own liberation struggle. This was the essence of Du Bois's "talented tenth" notion that is so often cited in the social science literature over the years. These biases and questions are balanced against a sense of hope and optimism about a people's ability to rise above their current circumstance. This was the conflict Du Bois wrestled with as he ultimately gave in to the personal despair regarding America's refusal, despite her pronouncements about "We The People . . .," to confront the race condition in America openly and honestly. This despair ultimately influenced his decision to leave the country and establish a new home in Ghana, West Africa.

Within Du Bois's work, one can see the psychic struggle to both achieve social progress, while simultaneously staying true to one's sense of identity and culture. This is the essence of the psychological and emotional skirmish persons of African descent struggle with, knowing that their Africanness was and is at the core of human authenticity. Du Bois's struggle in some respects is no different than the one African-descent people in contemporary America must face, including the late Michael Jackson. Parham (2009) writes that they (people of African descent) receive very little validation and affirmation for being their authentic Black selves. At the core of their being, they love their beautiful Blackness, but in certain situations, they learn to disguise it so as not to antagonize or make uncomfortable their White colleagues, neighbors, and/or social acquaintances. They wear it as a badge of cultural pride, and yet realize that doing so might antagonize their culturally different colleagues, resulting in restricted access to opportunities in the larger White world. They struggle with both self-imposed and socially imposed notions of invisibility. They confront what Parham (1989, 2009)has described earlier in this chapter as the essential question of: how one maintains a sense of cultural integrity in a world that does not support nor affirm your humanity as a person of African descent. It is this struggle that is so clearly captured in the Nigrescence writings of Thomas (1971); Cross (1971, 1991); Parham (1989); Helms (1990); Cross, Parham, and Helms (1998); Spenser and Markstrom-Adams (1990); Stevenson (1995); Swanson, Cunningham, Youngblood II, and Spenser (2009); and others, as they sought to describe the dynamics associated with the identity resolution process. Because we expect this emotional and intellectual "tug-o-war" to continue for some time to come, the topic is covered here in this fourth edition of *The Psychology of Blacks*.

THE PSYCHOLOGY OF NIGRESCENCE

If one can assume that the development of identity is a dynamic process, then movement from one set of attitudes or beliefs to another would be an expected outcome. In fact, a cursory look at the history of African Americans in this country clearly illustrates this phenomenon. Cross, Parham, and Helms (1998), in their comprehensive review of the Black identity development process, remind us that in light of the obsessive attempts at deracination (attempt to erase Black consciousness) by White people and White America, it comes as no surprise that within African-American history are accounts of Blacks who, having first been deculturalized, experience revitalization through a process of *nigrescence*. It is important to note here that nigrescence as a construct is derived from the French language, and literally means "to become Black." Nigresence models speculate that the identity development process is characterized by movement between various identity states and/or stages (Cross, 1971; Thomas, 1971; Helms, 1984; Parham, 1989). Cross (1971) introduced the description of the "Negro-to-Black" conversion experience by suggesting that the development of a Black person's racial identity is often characterized by his or her movement through five distinct psychological stages: Preencounter, Encounter, Immersion-Emersion, Internalization, and Internalization Commitment.

PRE-ENCOUNTER   In this stage, the traditional description characterizes the individual who is prone to view the world from a White frame of reference. He or she thinks, acts, and behaves in ways that devalue and/or deny his or her Blackness. The person has accepted a deracinated frame of reference; and because that reference point is usually a White normative standard, he or she develops attitudes that are very pro-White and anti-Black. Cross (1998) refers to this stage as one where the conditions for transformation and change are ripe. He suggests that at the center of the Pre-Encounter mentality be both an assimilation-integration philosophy that is linked to an attempt to secure a place in the socioeconomic mainstream, but motivated by a desperate attempt to insulate themselves from the implications of being Black.

ENCOUNTER   This stage is characterized by an individual experiencing one or many significant (shocking) personal and social events that are inconsistent with his or her frame of reference. For example, a Black person who views his or her race as not important and wishes to be viewed and accepted simply as a "human being" is denied access to living in an exclusive neighborhood because of skin color.

These encounters successfully shake a person's self-image of non-Black or "be like White" and make them vulnerable to a new interpretation of self in relation to the world. The Encounter stage appears to involve two phases. The first is a realization phase where an individual recognizes that his or her old frame of reference or worldview is inappropriate, and he or she begins to explore aspects of the new identity. The second phase (decision) occurs when the person, first cautiously, then defiantly decides to develop a Black identity. During this second stage, it is difficult to predict which specific encounter or how many encounters will be sufficient to instigate the psychic disruption that encounters bring. Parham (1993) has argued that the vulnerability to examine one's attitudes and beliefs about race will be influenced by the degree of psychological defensiveness present at the time of each encounter. If the degree of defensiveness is low, then the probability of change is increased. If, however, the degree of defensiveness is high, then many more encounter experiences may be necessary in order for a person to challenge his or her Eurocentric beliefs and attitudes.

IMMERSION-EMERSION   This stage represents a turning point in the conversion from the old to the new frame of reference. The period of transition is characterized by a struggle to repress or destroy all vestiges of the Pre-encounter orientation while simultaneously becoming intensely concerned with personal implications of the newfound Black identity (Cross, 1978). The person begins to immerse himself or herself into total Blackness, clinging to various elements of the Black culture while simultaneously withdrawing from interactions from other ethnic groups. Although the degree of overt manifestations of Blackness is high (i.e., Black clothes and hairstyles, attendance at all-Black functions, and linguistic style), the degree of internalized security about one's Blackness is minimal. At this stage, everything of value in life must be Black or relevant to Blackness. This stage is also characterized by a tendency to denigrate White people while simultaneously glorifying Black people (pro-Black/anti-White attitudes). Cross (1991, 1998) agrees that this stage represents the most sensational aspects of the identity development process, as it is the most disruptive of the stages. The emotional intensity required to both shake the vestiges of the old identity as well as that required to embrace the new identity is quite pronounced. Despite this emotional liability, through time and self-exploration, the individual is able to reconcile the various aspects of this transformative process and move toward a more crystallized picture of one's identity.

INTERNALIZATION This stage is characterized by the individual achieving a sense of inner security and self-confidence with his or her Blackness. The resolution of conflicts between the old and new worldviews becomes evident as tension, emotionality, and defensiveness are replaced by a calm, secure demeanor (Cross, 1978). This stage is also characterized by psychological openness, ideological flexibility, and a general decline in strong anti-White feelings. Although still using Black as a primary reference group, this person moves toward a more pluralistic, nonracist perspective (Cross, 1978). Having viewed the transformative process of nigrescence through a linear lens, it is tempting to believe that those who arrive at this stage have similar attitudes and beliefs. However, it is important to recognize that although internalized attitudes may correlate with a high salience to issues of race, not everyone who emerges with these attitudes will have the same salience for their Blackness. Some may express attitudes of Black nationalism, whereas others may see and relate to life in more multicultural terms.

CONTEMPORARY VIEWS

Although the nigrescence models by Cross (1971, 1978) and others (Thomas, 1971; Jackson, 1975; Williams, 1975) are helpful in illustrating both changes in attitude over time, and the within-group variability reflected in the consciousness of African Americans, they are also prone to limitations. Specifically, these models imply that although they are process in nature, their "development over time" focus is usually restricted to the late adolescence and early adulthood period in the life cycle. Consequently, although the stages articulated by Cross document how a person's racial identity can change from one stage to another (i.e., Pre-encounter to Internalization) during the later adolescent—early adulthood periods, they fail in their earlier iterations to detail how various stages of racial identity will be accentuated at later stages of life. In an article entitled "Cycles of Psychological Nigrescence," Parham (1989) presented a lifecycle nigrescence model based on a modification of the Cross stages. The first object of Parham's concern is pinpointing the earliest phase of life at which one is capable of experiencing psychological nigrescence (the process of developing a Black identity). He presupposes that the manifestations of identity during childhood are "more the reflection of parental attitudes or societal stereotypes that a youngster has incorporated" than the integrated, cognitively complex, identity structures found in adults. Consequently, Parham hypothesizes that it is during late adolescence and early adulthood that one might first experience nigrescence, and thereafter the potential is present for the remainder of one's life. Parham also notes in his writings that there is a qualitative difference between the nigrescence experience at adolescence or early adulthood, than, say, the nigrescence experience at middle or late adulthood, because an African-American person's concept of Blackness will be influenced by the distinctive developmental task associated with each phase of adult life. Perhaps the most profound issue Parham raises is not so much that aspects of the initial nigrescence episode vary with age; but having completed nigrescence, he sees the demand characteristics of each phase of adult development making more likely a person's recycling through the stages. From Parham's perspective, recycling does not mean the person reverts back to the old (Pre-encounter) identity and then traverses all the stages. Rather, he is inclined to believe that the challenge or trauma acts as a new encounter episode that exposes small or giant gaps in a person's thinking about Blackness, and the person recycles in order to fill such gaps. Thus depending on the nature of the challenge or the new encounter, recycling may mean anything from a mild refocusing experience to one involving a full-fledged Immersion-Emersion episode.

Another important advancement in Parham's (1989) writings is his recognition that a person's initial identity state is not restricted to Pre-encounter attitudes. This assertion represents a significant departure from the traditional nigrescence models presented by Cross, Jackson, and Thomas, which implicitly or explicitly suggest that one's racial identity development begins with a pro-White/anti-Black frame of reference or worldview. Parham speculates, for example, that if a young adolescent is exposed to and indoctrinated with parental and societal messages that are very pro-Black in orientation, the personal identity and reference group orientation initially developed by that youngster might be pro-Black as well. Contrary to the assumptions implicit in the original nigrescence models, we concur with Akbar (1989), who suggests that the process of identity formation that results from the positive encounters and affirmations of one's racial identity, rather than that which results from the negative encounter situations experienced in life, are a different and much healthier form of identity development. In fact, Parham (1989) is also clear in his assertion that African-American cultural identity is an entity independent of socially oppressive phenomena. This independent identity notion provides a critical extension of the original nigrescence theories that initially conceptualized Black identity and the affirmation of oneself as an African American as only a reaction to the oppressive conditions of White-American racism.

A third point of interest in Parham's model is his articulation that identity resolution can occur in at least three ways: **stagnation** (failure to move beyond one's initial identity state), **stagewise linear progression** (movement from one identity state to another in a sequential, linear fashion), and **recycling** (movement back through the stages once a cycle has already been completed). The Cross (1971), Jackson (1976), and Thomas (1971) models imply that nigrescence occurs in a linear fashion, with no other alternatives being proposed. More recent advancements in the nigrescence theory and research have both added to the expansion of specific stages as well as opened the model up to renewed criticisms. Cross (1991, 1998) has recognized that the original definitions of the Pre-encounter and Internalization stages may have been limited by their focus on single dimensions in each stage. In the case of the Pre-encounter stage, he now posits a continuum of racial attitudes that extend from low salience, to race neutral, to anti-Black. Thus, a person with Pre-encounter attitudes may acknowledge his or her Blackness while believing that it has little importance or meaning in his or her life (low salience), or he or she may express strong anti-Black sentiments as a way of denigrating the culture and distancing themselves from other African Americans who are perceived to be "too Black" for their personal comfort. With regard to the Internalization stage, Cross now takes the position that an individual's resolution of internalized attitudes will also vary, for example, from a monocukural focus (nationalistic) to one that is more multicultural in orientation. In either case, as with the Preencounter stage, it is important to remember that the nigrescence process does not evolve into a single ideological stance. Rather, there are a multitude of ways in which one's cultural pride and internalized identity may be expressed.

More recent additions in the nigrescence area have been promoted by Cross and Phegan-Smith (1996). In consolidating the nigrescence work of writers like Spencer, Stevenson, and Parham with other developmental theorists, they have advanced a model depicting the relationship between ego identity development and nigrescence. The model is based on the establishment of six sectors or periods that describe a life span scenario potentially influencing the evolution of one's ethnic identity. In each of the six life-span intervals, Cross and Phegan-Smith detail how African Americans embrace various aspects of their culture in reconciling the degree of salience ethnicity holds in their life.

Although work continues on advancing the nigrescence construct (Vandiver, Cross, Worrell, & Fhagan-Smith, 2002; Cross & Vandiver, 2001), including debating the merits of the concepts used and instruments employed to measure it (Cokley, 2007; Cokley & Chapman, 2009; Helms, 2007), it is also important to mention that the theory is not without its critics and detractors (Azibo, 1996; Stokes, Murray, Chavez, & Peacock, 1998), and that debate has continued to this day (Azibo & Robinson, 2004). Some of the critique continues to emerge from the orthodox African-centered school (i.e., Azibo) that apparently believes that the nigrescence construct lacks sufficient grounding in the cosmology of African-centeredness to be relevant, and more recently believes that the nigrescence process is "abnormal," and a sophisticated regression to a "deracinated psychologically misoriented misorientation" (Azibo & Robinson, 2004). Additional criticism suggests that the theory is anchored in the reality of African ethnic groups' experience with an oppressive French government (nigrescence is derived from the French language), thereby rendering it irrelevant to African-descent people in America. Adding to that debate, Cokley (2007) argues that psychometrically problematic instruments driven by rigid adherence to a particular ideology have slowed the study and advancement of the construct. Clearly, these debates will continue and deserve some attention for the way they interrogate the relevance of the construct, and the use of instrumentation and particular statistical analyses in understanding the measurement of racial identity. Unfortunately, some authors continue to adhere to questionable assumptions about whether individuals with internalized identity attitudes (as defined by the nigrescence stages) are somehow less Black, and do not prioritize the defense and promotion of African life and culture. Azibo (1996) and Azibo and Robinson (2004) fail to recognize that the oppression of African people is a global phenomenon related to the advancement of White supremacy. Therefore, whether you are in Europe, South Africa, the Caribbean, or America, the dynamics, we believe, are similar. When constructs like the nigrescence phenomenon emerge from the experiences of persons of African descent who happen to reside outside of the borders of the United States, they are no less realistic in their appraisal about the identity development process, particularly when it occurs within the context of social oppression. And, assuming that they are less committed to ideals and behaviors that align with a more African-centered lifestyle is at best questionable, and at worst, the height of arrogance to assume that there can only be one way to think and act as a person of African descent.

Equally interesting is the cyclical way in which themes of struggling with identity resolution, notions of invisibility, and psychological adaptation continue to appear on the landscape of the study of the psychology of African-descent people. Like Ellison's (1952) *The Invisible Man*, Franklin's (2006) analysis of the "invisibility syndrome" is right on target in describing both how society views persons of African descent and how they in turn experience the chronic assaults on their humanity. These assaults, or "microaggressions" as they were characterized by the psychological (Franklin, 1999) and psychiatric (Pierce, 1988) literature, further enhance the psychic tension and struggle African Americans face in seeking recognition, valuation, and validation for both who they are in the world and how they participate in their familial, social, occupational, academic, and even religious endeavors. The psychology of African-descent people continues to chronicle this struggle in the books, monographs, and journal articles being authored by numerous scholars.

In closing this chapter, we are also reminded that Leary (2005) also makes an important contribution to the African/Black psychology literature in her work on the *Post Traumatic Slave Syndrome*. In her text, which we cover more extensively in other chapters of this fourth edition, she chronicles the impact that racism, White supremacy, and social oppression have played in the lives of persons of African descent. Her theory builds on the work of others (Woodson, 1933; Akbar, 1992) by describing the patterns of psychological adaptation and survival skills Black folks continue to use, which represent residuals of past-trauma suffered by elders and ancestors in the Black community. Leary asserts that historical memories have been handed down to succeeding generations who continue to think, feel, and behave in ways that are both consistent with past generations of traumatized folks, and reflective of a psychological maladjustment that is detrimental to their future. The text seeks to provide the reader with greater insight into the African-American psyche, and the keys to aligning African thoughts, emotions, and behaviors with what is considered culturally congruent with the best of African traditions. Clearly, this whole notion of psychological retentions must be studied further, as African-American psychology seeks to understand the inner workings of the minds of African-descent people.

Summary

Achieving identity congruence in the face of racist and oppressive elements represents a significant challenge for most African Americans, not just entertainers and athletes. Undoubtedly, the achievement of congruence will be facilitated by several important propositions being promoted by contemporary Black psychologists. The first is borrowed from the ancient Africans and simply says, "Know thyself." Fundamentally, to know oneself (or one's nature) means to recognize, understand, respect, appreciate, and love those characteristics and/or attributes that make us uniquely African Americans. In addition, self-knowledge helps to dictate behaviors that ultimately support, sustain, and enhance our individual and collective beings as African Americans. Nobles (1986) asserts that in knowing one's nature, one is less likely to allow social and environmental conditions to become internalized, and in so doing, become the instruments of psychological maladaptation and dysfunction.

The second proposition is borrowed from Baldwin (1986), Kambon and Bowen-Reid (2009), and Akbar (1981, 2004), who suggest that a healthy African self-consciousness is probable if one's personality is nurtured in an environment of supportive personal and institutional systems. In their analysis, a healthy Black psyche is a prescription and a challenge. A prescription is a written (in this case) rule or law that outlines the necessary conditions to achieve a purpose or goal (identity congruence). Their prescription suggests the imperative to identify and utilize resources, networks, and institutions within the Black community that affirm and reaffirm our humanity as African Americans. Our parents, nuclear and extended families, schools, churches, social clubs and organizations, and other personal acquaintances must become the instruments by which we maintain congruence in African values and beliefs, and our primary sources of validation. The challenge is to recognize our collective responsibility to provide support and nurturance to persons and institutions within the Black community. Recognition of the sameness in ourselves and other African Americans and self-affirmation are natural outcomes when we extend ourselves to provide support, nurturance, and validation to others. Those who seek validation outside of their "community" will undoubtedly find identity congruence an unachieved goal. Functionally, this requires parents to not disguise but rather highlight those features of a child's physicality that define their beauty in all of its African splendor. From skin tones, facial features, hair textures, and body type, our children and adults must be told about how beautiful they are, and what a gift the CREATOR has blessed them with.

Lastly, Nobles (1986) also reminds us that ideas are the substance of behavior. Consequently, if our consciousness is culturally congruent, then our behavior should be focused on responding to our environmental realities in ways that help to enhance, maintain, and actualize our individual and collective beings as African Americans. In the African context of "being," the self is extended and collective, implying one's connections to others in the community, those yet unborn, and those belonging to the community of ancestors. It is critical to note, however, as Myers (1985) reminds us, that one's "being" did not automatically make one a part of the community, nor admit one to the position of ancestor at a later date (p. 35). Both roles required that each adopt a "proper" belief structure as evidenced through attitudes and behaviors. This is what is required of parents, teachers, mentors, Jegna's, or anyone who is interested in helping to properly socialize young children, and helping them develop a crystallized African-centered identity.

7

■■■

The Psychology of African-Centered Education

The challenges that confront the nation's system of education are significant, and yet people of all colors can no longer afford to engage these issues with attitudes that appear to perpetuate the status quo, or seem content with empty promises of "No Child Left Behind." The condition of our nation's schools; the growing disparities in educational achievement outcomes among culturally different students in general and African-American students in particular; the difficulty in lower income families accessing quality education; the scarcity of the best and the brightest college graduates who pursue teaching as a career; the lack of affordability for the middle, working, and lower classes; and the recurring debates about affirmative action in higher education mandate that these issues occupy a more central place in the discourse of our nation's domestic priorities. It is the premise of this fourth edition that African-American psychologists and others must speak boldly and clearly about these issues as well.

It is no small irony that this continuing debate around education takes place amid yearly celebrations when we honor the memory and legacy of individuals like the Reverend Dr. Martin Luther King Jr., who himself was a strong proponent of education. Consequently, it raises a question for each of us, much like Parham (2006a) has done, about how to honor and give proper respect to the man they call the "dreamer" and the "prince of peace." In his classic 1967 essay entitled "A time to break silence," Dr. King spoke out against the war in Vietnam, arguing that there comes a time when silence is betrayal. In his life, he challenged what he called the corruptness of an American government that spent more money on war and machines of destruction than on educating or feeding children. In a similar way, those who are committed to the psychological and educational growth and development of African-American children and adults cannot properly honor his legacy, and the principles of a human development we pretend to embrace, and remain silent about the military, social, political, and economic injustice that continues to plague our nation in 2010 and beyond. The discipline of African-American psychology must approach this dilemma by not only addressing the dynamics of educating African-American children and reforming schools, but also developing a platform that speaks to the need to reverse this trend of more money spent on a war in Iraq and Afghanistan than on educating children, fully funding schools, recruiting and properly compensating the best and brightest teachers, developing curriculum that both educates and excites our children, and youth mentoring programs.

NO CHILD LEFT BEHIND

In the first, second, and third editions of *The Psychology of Blacks,* White (1984); White and Parham (1990); and Parham, White, and Ajamu (1999) painted a dismal picture of the educational system, and the progress, or lack of, African-American youngsters were making in it. They introduced us to the notion of the "conveyor belt theory," suggesting that educational pursuits for many children and adults were tied to an implicit social contract where length in school was related to an increased range of choices and options in life. They also contended that the longer a student remained on the educational conveyor belt, the more informed and smarter he or she ought to be. Their collective statements of the problem generally suggested, however, as documented by the educational research of the 1960s and 1970s, that the longer Black children remain on the educational conveyor belt, the farther behind they fall. A more contemporary update of the academic progress and achievement of African-American youngsters reveals some slight change from the dismal reports of the 1960s through the late 1980s. A series of reports on the American educational system appeared in the early 1980s (National Commission on Excellence in Education, 1983; Goodlad, 1984; Task Force on Education and Economic Growth, 1983), and all commented on the overall failure of the educational system in preparing America's youth. To quote from *A Nation at Risk,* the most heralded report at the time:

> We report to the American people that while we can take justifiable pride in what our schools and colleges have historically accomplished and contributed to the United States and the well being of its people, the educational foundations of our society are presently being eroded by a rising tide of mediocrity that threatens our very future as a nation and a people.

To support this claim, the report sited, among other data, that 23 million adults were functionally illiterate, that there had been a decline over 17 years in SAT scores (a 50-point average decline for verbal scores, a 40-point average decline for mathematics); and that according to standardized tests, high school students were achieving at lower rates than they were some 26 years prior when Sputnik was launched. The academic profile of minority youth, particularly African Americans, was especially disturbing. Nearly 60 percent of African

Americans had completed high school, whereas only 12 percent were reported to have completed four or more years of college. The reports further indicated that African-American youngsters typically lagged behind their Anglo mates on almost every objective index of academic achievement. Most reports concluded that on standardized tests, average achievement scores of African-American youngsters in all subject areas are generally one standard deviation below their Anglo age-mates. In addition, the National Assessment of Education Progress (NEAP) measured achievement of youngsters at ages 9, 13, and 17, in seven content areas, including reading-literature-comprehension, music, art, citizenship, social studies, science, and mathematics. In tests administered from 1975 through 1982, African-American youngsters, in each age category, scored several points below the mean in each of seven content areas (NAEP, 1983).

Data from the NAEP's 1996 report, some thirteen years later, revealed that the gaps between African-American students and their White counterparts narrowed. Specific progress was noted in the areas of science, mathematics, and reading. However, the trend in writing continues unchanged (NAEP, 1996). Although the progress in certain areas was noteworthy, the factors that contributed to these trends were worth mentioning as well. National Center for Educational Statistics (NCES) data indicate that many African-American parents were involved in their children's education and actively participated by attending school events and by helping their children with homework assignments. For example, 1996 data indicate that 86 percent of African-American students reported having parents who attended scheduled meetings with their teachers, whereas almost half reported having parents who assisted with homework assignments at least three times per week. It is also clear from the data that African-American children seem to start their educational lives with cognitive, sensory, and motor skills equal to their Anglo age-mates, yet academic achievement levels for them seem to decrease with the length of time they stay in school. One of the culprits seems to be a family's socioeconomic status. It would not be uncommon to find, for example, that African-American children have fallen from one to three grade levels behind their White peers by the time they are in high school. African-American youngsters also seem three times more likely to be labeled as educable mentally retarded and to be enrolled in remedial educational programs. They are also half as likely to be enrolled in programs for gifted students when compared with their White counterparts.

The illiteracy rate for African Americans (44 percent) was more than two and one-half times that of Whites. Their high school dropout rates also continued to be high. Entrance rates into college for African Americans also decreased over the decade as well. In the late 1970s, slightly over 50 percent of African-American high school graduates entered college. By the early 1980s, the proportion of African Americans entering college had dropped to 36 percent. In California, for example, less than 4.5 percent of Black high school graduates were eligible for normal admission to a University of California school, and less than 11 percent were eligible for normal admission to one of the nineteen California State University campuses (California Post-Secondary Education

Commission [CPEC], 1988). The trend for African Americans finishing high school and entering college in the 1990s seemed to be on the increase. NCES data indicate that as of 1996, 87percent completed high school, whereas 56percent of those African-American students completing high school enrolled in college by October of that same year. Data also indicate that the percentages of 25- to 29-year olds finishing four or more years of college have risen to 16percent in 1997 (U.S. Department of Education, 2006).

In the earlier editions of this text, it was also pointed out that many African-American youngsters attended schools that were "in crisis." Several reports documented a growing number of cases of violence (e.g., student-student, student-teacher) and vandalism. Many of these same schools also had fewer experienced teachers and less-than-adequate teaching equipment and facilities. More recent data seem to suggest that similar factors continue to hinder educational achievement in the 1990s and 2000s, but that school location may have an impact as well. Most African Americans attending schools are located in the urban centers of this country. Teachers at schools in urban areas appear more likely to report the following: student apathy, drug use and abuse by students and some parents, student pregnancy, classroom discipline problems, weapons possession, and absenteeism (U.S. Census Bureau, 2000).

The educational attainment profile of African-American youngsters in the 1980s and 1990s was only slightly better than in previous decades, but still somewhat distressing. The continued travesty of this situation was all too apparent and the prospects of any positive, substantive change occurring in the near future was even less promising. Yet, taken collectively, these were the precise social and educational conditions under which the majority of African-American children live and were educated. Thus, it was clear that too many children, especially those of African descent, were being left behind, or otherwise forgotten in the realm of our nation's educational policies and practices. This is the challenge the country faced as the new millennium began.

NO CHILD LEFT BEHIND (NCLB)

"Leave no child behind (NCLB)." That was the motto the George W. Bush Presidency (2000-2008) trumpeted during the early years of his administration's national education policy that called itself trying to reshape the future of school children all across this nation, including African-American youth. The slogan, in and of itself, sounded reasonable, as then President Bush selected Education Secretary Margaret Spellings to trumpet this call to action. Higher standards, increased accountability, renewed interest on long neglected disadvantaged urban schools, parental options to redirect kids to alternate schools using vouchers, and incentives to do the right thing, were all part of the policy that aimed to address the problems that have plagued primary and secondary education for decades. While some elements of the African-American community were prepared to support any initiative that would promise to help ensure a proper education for their children, the policies of the Bush administration did raise several concerns among parents, teachers, as well as psychological service providers in the Black community who provide mental health and counseling support for our nation's schools. These include:

- The unfunded mandates that are long on accountability but short on financial resources to support our nation's schools, that characterized the NCLB policies

- Differences in per pupil spending between affluent schools and their less affluent counterparts, who despite their shortfall of resources, are held to the same standards of accountability

- The potential for vouchers that redirect children and families away from lower performing schools to contribute to the dismantling of public education

- The disproportionate numbers of African-American children in special education classes

Given these observations, what does the data show in recent years? The National Assessment of Educational Progress (NAEP) data from 2004 is contained in and quoted extensively in the 2009 "Condition of Education" (COE) report issued by the U.S. Department of Education's NCES, and the report issued in 2006. The COE is a congressionally mandated report that provides an annual portrait of education in the United States on some 46 indicators, including data broken down by race and ethnicity. In the area of reading, as in other categories, scores are compared at ages nine, thirteen, and seventeen. The data reveals that much like the scores from decades ago, reading scale scores are statistically lower for African Americans in all age categories, when compared to their White counterparts.

RACE	AGE 9	AGE 13	AGE 17
African American	200	242	264
White	226	266	293

In the domain of scale scores in mathematics, the data reveals the following trends, indicating statistically significant lower scores for African Americans when compared with other White students:

RACE	AGE 9	AGE 13	AGE 17
African American	224	262	285
White	247	288	313

Other data highlighted in the report discussed issues of preparation for college and SAT. Over the last decade or more, considerable emphasis has been placed on students participating in advanced placement (AP) courses as a way to better prepare for college, and make their applications more competitive. However, the NAEP data indicates that significantly fewer African-American students were taking and completing advanced placement courses, particularly in math and science. For example, 39 percent of Asian students, versus 20 percent of White, and only 11 percent of African Americans took courses in physics and chemistry. Similarly, only 5 percent of African Americans compared with 33 percent of Asians took courses in calculus. These data suggest that using this marker, there was no significant change for African-American students between 1998 and 2004 in completing advanced placement courses. In addition, there was a slight increase in the numbers of African Americans taking the SAT test over the past decade. However, data reveals that there continues to exist a gap of approximately one standard deviation (1 SD) between the verbal and math scores of African-American and White students (mean score is 500, with a standard deviation of 100). Verbal scores were 434 for Black students versus 527 for Whites; while scores in the quantitative domain were 429 for Blacks compared with 536 for Whites. Interestingly, while the achievement gap does not appear to be closing, despite the No Child Left Behind initiative, the rate of suspension from schools continues to impact African-American students disproportionately. Data reveals that suspension rates for African-American elementary and secondary students exceeded students from all other races, and the percentage of students who were retained for repeating another year at the same grade level was also high for African Americans. However, despite the suspension and retention rates, the 2006 data from the digest of Educational Statistics shows that dropout rates for African Americans declined from 14 percent in 1998 to 11 percent in 2006, both down from a high of 24 percent in 1975. Lastly, the percentage of students earning advanced degrees remained relatively constant, with 15 percent taking some college courses, 5 percent earning an associates degree, 14 percent earning a bachelors degree, 5 percent earning a masters degree, 1 percent earning another professional degree, and less that 1 percent earning a doctorate degree. Thus, if college degrees are the standard and measure of potential for upward mobility and employment viability, approximately 14 percent of African Americans have at least a BA degree or higher, while a staggering 51percent had no college education whatsoever.

TESTING VS. TEACHING

Within the eight-year rein of the Bush administration, the nation appeared to become even more obsessed with demonstrating the viability of particular educational strategies to produce positive results. In addition to initiatives like former corporate and military leaders, and even municipalities and state government managing large school systems, too many schools have reduced measures of accountability and "average yearly progress (AYP)" to performances on national tests, rather than really exploring what our children are learning everyday in classrooms all across this country, and how that knowledge base helps to guarantee brighter futures for these students. The challenge here, as Lipman (2002) points out, is that certain elements of the educational experience are sacrificed in schools that become preoccupied with the performance of their students on these national assessments. Specific elements of the educational experience that do get minimized include programs in music and the arts, initiative to develop stimulating curricula and innovative instructional methodologies, as well as the more personable dynamics of a teacher's relationship with their students. While the authors of this text are in favor of measuring competence and proficiency in all subject areas, concern must be expressed about any educational methodology that simply teaches young people to take and pass a test, rather than helps first assess the ways in which our children learn best, and then implements these strategies and techniques in classrooms across this nation. Thus, we are in favor of any strategy that helps to: properly train and empower teachers, increase levels of compensation for them to attract the best and the brightest, implement instructional methodologies that are culturally based, modify curriculum offerings to include more culturally enriching content, resist tendencies to classify children as uneducable or less than capable of learning, and contribute to the general and specific academic growth of African-American students.

EDUCATIONAL INNOVATIONS FROM THE OBAMA ADMINISTRATION

As we watch the Obama Administration consider its own education policy in 2009-2010, select Arne Duncan as its own education champion to occupy the Secretary of Education post, and decide whether or not to support or dismantle the NCLB initiative (which is a reauthorization of the Elementary and Secondary Education Act of the 1960s), the advocacy domain of African Psychology needs to go on record as opposing unfunded mandates, advocating for an equitable distribution of resources across all school districts, advocating for more systematic and culturally congruent ways to test and assess our children with instruments and methodologies that are strength-based, and opposing any attempt to dismantle public education. In making such considerations, the Obama Administration must confront the policies of the prior administration that some now consider a colossal failure. And yet, even with the critiques that are now directed at the Bush Administration's No Child Left Behind policy, we believe that credit must be given for two central themes of that legislation. These include a focus and spotlight on the incredible disparities in achievement rates between African-American children and their other racial counterparts, and the insistence on accountability that now permeates every aspect of the nation's educational policies.

It appears that as of the writing of this fourth edition, they are off to a great start. First, the Obama Administration and Secretary Duncan have made more federal dollars available to states and school districts through their stabilization funds, anchoring specific programs entitled "Race To The Top" and "Innovation and What Works" (three iii's funding). They have set out an ambitious agenda contextualized by a recognition that they have a "historic moment" to make change and improve low-performing schools that will last beyond the Obama Administration's tenure in office. The four pillars of their educational plans include: improving instruction and standards of accountability; recruiting, retaining, and supporting effective teachers and ensuring that they are distributed across school districts; reforming and transforming struggling schools; and making sure that all of their efforts are conducted in a climate of transparency around outcome data, spending, successes, and things that need improvement. Their focus appears to be aimed at all children and schools, but with particular emphasis on those students and districts where funding has been low, educational resources are inequitable, and achievements are in need of dramatic improvement. This text wants to support those aims.

In addition, as the Obama Administration decides what role the federal government will play in the reforming of our nation's schools, and reversing the underachievement trends for African Americans, they will also have to wrestle with the notion of decentralizing control of programs and funds to individual states. This posture implies that states will be equitable in distributing resources to communities in need. They would have people in the broader African-American community forget that most of the progress they have made in education, civil rights, and criminal justice has been because of federal intervention, when the states couldn't get it right. Only time will tell whether states can actively contribute to policies and practices that provide real and substantial reform to schools, while the federal government will have to meet its own yardsticks for measured progress.

THE CHALLENGES OF EDUCATION BEYOND 2010

Perhaps no other endeavor is more important to a people or a society than the education of its youth. After all, our youth represent our individual and collective hope for the future. Historically, the success and continued vitality of any society has been predicated upon its ability to prepare future generations for varied life challenges. Consequently, education has been the primary method employed by societies in orchestrating the successful development of future generations for their societal roles and responsibilities. It is our belief that the foundation for the educational success of our youth has been predicated upon a collaborative relationship between the home, the school, and the community. Unfortunately, this collaboration is nonexistent in many communities across this nation, and consequently our children suffer because of it. One has only to examine the academic profile of African-American youth presented earlier in this chapter to realize this truth.

ACADEMIC PROFILE CAUTIONS

Most profiles of the kind reported herein, however, need to be viewed with some caution. These kinds of statistical summaries, although useful, often fail to provide a balanced picture. The academic achievement profile of African-American youngsters just presented, for example, says little about those youngsters who are in fact succeeding academically. Many of these youngsters are reared in the same environment within which many of their African-American peers are failing, yet some are succeeding at rates equal to, if not in excess of, their White peers. What factors contribute to the differential academic success

rate of African-American youngsters given that all of them are essentially products of the same environment? Perhaps an understanding of the correlates of
achievement might provide us with an answer of these questions. Parham,
White and Ajamu (1999) have identified six correlates of achievement that they
feel are key to the academic survival of African-American youth, which were
presented in our 1999 third edition. In this fourth edition, we continue to embrace these variables as central to the academic achievement of African-
American students.

CORRELATES OF ACHIEVEMENT

Identifying the correlates of positive and negative achievement for the African-
American youngster remains a central focus for those concerned with the educational achievement of African-American students. These variables or factors
are key to any discussion about education for they invite scholars and advocated alike to make attribution about why things are the way they are, and what
might be done to improve the condition of education in this country. The list of
factors that potentially correlate with (either positive or negative) academic
achievement is almost endless. Yet, several factors are more consistently identified as contributing to or inhibiting academic achievement in Black youngsters.
White and Parham (1990) and Parham, White, and Ajamu (1999) have suggested that these factors include self-concept, value orientation, teacher expectation, family composition, poverty, and parent educational attainment. In this
fourth edition, we would add academic achievement motivation, and personal
and academic self-efficacy.

Academic Achievement Motivation

Achievement motivation, as originally defined by McClelland (1961) and more
recently by Graham (1994), relates to those personal factors that motivate a
child to compete and achieve in his/her academic endeavors with a standard of
excellence. Unlike the research of old that focused on locus of control (Rotter,
1966) and success expectations (Rosen, 1959), however, Hudley (2009) advances the need to abandon such research and argues persuasively that constructs such as self-beliefs like self-concept and self-efficacy, combined with an
individual's perceptions about barriers to success, account for higher percentages of the variance in explaining the academic achievement question. In that
vein, while it is important to acknowledge environmental factors that impact a
child's willingness and urge to excel, we are not willing to surrender the construct of motivation to the realm of the external. For us, this concept of motivation, and achievement motivation in particular, is an internal construct particular to each and every child. Achievement motivation emerges naturally, as a
child pursues his or her own inquisitiveness about the nature of things, the interaction with people, and the application of knowledge that can be used to address situational and life circumstances. It can be reinforced by those significant
others in a child's life, who acknowledge the child's efforts to pursue a particu-

lar goal or outcome, and celebrate the child's success on a given task. The task of parents in this regard is to help their children remain excited about learning; knowing that with each element of new found knowledge, and the delight that child displays in acquiring that information, there is an element of personal satisfaction in achieving that task that will naturally reinforce the desire to achieve and excel to higher and higher goals.

Self-Efficacy

Efficacy, in its basic form, is really about confidence. It answers the question of how confident a child is in knowing that they can successfully complete or accomplish a task. In some respects, the issue is not simply about accomplishing a task per se, but rather completing that task at a particular level consistent with what that individual was striving for. Efficacy beliefs are an important construct, given the relationship that has been determined to exist between it and academic constructs such as grade point average, and even the process of transitioning from grade school to middle school. Apparently, research has demonstrated that for African-American children, self-efficacy significantly predicts the level of academic achievement in sixth-grade students, particularly as they prepare for and transition to middle school (Gutman & Midgley, 2000). It is also important to note here that academic self-efficacy is impacted by gender, as studies show that efficacy beliefs are much stronger predictors of high school females of African descent than their male counterparts. Irrespective of that qualifier, however, it is important for parents to ask themselves the question of how they can boost the confidence of their primary-, middle school-, and high school-aged children. Talking to them about success is important. Helping them demonstrate success on certain tasks is important. And yet, the central theme we believe it is important to get across to children is that real confidence does not come from an over abundance of self-esteem; rather, it comes from an absence of a fear of failure. In addition, creating and sustaining an environment where the home, school, and community are all involved in expressing messages of optimism, and confidence in a student's ability to master a given task will go a long way toward helping that child develop a sense of self-efficacy.

Poverty

Among the variables that significantly impact our children and their educational achievement is the issue of poverty. Recent data now available indicate that nearly one in four African Americans (24.3 percent) continued to live in poverty during the fiscal year 2006 (U.S. Census Bureau, 2008). Research also indicates that poverty rates disproportionately impact African Americans with 57 percent of children lived in low-income families. This figure is nearly twice the rate for White children (34 percent) nationwide. When accounting for children up to the age of 18, one-third (33 percent) of African-American youth lived in poverty, compared to a national average of 9.8 percent.

The recitation of these statistics is distressing when one considers how far-reaching the impact of poverty can be. Fields (2003) reinforces data from the

Children's Defense Fund of the middle 1990s, which found that children living in poverty were more likely to be classified as children with learning disability and to experience educational failure when compared to more socially advantaged, non-poor children. It is also important to note that according to research data, nearly one in five of these poor children will experience homelessness during their lifetime, putting them at further risk for educational failure and dropout, drug use and abuse, and diminished employment opportunities. These data continue to support the analyses provided by many researchers, who also assert that achievement scores nationally show a strong correlation between low achievement and higher concentrations of poverty, particularly in urban areas.

Self-Concept

Another variable that undoubtedly influences the achievement aspirations of Black youngsters is self-concept. Yet, exactly how self-concept impacts achievement aspirations yields debatable answers. Psychologists and sociologists have argued that the self is found to be in direct relation to how a person thinks others perceive him or her (Mead, 1934; Rogers, 1961). Thus, a person in our society validates his or her identity through the evaluations of significant others. If the notion of necessary external validation is accurate, it seems reasonable to assume that the achievement aspirations of Black youngsters would be influenced by evaluations by significant others in the child's life.

Although such an assertion might be reasonable, researchers have had difficulty agreeing on from where the child's source of validation is derived. Some research suggests that validation and approval are derived from the Black community (Banks & Grambs, 1972; Barnes, 1972; Norton, 1983). Unfortunately, the larger body of research suggests that approval is sought from the dominant White culture (Kardiner & Ovessey, 1951, 1968); and because of the negative attitudes perpetuated by the larger White society, positive achievement by Blacks was not an unexpected outcome.

Investigations of the Black self-concept and self-esteem have generally assumed that every aspect of Black life is a reflection of the group's castelike position in the dominant society, and that Black Americans are incapable of rejecting the negativistic images of themselves perpetuated by the dominant White society. The prototype for these studies was presented by Clark and Clark (1940, 1950) in an investigation in which they found that Black children preferred White dolls to Black dolls. They concluded that the children's White doll choice was a reflection of their group self-hatred. Other studies followed (Goodman, 1952; Morland, 1958) that similarly pointed out the tendency for Black children to identify with and/or prefer White skin, White dolls, and White friends. These identity problems, the literature suggested, were linked to problems of self-evaluation. In addition, the literature further pointed out that Black people's assignment to second-class status, together with White racists' insistence on Black people's innate inferiority, no doubt was instrumental in creating doubts in Black people concerning their own worth (Arnez, 1972).

Several authors have sought to explain this self-hate phenomenon by hypothesizing that Black people's hostility toward the oppressor was so threatening that repression of hostile feelings was the only means by which they could deal with their feelings (Kardiner & Ovessey, 1968). In turn, the repressed hostility was redirected internally, and thus stimulated self-hatred. Other attempts were made to explain Black self-hatred by pointing out Black people's simultaneous feelings of hatred of the oppressor and desires to imitate him or her, thus resulting in feelings of self-hate, confused identity, and the like (Kardiner & Ovessey, 1951). It was, in fact, Kardiner and Ovessey (1951) who clearly exemplified this negative analysis of Black subgroup status when they asserted,

> The Negro has no possible basis for a healthy self-esteem and every incentive for self-hatred. The basic fact is that the Negro's aspiration level, good conscience, and even good performance are irrelevant in face of the glaring fact that the Negro gets a poor reflection of himself in the behavior of Whites, no matter what he does, or what his merits are. The chief distinguishing factor in the Negro is that he must identify himself with the Negro, but this initiates the compensatory identification with the White (person) who is also hated. (p. 297)

Dansby (1972) suggested that an example of this "identification with the aggressor" or imitation of Whites could be seen in Black people's use of cosmetic products to make themselves appear White (i.e., straightening hair or lightening skin tones). In addition to these behavioral examples, the literature was replete with studies describing this identification with the oppressor phenomenon. Bayton, McAliste, and Hamer (1956) described minority group persons as tending to idealize the majority group, thus contributing to their own self-rejection. Also, Pettigrew (1964) cited a large body of psychological literature that demonstrated the power of role-playing on conceptions of self. He postulated that Blacks had played the role of "stupid," "slow," and "inferior" to appease the White power structure to the detriment of their own self-esteem and integrity.

Wyne, White, and Coop (1974) has also addressed the consequences of this role-playing behavior. He asserted that when the minority tends to use the majority as an emulative reference group, as Blacks have done, the result is usually that the minority tends to adopt those behaviors and beliefs about the self that they feel the majority holds to be desirable. Wyne concluded that the effect becomes a self-fulfilling prophecy, reinforcing the prejudiced feelings and beliefs of the majority.

What might be added to the observations by Pettigrew (1964) and Wyne, White, and Coop (1974), however, is the possibility that such role-playing may also hinder attempts by researchers to perceive, understand, and/or interpret the nature of Black self-concept. Both authors seem to suggest that Black people have often felt it necessary to conceal their true selves in order to survive in a racist social order. Ames (1950) speaks to this phenomenon of "role-playing" or "mask wearing" as he states, ". . . got one mind for White folks to see; another for what I know is me." Although explanations and observations of this tendency to disguise oneself appear less frequently in the literature, they do provide additional data through which to evaluate studies on the Black self.

As the above studies indicate, it was common for White and Black social scientists to write and reiterate that Black people, in general, have had a negative self-concept. Furthermore, these tendencies toward negative self-conceptions have been linked to phenomena such as identification with the aggressor, over-assimilation, and low achievement.

In contrast to the low self-concept/low achievement-oriented studies of the past, more contemporary research cites evidence that, indeed, African-American children do have positive racial self-concepts (Powell & Fuller, 1970; Soares & Soares, 1969). In fact, Powell (1973) concludes that the concept of low self-esteem in Black children should be disregarded in light of several extensive literature reviews (Wylie, 1978; Rosenberg, 1979; Weinberg, 1977) that revealed (1) little or no differences in self concept between Black and White children, and (2) higher self-esteem scores in Black children.

The low self-concept conclusion of the past has also been questioned by challenging the notion that Black children agree with and internalize the negative evaluations of them promoted by the larger society. On the contrary, several studies have indicated that African-American children do not believe or agree with negative stereotypes about themselves or that they are inferior (Brigham, 1974; Campbell, 1976; Rosenberg, 1979). Accordingly, what has been overlooked is the minimization of the role of the oppressor (in influencing self-images), and more specifically, the adaptive strengths of the African American (child). Consequently, social scientists, teachers, and students themselves must come to grips with the fact that positive academic achievement among Black children is not only a possibility, but also a realistic expectation.

Although the debate over the disposition of the Black child's self-concept may be temporarily suspended, the notion that a child's sense of self influences his or her academic achievement appears to be unanimous. If such is the case, how can the community contribute to the development of a healthy self-image? We believe that parents and immediate family must provide reinforcement for a child's self-image by instilling a sense of pride, and by acting as a filter for the negative images a child is exposed to. Parents and schools must play a role in communicating both expectations and encouragement for achievement, and constant praise and reinforcement for a child's mastery of various developmental and educational tasks. Children must also be assisted in identifying and participating in positive peer relationships and group activities that reinforce a positive sense of self. Each of these influences, together with other community resources (churches, parks and recreation, business leaders), must collaborate to reinforce for the African-American child principles of self-affirmation and self-determination. Other suggestions for enhancing self-concept were provided by Powell (1985) in her study on the effects of school desegregation on the self-concepts of Black children. Her investigation concluded that in order for self-concept of children in various schools to develop in a normal pattern, several criteria seem to be necessary. Those factors included: (1) maximum participation by parents and teachers, (2) mores and values of the home reinforced in the immediate community and school, (3) Black culture and lifestyles reflected in the educational curriculum, and (4) academic achievement being encouraged regardless of social class.

Value Orientation as a Correlate

Thomas (1967) defines values as a normative, conceptual standard of desired behavior that influences individuals in choosing among personally perceived alternatives of behavior. Values are believed to influence ways in which people think, feel, and behave (Kluckjohn & Strodtbeck, 1961). As such, values may also influence academic achievement of Black youngsters. Much of what a Black youngster comes to value positively and negatively in the world is influenced by what significant others in his or her life value as well. Typically, values of specific ethnic groups are transmitted from generation to generation in ways that allow cultural traditions to continue and self-actualizing behavior to flourish. Occasionally, however, perceptions that culture-specific values are less functional than values of other cultures force many Black youngsters to abandon traditional African-American values in favor of Eurocentric ones. One consequence of this phenomenon is the adoption of many behaviors that are perceived as functional but ultimately prove to be self-destructive to the individual and the community. Nobles (1980, 1986) helps to clarify the relationships between personal values and academic achievement by suggesting that ideas are the substance of behavior. Essentially, Nobles implies that the development of a strong desire to achieve academically and behavior directed toward that goal attainment are facilitated by a conceptual grounding in the philosophies of African culture.

The notion that education is a necessity for survival and advancement of one's people and oneself is a value that must be promoted by significant others in the child's life. We believe that academic achievement in Black youngsters occurs when achievement is encouraged and supported by the community at large. Families, schools, churches, community organizations, and peer groups must come together in a collective voice and support efforts toward excellence.

In absence of a unanimous consent for this idea, there must be enough support from particular significant others in the child's life, in order for that value to be internalized and practiced by the youngster.

The present authors would also argue that academic achievement is stifled when motivation to achieve is nonexistent and the desire to achieve is challenged by environmental obstacles that prevent goal attainment. If the Black community is to be the reference point around which Black youngsters seek validation and support, then the community must also accept the challenge of eliminating those barriers that prevent Black youth from achieving academically. Ironically, the very institutions that are supposed to encourage achievement are the ones that hinder it. Nowhere is this example clearer than in some of our schools.

Primary and secondary educational institutions have become havens for drug abuse, gang violence, extortion, and misconduct. Many youngsters are more concerned with mastering the intricacies of selling drugs for profit than they are about learning the intricacies of reading, writing, and counting. The idea of making large sums of money without much work proves to be a powerful distracter to many youth. Clearly, there is a deterioration of African values when the attainment of wealth and material possessions at any cost are valued over the uplifting of one's people.

However, there are many youngsters who emerge from what is perceived to be negative environments with the determination to succeed in life's endeavors. We believe that youngsters who make it, and who are successful in achieving academically, manage to remain focused on an ideal of self-determination. They develop the will and intent to succeed in spite of negative elements and seemingly insurmountable obstacles in the environment. Indeed, it is the child himself or herself who must choose a commitment to excellence over destructive distractions. Having said this, however, we do recognize that individual choices are influenced by elements in the environment that shape the way our children process information and make sense out of their world.

Kunjufu (1986) suggests that values are the foundation for motivation, which in turn influences one's behavior. He further asserts that values are developed and nurtured through exposure to information. If Kunjufu's assertion is at all correct (and we suspect it is), then some analysis of the types of information our children are receiving (or not receiving) is in order, and may help to crystallize how incorporation of values influence achievement of Black youngsters.

Exposure to massive amounts of television on a daily basis has been identified as one of the prime socializers of African-American youngsters. In subtle and some not-so-subtle ways, our children's value systems are being influenced and shaped by what they visually and auditorily absorb from that medium (Berry, 1982). This realization is compounded by the notion that Black children devote a disproportionately high amount of time to television viewing (as high as 6 hours per day), and like other children are likely to believe that television accurately reflects life as it really is or should be (Greenberg & Dervin, 1970). Berry (1982) helps to further clarify the question of television's influence on the development of values and the desire to achieve by asking two questions. First, television depicts levels of academic and occupational attainment. To what extent does television convey to African-American children the concept that they can be successful only in a (Black) environment, and to what extent must aspiration for broader occupational and academic positions in a multicultural world be limited?

Second, television occupies a prestigious position in our society and for some young people, it tends to validate and add glamour to the roles being played. To what extent are children patterning their behavior and establishing personal attitudes (and values) from television characters who may not be wholesome role models? Children are being exposed to images and role models who depict the Black community in very negative ways. Images of street-smart children and adults who will do whatever it takes to "get over" (lie, cheat, steal, murder, sell narcotics) are very inappropriate. Images of Blacks being confined to low-status jobs and being prevented from exploring a wider variety of career options are also inappropriate, and may be especially damaging to a child's achievement aspirations. Scenarios that promote money, status, material possessions, and sexual exploits as measures of manhood and womanhood are extremely destructive.

In many cases, the Black community has reacted strongly to these negative portrayals of Blacks on television by calling for a change of venue. Yet, the very community that demands that television images change fails to realize that the validation for our children adopting these negative stereotypes and portrayals is being provided in and by the community itself. Street corners are filled with dozens of individuals who have simply given up on life and feel helpless to change their condition. Parents also fail to support their children in their educational pursuits in a number of ways. If exposure to information is to remain as a prominent influence on values, and values in turn influence behavior, then manipulating the type, amount, and quality of information our children receive will help them develop a value system that is more consistent with their African culture. Such values might include, for example, the principles of *Nguzo Saba* (Karenga, 1976), which are part of the yearly Kwanzaa celebrations, which take place between December 26 and January 1 of the annual holiday season. These annual celebrations continue to be celebrated in families across this nation and are even beginning to penetrate the halls of primary, middle, and secondary schools over the past decade of this new millennium. These include

Umoja—Unity

Kujichagulia—Self-determination

Ujima—Collective work and responsibility

Ujamaa—Cooperative economics

Nia—Purpose

Kuumba—Creativity

Imani—Faith

Presentation of, and teaching about, African-Centered value systems continues to be an important strategy in helping our children develop the will and intent to achieve.

Teacher Expectations as a Correlate

Teacher expectations is yet another correlate of academic achievement that spawned wide scale interest among researchers. The bulk of the studies suggesting that teacher attitudes and expectations affect a child's school performance began to appear in the late 1960s and early 1970s, when Rosenthal and Jacobson published their now classic study, *Pygmalion in the Classroom* (1968).

At the heart of the Rosenthal and Jacobson experiment was a belief that teacher's expectations would significantly affect the learning of a group of socially and racially mixed elementary school children whose teachers were told possessed special intellectual talents. The teachers were also told that these "talented" children would show marked intellectual improvement by the end of the first few months of the experiment. The results confirmed the experimenter's prediction in that these intellectually talented students scored significantly higher than the control group on measures of IQ.

In explaining their results, Rosenthal and Jacobson speculated that teachers are especially attentive to students who are expected to show intellectual promise. These students are often treated in a more encouraging manner, and teachers tend to show increased tolerance and patience with the child's learning process. The converse is true for students perceived to be less intellectually gifted. When students are not expected to make significant educational gains, then less attention and encouragement is given to them.

Several other studies (Beez, 1969 Palardy, 1969; Rothbart, Dalfen, & Barrett, 1971; Rubovitz & Maehr, 1973) documenting the teacher expectancy effect came on the heels of the heralded "Pygmalion" experiment. In a study conducted by Beez (1969), for example, faked psychological dossiers that described "high-ability" preschool students in favorable terms and "lower-ability" preschool students in less favorable terms were given to teachers who worked with these high- and low-ability preschoolers on simple word learning tasks. As predicted, high-ability preschool students learned more words than their low-ability peers. This differential in performance among the preschool students, according to Beez, was attributable to, at least in part, the expectations of the students held by teachers of both groups.

Palardy's (1969) study examined the differential perceptions of teachers and wondered what effect these perceptions would have on boys and girls learning to read. Despite every child receiving above-average reading pretest scores, boys taught by teachers who perceived their ability to learn to be as good as girls learned as good as girls. Boys taught by teachers who perceived their ability to learn to be lower than girls were outperformed by girls. The Rubovitz and Maehr (1973) investigation took a slightly different slant in that differential teacher expectations with respect to student's race and learning ability were of interest. A group of four mixed-ability eighth-grade students (two African-Americans and two Anglos) were assigned to 1 of 66 women teachers (creating 66 teacher-student groupings), and two of the four students in each group (one African-American and one Anglo) were randomly given high IQ scores. The experimenters found differential teacher expectancy effects in predicted and unpredicted directions, and the student's race proved to be a very salient factor. African Americans, both gifted and nongifted, received less favorable treatment than gifted and nongifted Anglos. In rank order, increased attention and encouragement were given to gifted Anglos, nongifted Anglos, nongifted African Americans, and gifted African Americans. In essence, African-American giftedness was penalized with less attention and praise, whereas Anglo giftedness was rewarded. By way of balance, it should be pointed out, however, that not all teacher expectancy studies resulted in a finding consistent with the investigations just cited. The Claiborn (1969) and Fleming and Anttonen (1971) studies are cases in point. Both involved the usual teacher-student grouping, and expectations of students' intellectual talent (or lack thereof) were shaped using fake data. Posttest results in both studies failed to show greater relative gains in learning between experimental and control groups.

PARENT EDUCATION ATTAINMENT

The relationship between a child's educational achievement and poverty is even more pronounced when one considers the effects of a parent's educational background. The high poverty rate of children in families in which the parent has less than a high school degree results in part from lower wages paid to those without college degrees (NCES, 1997). The disproportionate impact on African-American families can be seen in rates nearly four times higher when compared to White families. The NCES estimates that in 1995, 16 percent of African-American parents had not completed high school compared to just 4 percent for White parents.

Family Background as a Correlate

Historically, many social scientists have attempted to answer the question of academic achievement in Black youngsters by assuming that the environment negatively impacted the child. That is, it was assumed that low achievement was related to an absence of supportive attributes external to the child himself or herself. The chief scapegoat in these studies appears to have been the family.

As early as the 1930s, research sought to document the consequences of poverty on the perceived instability, weakness, and disintegration of the family (Frazier, 1939). Not surprisingly, much of the research that followed attempted to validate these prior assumptions about the pathological Black family (Moynihan, 1965; Rainwater, 1970) Moynthan (1965), for example, characterizes the family as "tangled and a web of pathology."

Similarly, Rainwater (1970) suggested that the functional autonomy of the Black family reflected destructive features that expressed themselves in violent, repressive, and depraved lifestyles. These studies went on to further suggest that this disorganized family contributed to personality, social, cognitive, and mental deficits in Black children.

By and large, the family variables that were identified as culprits included low socioeconomic status, a matriarchal family structure, and a lack of educational resources (Clark, 1983). Assuming these factors are absolutely essential in promoting academic achievement in some youngsters, perceived low achievement by Blacks came as no surprise. Explaining positive achievement of Black youth who are nurtured in a supportive environment has been a recent, albeit infrequent, focus in the literature. For one thing, crediting the Black family (supportive or not) with helping to develop and promote achievement ideals occurs on too few fronts.

Images of the pathological and disorganized family have begun to change over the past decade, however. In some respects, the formation of positive family images has been assisted by researchers who understood that previous characterizations of the unhealthy Black family were in part influenced by biased assumptions and conclusions of the previous researchers themselves. Not surprisingly, then, these latest studies (Billingsley, 1968; Hill, 1971; Ladner, 1971; Stack, 1974 have served as a reaction to previous Black family research by criticizing previous research efforts, and by attempting to explain family dynamics and composition in a way that highlights strengths of the family. For example, Billingsley (1968) cautions researchers against classifying the "Black family" as a single entity, rather than recognizing that, indeed, there is not "one" description that accurately characterizes the Black family of today. Similarly, Hill (1971) presented strengths or factors that have helped Black families to sustain themselves under less than ideal circumstances. These include strong orientations to work, religion, and achievement; strong kinship bonds; and role flexibility by family members.

Recent studies on the Black family have continued to substantiate the work by Billingsley, Hill, and Ladner by isolating those factors that help modern-day Black family members in meeting their needs (McAdoo, 1986; Nobles, 1986). Although these studies have been successful in characterizing the Black family as a vehicle that presumably helps to foster academic achievement in Black youth, they (studies) have been limited in their ability to explain exactly how achievement is supported and encouraged. One of the most important studies to emerge in the literature over the past thirty years that attempts to explain this phenomenon was conducted by Clark (1983). Clark attempted to answer the question of why poor Black children succeed or fail in his book on *Family Life and School Achievement*. Essentially, in his ethnographic study conducted in a major Midwestern city, he compared and contrasted five high-achieving with five low-achieving students, and identified parenting and child development strategies used by each family. He concluded that parental dispositions and interpersonal relationships with the child are the main contributors to a child's success in school. Perhaps the most profound statement made in Clark's research effort is that communication and quality of interaction are more important than sociodemographic variables (i.e., family composition, income status) in predicting high achievement in Black youngsters. It is our contention, however, that although quality of interaction between parent and child is an important component in school achievement, we cannot overlook a youngster's willingness and motivation to respond to supportive environmental cues. Indeed, motivation is a characteristic that emerges from within the child himself or herself.

EDUCATIONAL CHALLENGES FOR THE NEW MILLENNIUM

One of the most important challenges facing African Americans as we end the first decade of the new millennium is to reexamine the purpose of education. In many corners of our communities throughout this nation, education has been linked to one's career aspirations. Thus, the purpose of education in the minds of too many young people and their parents is to secure the best possible job or career position with the ultimate intent of securing greater access to wealth and possessions. Too many of our families have joined the race for higher scholastic achievement (i.e., SAT and ACT) scores and admission to prestigious colleges and universities at the expense of some equally important ideals. Be clear that we do not argue against preparing ourselves to compete with society's standards of excellence. However, if our purpose for education is relegated to these academic pursuits alone, then we miss something very valuable about education in an African-centered context.

Hilliard (1997), in his text entitled *SBA: The Reawakening of the African Mind,* reminds us that in ancient, historical, and contemporary African societies, education emphasized the process of socialization Thus, the education a student received was intrinsically linked to one's personal development and transformation. This transformation not only led to a more enlightened self, but also helped each student explore a deeper relationship with the Divine, commit to a set of cultural values (i.e., MAAT, which is defined as a code of conduct and standard of aspiration for the Ancient African Egyptians) that were life-affirming principles, and explore ways of achieving maximum congruence between thought and behavior.

In a similar way, our educational practices need to reengage the process of socialization such that we prepare current and future generations of students and teachers to have more enlightened minds, more spiritually principled values, and more culturally congruent behaviors that contribute to the individual and collective uplifting of African people. Although we also recognize that African-descent people control few, if any educational institutions (particularly at primary and secondary levels), our task is to convert those institutions that do exist in our communities into centers for the socialization and transformation of our people. In that way, our communities and our families help facilitate the transmission of culture and guide the transition from personhood to peoplehood.

We have attempted to point out in this chapter that the academic achievement of African-American youngsters, generally speaking, continues to be less than satisfactory. If one looks at the data presented and concludes that educational and academic achievement is a hopeless enterprise, then the future of African-American educational achievement is bleak indeed. If, however, one views the data with concern and uses them as an opportunity to make a difference, then there are some additional challenges that face school systems, the African-American community, and indeed the students themselves as we move into the next decade beyond 2010.

There also is the question of role definition, which requires all of us, including those in the psychological community, to ask ourselves whether or not we define our roles as educators in terms of function, or in terms of needs of our students. Defining our roles in terms of function relegates educators to certain activities (lecture, answering questions, office hours, grading tests). Defining a role in terms of the needs of students, however, requires that educators become a barometer of student needs such that one learns to translate student needs into social change.

Educators may also have to assist parents and provide them with some feedback on how best to support the intellectual growth and development of their children. In our experience, we have found that parents make several critical errors when it comes to educational achievement in their children. Clark (1983) was very clear in articulating these factors and included among these are

1. Failure to review lessons with children who are completing homework assignments.

2. Failure to insist that homework be completed before engaging in any extracurricular activities (including television).
3. Failure to articulate parental expectations regarding their child's academic performance to the teacher, and insisting on periodic review.
4. Failure to provide guidance when viewing television programming with their children.

This obviously raises questions about the impact of parenting styles on the achievement rates of African-American children. At best, we can say that the research in this area is inconclusive. While Culp, Hubbs-Tait, Cuilp, and Starost (2001) suggested that styles high in parental control and harsh punishment were linked to lower academic achievement, other research has shown that this link is not the same for African-American children, in the same ways that it was more predictive for White youth. More recent studies have reported that parenting practices and beliefs, as indicated by visiting libraries, helping children learn the alphabet, increased contact with teachers, reading with one's child, and academic expectations do have moderate effects of school performance in Black children (Aikens & Barbarin, 2008). Other studies have also explored the impact of "neighborhood effects" on children's academic performance, and concluded that a disadvantaged neighborhood, as characterized by poverty, family disintegration and disruption, and high turnover, might be related to lower rates of pro-social and personal competence, grades, and educational expectations, and higher rates of problem behaviors. In spite of these more recent studies, we continue to be persuaded by a profound study published some twenty-seven plus years ago by Reginald Clark (1983).

In that text entitled *Family Life and School Achievement: Why Poor Black Children Succeed or Fail,* Reginald Clark (1983) points out that it is not family composition, but parental disposition, that provides the most important influence on a child's school achievement. He writes that there is a strong correlation between family expectations for youngsters and those youngsters being high achievers. The four parental dispositions observed by Clark include:

1. Parents' willingness to put their children's growth and development above their own.
2. Parents who believe that schools cannot do and teach everything to their children; consequently, parents take personal responsibility for assisting their children in developing skills needed for success in the classroom.
3. Parents who believe that children are personally responsible for pursuing knowledge and consequently expect regular classroom attendance and active participation in classroom activities. Such a practice also provides parents with a daily monitor of a child's academic progress.
4. Parents who routinely emphasize that their children should exceed their own goal attainment, and even consider pursuing secondary training beyond what they personally received. Active involvement by parents is not only beneficial to a child's cognitive growth, involvement also helps to strengthen the emotional bond between parent and child.

Another challenge before us is how to extend opportunities for learning and cultural socialization beyond the halls of academia. The problem is that beyond this realm, many people in the African-American community do not take advantage of the learning opportunities available, nor do they occupy institutions of higher education in large numbers. As such, any educational mission involving the resocialization of our people cannot be restricted to those who occupy academic institutions. Rather, we who are in education must be aggressive in our attempts to support the development of partnerships and collaborations with other community interests such that the masses of African-descent people begin to gain access to the knowledge that will assist them in achieving the liberation they so desperately seek. The key, however, is to help people understand the difference between education and training, for if African-descent people's minds are only trained to develop skills in support of other people's communities and livelihood, then we have not done our jobs well. Indeed, the role of African-American psychologists and educators is to help our people become more enlightened such that their knowledge is used to enhance the survival and collective well-being of themselves and others in their communities.

Another challenge facing African-American people and youth in particular is the need to more critically examine and hold accountable the institutions that educate our children. If we listen to our youth and family constituents, it is clear to us that many of the difficulties and challenges that our young people face on a daily basis have less to do with individual obstacles and barriers and more to do with systemic/institutional ones. As a consequence, we have little hope of affecting the educational endeavors of our young people if we cannot in turn impact the educational institutions that we trust with the intellectual growth and development of our children. Thus, we would like to propose that each community across this country develop a regional report card that would be issued jointly by a coalition of community interests as we analyze the degree to which school systems throughout the country are effectively meeting the needs of our children. This "institutional report card" might take the form of a regional survey that would be administered to various school districts throughout a particular locale as a way of measuring those variables that both impede and/or facilitate the educational success of African-American children.

Obviously, the development of an institutional report card instrument will require extensive time, professional expertise, and unique sensitivity to the issues impacting our youth in school systems throughout this nation. However, we believe that a team of individuals could be persuaded to pull their collective expertise in developing such an instrument. For example, we might propose that a regional report card would evaluate school districts on seven content areas. Those areas would include the following:

1. **Faculty/Staff Composition**
   - percentage of teachers who are African American
   - teachers certified to teach particular subject matter
   - teachers trained to work with African-American children via multicultural education

- the extent to which professional development opportunities are available in that particular school system

2. Curriculum
- availability of African-American history
- the degree to which the school district integrates African-American content into the curriculum
- the degree to which the district sponsors schoolwide programs designed to foster a sense of cultural pride and affirmation
- cultural celebrations that are designed to highlight and identify the unique aspects of African-American culture and traditions

3. Methodology
- instructional method (active versus passive learning)
- technology

4. Special Education
- What are the criteria for placement?
- What is the percentage of African-American children enrolled?
- How does the individual education plan (IEP) benefit learning?
- What is the congruence between traditional educational curriculum and the special education curriculum?
- What services are offered for those persons classified as needing special education?

5. Gifted Education
- What are the criteria for placement?
- What is the percentage of African-American children enrolled?
- How does the IEP benefit learning?
- What services are currently offered for gifted students?

6. Administration
- To what degree do the policies and practices of this institution positively impact African-American children and families?
- To what degree is the leadership sensitive to the needs of the African-American community?
- To what degree is the administration knowledgeable about the educational needs of African-American children?
- What are the graduation rates from each category of instruction?
- What are the dropout rates from each category of instruction?
- What are the discipline rates?
- What percentage of students obtains college admissions?

7. Parental Involvement
- What is the percentage of African-American parents attending back-to-school nights?
- To what degree does this school system develop and utilize parental advisory boards?
- To what degree does this school system outreach to parent groups?

The development of a regional or local report card might accomplish several things in the desire for better educational practices:

1. It would assist in the development of collaborative partnerships between home, school, and communities.
2. It would help concerned community interests call attention to the educational needs of our youth.
3. It would help to standardize the way in which communities across the country *assess* the quality of the educational experience that African-American youth receive.
4. It provides a measure of accountability for school systems around the country and serves as a barometer for progress on issues identified as paramount in a particular year.

PROMISING PRACTICES

Holding schools more accountable for how they educate our children is certainly an important goal. However, the responsibility for properly educating our children must be shared by our families and communities as well. Educational success in the new millennium will depend on how effective African-Americans are at developing collaborative relationships and community partnerships.

An example of such a collaboration exists in the southern California region of the country where the first author of this text, through his membership in the 100 Black Men of America's Orange County Chapter, has helped to develop a promising program. Parham (1994, 2006) believes that student success depends on a cooperative relationship between the home, school, and community. In attempting to reconnect this "triangle for success," Parham and his colleagues developed the *Passport to the Future Program*. The Passport program is a four-year sequential experience where each year, ninth-grade high school students and their parents are invited to participate in the educational support initiative. Invitations to participate are extended through the high school principal, who gives his or her endorsement of the program and the 100 Black Men to the parents.

Students who are accepted in the program are exposed to curricular and experiential activities that include:

- a Rites of Passage program in the ninth grade
- a Mentoring program in the tenth grade
- a Personal and Leadership Development Program in the eleventh grade
- an Apprenticeship/College Preparation Program in the twelfth grade

Through Parham's instruction, and that of other instructors, students are reminded that in a society that awards privileges based on chronological age, criteria for manhood and womanhood cannot be restricted to such simplistic attributes. It is true that youth can obtain a work permit at 14 years of age, a driving permit at 16, can vote at 18, and consume alcohol and gamble at 21. But does that make them men and women?

The *Passport to the Future Program* supports a more African-centered perspective by suggesting that manhood (and by extension womanhood) is status earned by mastering several fundamental areas of skill, knowledge, and experience. Parham has recommended that these areas include self-awareness, history, relationships, skill development (career development, conflict resolution and anger management, economic empowerment, communications, and health and wellness), leadership, and community service. Although this list is far from exhaustive, it will provide you with an example of criteria more relevant than age.

Having reviewed the six areas of mastery and the four levels of intervention (ninth through twelfth grades), you can see how this six (areas of mastery) times four (levels) matrix can be used to construct a model of educational intervention and resocialization of African youth.

Table 7.1 provides a more detailed diagram of the program.

Classes are held every other week in the local school site during the school year. By combining the talents and expertise of the community (100 Black Men), together with support from the home and the school, initiatives like these provide an important supplement to the education our youth typically receive. The Passport Program promotes the idea that African-American students learn best and contribute more in an active, participatory, instructional environment where African-centered values, history and heritage, and collective responsibility are emphasized. By combining the psychological expertise and youth development interests of the community with the dream and aspirations of the home and school, this community is taking an active role in preparing African-American youth for the future. Not surprisingly, this Passport Program has grown in its visibility, and over the past ten years, has been encouraged to expand its scope. Taking the program to scale required that all elements of the program be transferred onto a CD formatted disk that can be used in communities outside of Southern California. This expended version of the Passport Program is now known as *THE BAKARI PROJECT* (Parham, 2007). The name Bakari is a ki-swahili word, which when literally translated, means "one who will succeed." This mantra is now being used in several locations around the country, the most recent of which has been in San Luis Obispo California, in conjunction with the university, community, and County Probation Department. In this program, the Bakari curriculum is being taught to youth offenders who have had contact with the criminal justice system, and are currently on probation. While time and evaluation data will tell if the program achieves a similar success to its Southern California counterpart, what is clear is that the "triangle for success" concept is helping to foster collaborations between families, schools, communities, and even the criminal justice system.

An African-Centered Ideology

In addition to increasing reading, writing, and math proficiency, our revised educational activities and policies must begin with some basic assumptions:

- Positive educational outcomes are facilitated when there is a **triangle for success** that includes the home, school, and community all working in partnership.

TABLE 7.1 Bakari Project Model Chart

	Self Awareness/Spirituality	History	Relationship	Skill Development	Leadership	Community Service	Validation Market
Rites of Passage							
Mentoring							
Personal Leadership Development							
Apprenticeship College Prep							

- **Mental liberation** is a critical focus of any educational program for African-American children. Curriculum must be modified in ways that teach them how to critically analyze information they receive and sift through falsehood to find hidden truth. Schools cannot continue to assault the humanity of our children and then expect that they will excel in spite of a negative learning environment.
- Young adulthood must be defined by **mastery,** not by age. Instruction for students should be anchored in the African-centered belief that students must master certain fundamentals of prerequisite knowledge and skills in order to meet the test of intelligence.

Those areas should include self-awareness, history, relationships, skill development (career development, conflict resolution and economic empowerment), leadership and community service (five hours a week). The end of the school year should require an additional challenge for the school children by requiring them to demonstrate their mastery of these didactic and experiential modules in an African-centered ceremony.

The Reciprocal Nature of Education and Health Care

A final thought in this chapter on education of African-American children is reserved for an opportunity to advocate for a shift in one of this nation's social policies. This relates to health care. Clearly, the discipline of African psychology, as evidenced by the writings by several of its scholars (Parham, White, & Ajamu, 1999; Neville, Tynes, & Utsey, 2009; Belgrave & Allison, 2010), supports and encourages academic excellence. Yet, it is important to recognize, as Parham (2009) has articulated, that you cannot have academic excellence without academic wellness. Given what we believe is the deplorable condition of education generally in the African-American community nationally, African-American student's educational achievement should become the civil rights issue of our time. The challenges faced by the growing achievement gap, the condition of our nation's schools, and the low graduation rates coupled with the deplorable college eligibility index are all topics that should occupy a central place in the discourse of African-American psychologists and our national debates on education. And yet, it is difficult to imagine a child taking maximum advantage of the educational resources in any school or academic environment without embracing and owning a sense of what Parham (2009) calls academic wellness.

Wellness begins with a recognition that individuals must commit to lifestyle choices that promote healthy minds, bodies, and spirits. However, making decisions to pursue healthy lifestyles is not simply an intellectual exercise, nor should it be a practice restricted to a privileged few who can afford to support such a commitment. Rather, it requires, among other things, that all citizens, even those who live at the economic margins of society, have access to preventative and urgent care treatments that address the myriad of physical and psychological ailments that intrude into people's life. Owing to a combination of genetic and environmental realities, each of us, and especially our children, is saddled with a vulnerability index that makes us prone to certain illness and disease. For some, it is wrestling with an occasional common cold; for others, it means confronting the debilitating effects of a chronic disease (e.g., asthma) that must be controlled with medical treatment and pharmacological medications. If children and their families are blessed with a health care plan and can afford to access it, then the interruptions to their educational routines can be minimized. If, however, children and families have no health care insurance, little money for out-of-pocket medical expenses, prescriptions or even over-the-counter remedies, and restricted access to providers who can manage their medical conditions, then they are likely to sacrifice their educational pursuits in an effort to cope with their medical ailments.

This is the condition that too many children in our nation, especially those in the African-American community, find themselves in. One has only to examine the data to confront this terrible reality. A disproportionate number of African-American children live in poverty, which negatively influences health status and access to medical care. Data from national health statistics indicate that African Americans have lower rates of mothers accessing prenatal care, higher rates of infant mortality, higher rates of mal-nutrition, and low birth weight. They are disproportionately impacted by childhood illnesses like diabetes, ADD and ADHD, and obesity. They are much less likely to be immunized for influenza, and carry a 60 percent higher asthma prevalence rate when compared with their White counterparts. This statistic in particular is alarming because as far back as 15 years ago, African-American children were four to six times more likely to die from asthma-related complications when compared to their White counterparts. In addition, asthma was the leading cause of medical absenteeism from school in African-American children, and a significant contributor to home confinement in African-American working adults.

Clearly, students must be at their healthy best to participate fully in the promise of education. However, the growing disparities in health outcomes, the lack of health care, and the plague of illnesses that disproportionately impact the African-American community make education and health care reciprocal partners in the debate on how to secure brighter futures for our nation's children. The discipline of African psychology should be a strong voice in advocating for the educational achievement of our children. However, in doing so, they and we must also echo loudly and clearly our support for the health care reforms and initiatives that are currently being debated across this nation. For in doing so, we understand that academic excellence is facilitated by academic wellness, and our children need strong minds, healthy bodies, enlivened spirits, and clear aspirations that are nurtured in a supportive environment if they are to fully realize the promise of a brighter future.

Summary

The achievement rates of African-American youth and the condition of our educational system nationally demand that educators and even psychologists rethink both how and why we educate young generations of Americans. Consequently, as we close this chapter on education, it begs the question about how our nation and local communities need to rethink building an educational system of instruction, pedagogy, instructional methodology, and accountability that might last for eternity. In proposing this "building for eternity" concept within the context of education, we borrow this application from Parham (2007) as he continues to advance this perspective.

IMAGE 7-1   Educational Pyramid, Building Blocks

In utilizing Parham's adaptation, we are clear as he has been about the assumptions that we make. These include:

- Educational excellence is not simply related to high test scores and achievement levels, but is also related to how the human spirit is illuminated and how the human potential is cultivated

- Learning is a shared activity that is enhanced when it is reinforced at every level of society

- There is a triangle for success that facilitates the academic achievement of young people who are marginalized in the educational system

- The purpose of education should never be related to the acquisition of employment

The building blocks of a better educational future begin with **strong conceptual anchors.** These include: a strong foundation that challenges the mindset of our children; questions about what achievement is and what is the real purpose of education; a strong belief in the possibility of human transformation (such that irrespective of how Black children have performed in the past, their educational lives can be transformed); a definitive statement about who is capable of excellence; knowledge of culture at the deep structure level (difference between surface understanding and deeper insight), and how culture should inform instructional methodologies; and congruence between home, school, and community such that the triangle for success is connected rather than disconnected.

The second layer of building a stronger education future involves a commitment to a particular set of values. Among those that need expression, we advance the ideas that there is a need to develop an aspiration to harmonize with divine intent (in accord with

Building Blocks of Educational Excellence

- Strong belief in the possibility of human transformation
- Strong foundation that challenges the mindset of our children
  - What is achievement?
  - Who is capable of excellence?
- Knowledge of culture at the deep structure level (difference between surface understanding and deeper insight), and how culture should inform instructional methodologies
- Congruence between home, school, and community

IMAGE 7-2   Conceptual Anchors, Building Blocks

Building Blocks of Educational Excellence

- Aspiration to harmonize with divine intent (in accord with the nature, aim, and purpose of our creation)
- Education is a fundamental right of each human being that must be respected with a commitment to excellence
- Education is an investment we make in ourselves on behalf of those who came before us and will come after us
  - Self reliance vs. instructional dependence

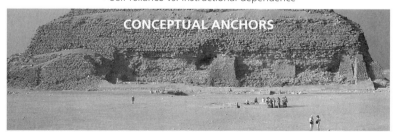

IMAGE 7-3   Values, Building Blocks

the nature, aim, and purpose of our creation); that education is and should be treated as a fundamental right of each human being that must be respected with a dedication to excellence and a commitment to provide the necessary resources; that education is an investment we make in ourselves on behalf of those who came before us and those that will come after us; and that self reliance and personal motivation are a posture worthy of pursuit, as compared to instructional dependence and externalizing responsibility and blame.

A third building block of educational excellence involves recruiting, cultivating, compensating, and retaining the best and brightest teachers. However, these activities must be anchored in a commitment to help teachers develop the cultural competencies necessary to properly teach our children. The core areas of competence include awareness, knowledge, and skills.

In the area of *AWARENESS*, teachers and students must do a better job of understanding and managing the biases and assumptions they bring with them into the classroom each day. With respect to *KNOWLEDGE*, teachers must be particularly in tuned with a student's history and culture, the within group variability and between group differences they represent when compared to their different ethnic and racial counterparts; and knowledge about the educational disparities that exist between Black and other students, and how you as an educator can improve on them. With regard to *SKILLS,* we believe that teachers and administrators will need to develop core competencies that involve connecting with students in authentic ways, administering culturally competent assessments and evaluations that have been normed and standardized on Black children, engaging in behaviors that provide for the installation of hope while also igniting passions for learning; and enlisting the support of students to participate in their own knowledge acquisition.

The fourth building block for educational competence requires a level of social advocacy competencies that aligns with a spirit of individual and community empowerment. However, we are advising that if building for eternity is the ultimate goal, then advocacy must traverse the landscape between the individual, institutional, organizational, and societal levels of intervention.

Building Blocks of Educational Excellence

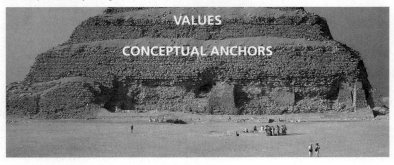

COMPETENCY DIMENSIONS

SKILLS: Connecting with students, competent assessment and evaluation, installation of hope, igniting passions, enlisting support of students to participate in their own knowledge acquisition.

KNOWLEDGE: A student's history and culture, within group variability and between group differences, educational disparities and how you as an educator can improve on them.

AWARENESS: Teachers and students who understand the biases and assumptions they bring with them into the classroom.

VALUES

CONCEPTUAL ANCHORS

IMAGE 7-4 Competency Dimensions, Building Block

Building Blocks of Educational Excellence

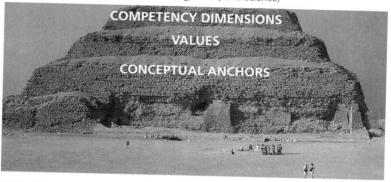

DOMAINS OF ADVOCACY

- SOCIETAL (advocate for public policy that addresses disparities in education [access, funding, resources, and environment])
- ORGANIZATIONAL (hire and train more culturally competent teachers, staff, and administrators)
- INSTITUTIONAL (advocate to change the culture of education from what it has become)
- INDIVIDUAL (personal accountability, a commitment to ground self in basics of reading, math, and science)

COMPETENCY DIMENSIONS

VALUES

CONCEPTUAL ANCHORS

IMAGE 7-5 Advocacy, Building Blocks

Regarding SOCIETAL interventions, psychologists, parents, community members, and educators themselves must advocate for public policy that addresses disparities in educational access, funding, resources, and school physical plant environment. With respect to ORGANIZATIONAL advocacy interventions, there must be concerted efforts to recruit, hire, and train more culturally competent teachers, staff, and administrators. There must also be concerted efforts to distribute high- functioning teachers and administrators throughout school districts, rather than have groups of them clustered in one or a few schools. Simultaneously, there must also be some attention paid to moving poor-performing teachers out of classrooms where their efforts at teaching African-American children are doing more harm than good. Where INSTITUTIONAL advocacy is concerned, efforts must be employed to change the culture of education from what it has become, to what it should rightfully be. In our minds, the purpose of education should not be relegated to securing the best and most profitable job or career position. Rather, the purpose of education is about the cultivation of the human spirit and human potential in all of its aspects. With regard to INDIVIDUAL levels of advocacy, each member of a community and family must engage in a greater level of personal accountability. In this aspect of advocacy, parents, teachers, administrators, community members, and legislators cannot shoulder the lion's share of responsibility, and somehow absolve students of their duties and obligations. Accordingly, each student must make a commitment to ground themselves in the basics of reading, math, science, and language arts, and commit to compete in the classroom with a standard of excellence that is commiserate with the same effort and initiative they employ on the playgrounds and in social situations in their communities.

Building Blocks of Educational Excellence

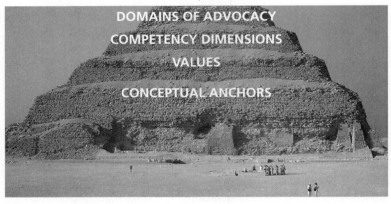

LIBERATION

Freeing ourselves from the psychological incarceration that impacts our:

- SPIRITUAL (abandon negative energy)
- BEHAVIORAL (stagnation)
- EMOTIONAL (fear of failure, low esteem, apathy)
- INTELLECTUAL (acting white, valuing potential

DOMAINS OF ADVOCACY

COMPETENCY DIMENSIONS

VALUES

CONCEPTUAL ANCHORS

IMAGE 7-6 Liberation, Building Blocks

Finally, building for eternity in the area of education involves the domain of liberation. In this respect, psychologist's roles are particularly salient, for most of the liberation struggle is decidedly more mental than physical. With respect to liberation, our youth must be assisted with freeing themselves from the psychological incarceration that impacts their SPIRITUAL (abandon negative energy), BEHAVIORAL (stagnation with little

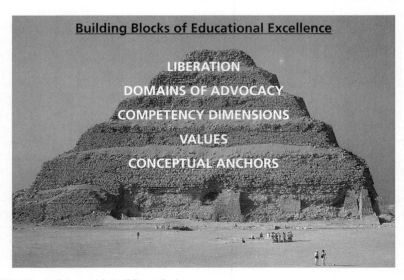

Building Blocks of Educational Excellence

LIBERATION

DOMAINS OF ADVOCACY

COMPETENCY DIMENSIONS

VALUES

CONCEPTUAL ANCHORS

IMAGE 7-7 Full Pyramid, Building Blocks

Building Blocks of Educational Excellence

Education is the passport to the future,
for tomorrow belongs to those who
prepare for it today.
Malcolm X

IMAGE 7-8   Malcolm X

movement or progress toward legitimate educational goals), EMOTIONAL (fear of failure, low esteem, apathy, and low frustration tolerance), and INTELLECTUAL (acting white, valuing potential) aspects of their personalities. This building block is particularly important, because we continue to cling to the notion, as mentioned earlier in this text, that the biggest challenge our youth face is not drugs, gangs, violence, poverty, racism, or White supremacy; rather, it is the need for mental liberation.

This is the important work that psychologists must do in helping to secure a brighter future for our nation's African-American youth. If and when communities can come together and organize an educational institution and system around strong conceptual anchors, culturally congruent values, sound competency dimensions, empowered domains of advocacy, and a mindset toward liberation, then it has the makings of a structure that will last for eternity.

Finally, we end this chapter with a quote from one of the African-American community's greatest leaders who ironically had no higher education degrees or letters behind his name. However, he knew the value of education. Thus, in the spirit of not simply worshipping personalities in deference to embracing principles, we leave you with a quote from Brother Malcolm X. He reminds us that education is the passport to the future, for tomorrow belongs to those who prepare for it today.

8

Mental Health Issues Among African-American People

Since publishing the third edition of this text in 1999, much has occurred in the field of mental health. There are new advances in treatment interventions, including psychopharmacology and therapy, as well as new sensitivities about how to confront the challenges of coping with mental illness in people's lives. Even as we have now ushered in the Obama Administration in Washington, with promises or a more robust, accessible, and affordable health care system, questions still linger about how the administration's policies will impact the services available and rendered to African-descent people, whose mental health needs have long been the subject of health disparities discussions. Access to care in traditional outpatient clinics versus emergency room visits has been one of those concerns, and this trend among persons of African descent continues to raise questions about how to best handle this element of mental health disparities echoed in the Surgeon General's Report on Mental Health (2001) and the National Healthcare Disparities Report (2003). The impact of new pharmaceutical drugs on the biochemistry of African-American patients has been a concern as well. Still another is the individual and group therapeutic treatment interventions that have been delivered to African-American children, adolescents, and adults, and whether such is done in culturally sensitive ways with professionals who themselves are deemed culturally competent. In truth, there may be more access, there are new medications that show promise across racial groups, and the new wave of cultural competence training is impacting the profession of counseling and psychology, if only in the ranks of graduate student and post-doctoral trainees. Thus, while there is cause for legitimate celebration at some of these advances, it is necessary to view some of these innovations with caution, particularly as they relate to persons of African descent. In this chapter, Parham reminds us, as he has in the past (2002) that: *healing is therapeutic, but not all therapy is healing.*

Throughout the discipline of psychology, there continues to be a restless tension as professionals struggle with the notions of cultural competence and how a clinician can prepare himself or herself to intervene effectively with culturally different populations. Clearly, the discipline of African-centered psychology has been a primary instigator in these debates through its writings (White, 1984; Myers, 1988; Akbar, 1994; Parham, White, & Ajamu, 1999; Belgrave & Allison, 2006, 2010), advocacy (i.e., the Association of Black Psychologists [ABPsi]), and training. In fact, since the writing of the last edition of this text, the ABPsi has begun to lead the way in cultural competency training, having initiated the African Psychology Institute (2005), which now meets and trains experienced and neophyte clinicians and academicians in the foundations of African-centered psychological perspectives. This practice occurs each year at ABPsi's annual convention where persons from all across the country and the world come to be trained at the INTERNATIONAL CONGRESS ON LICENSURE, CERTIFICATION, and AND PROFICIENCY IN BLACK PSYCHOLOGY. Beyond the perspective that traditional psychology is sometimes inadequate when applied to African Americans, there has been a challenge over the last decade to more clearly delineate an authentic, workable theory of mental health for people of African descent, and the ABPsi has picked up that baton.

This ABPsi Congress is a welcome addition to the discipline because in discussions, lectures, and training workshops throughout the country Parham (1997, 2002) and others (Constantine, Redington, & Graham, 2009) have argued for more cultural specificity in psychological theories and constructs, as well as treatment methods regarding African Americans. Their assertions have been grounded in the assumption that as "mental health" professionals, it is difficult to facilitate psychological health if one has no idea of what constitutes being mentally healthy for African-descent people. Certainly, the definitions advanced by traditional psychology have been and continue to be inadequate to describe the life space and life experiences of African Americans. Thus, a more comprehensive and compelling definition of African-American mental health is now available to be studied, understood, and critiqued.

Like previous editions, our discussion will begin with an exploration of the questions "What is mental health?" and "How is mental health operationalized in the Black community?" The chapter will continue with discussions about historical trends, therapeutic prognosis, help-seeking behaviors in African Americans, specific mental health challenges, and the discussion of the dynamics and therapy involved in working with an African-American client. This chapter will conclude with a brief discussion of training issues as they relate to mental health professionals delivering service to African-American clients.

MENTAL HEALTH OR MENTAL ILLNESS: A QUESTION OF PERSPECTIVE

Despite considerable disagreement regarding what constitutes mental health and/or mental illness, most mental health professionals generally assume that a state of mental health exists when individuals are mentally free of the psychological ailments and/or distortions that negatively affect cognitive, emotional, and behavioral abilities, or in some way impede an individual's growth and ability to reach his or her full potential; and when one feels his or her life has moved, is moving, or has the potential to move in a meaningful direction. Speight, Blackmon, Odugu, and Steele (2009) and Belgrave and Allison (2010) provide good summaries of the mental health definitions that have been so pervasive in the psychological literature for decades. These models tend to align themselves with perspectives that see certain personal characteristics as indicative of healthy functioning. Johada (1958) emphasized positive attitudes toward oneself, sustained growth and development over time, accurate and realistic perceptions of reality, and the ability to adapt to one's environmental circumstances. Lazarus and Fay (1975), in surveying various models of mental health, concluded that characteristics common to mentally healthy persons were a strong sense of reality, the capacity to extend love to others unconditionally, comfort with who one is, and developing a level of independence and autonomy. Even the U.S. government's definition, as offered through its Office of Health and Human Services, emphasizes achieving desired outcomes on specific tasks, developing meaningful and rewarding relationships with others, the capacity to manage change, and the ability to successfully confront life's adversities (U.S. Department of HHS, (2001))

Belgrave and Allison (2006) also provide a characterization of mental health, observing that some definitions tend to align with various theoretical orientations prevalent in schools of psychotherapy. The corresponding definitions then tend to assume that maladjustment (or mental illness) occurs when there is some deviation from the normal course of development proposed by that theoretical orientation. For example, psychodynamic perspectives tend to emphasize disruptions in childhood around critical tasks that create unresolved issues that manifest themselves in adulthood neuroses. More behaviorally oriented perspectives tend to emphasize how particular stimuli serve as reinforcement to influence behaviors in directions that are healthy and unhealthy. Gestalt approaches tend to emphasize the person-environment interaction, where "creative" and "non-creative" adjustments people make in meeting daily needs are the results of healthy or unhealthy psyches. Cognitive-behavior approaches, in contrast, focus on the thoughts and ideas one has about self, others, and situations, which contribute to the satisfaction one feels or the emotional distress one experiences. Biological-psychological-social schools emphasize the role of one's body and brain in facilitating and/or inhibiting effective functioning. While these perspectives are interesting, they fail to incorporate, as Neville, Tynes, and Utsey (2009) and Belgrave and Allison (2006, 2010) rightly point out, issues of culture into their foundation, and as such, are rendered less potent when considering the construct of mental health in an African-centered context.

In the first, second, and third editions of *The Psychology of Blacks,* White (1984); White and Parham (1990); and Parham, White, and Ajamu (1999) discussed the notion of mental health for Black people. Among other things, they concluded that a psychologically healthy Black person is one who interprets the African-American ethos into his or her own life space. As Ani (1994) explains, that ethos refers to the emotional tone of a group of people. It represents an emotional bond created by shared cultural heritage and life experiences. A healthy person is also psychologically open to self and able to relate to others, is resourceful, inventive, imaginative, and enterprising in his or her approach to life. White and Parham (1984), and Parham, White, and Ajamu (1999) also contend that mental health for Blacks requires that a person be centered in, grounded in, or otherwise in touch with one's African-American makeup, with a foundational identity, a healthy self-esteem, and a collective sense of consciousness.

The importance of their assertion is underscored by the assumption that what constitutes mental health for Blacks needs to be understood in the context of one's own culture. Belgrave and Allison (2006, 2010) also make this point as they review bio-psychosocial models and additional African-centered perspectives in mental health and mental disorders. Traditionally, Eurocentric standards of what constitutes mental health are often inappropriate for Blacks because they are based on the philosophies, values, and mores of Euro-American culture, and they use these variables to develop normative standards of mental health based only on Euro-American culture. Thus, what constitutes sane or insane behavior, mental health or mental illness, or normal or abnormal behavior is always in relation to a White normative standard.

In the second and third editions of this text, White and Parham (1990) and Parham, White, and Ajamu (1999) reviewed some of the work of African-American scholars who began to articulate their own definitions of what constitutes mental health and self-actualizing behavior for African-American people (Akbar, 1981; Parham & Helms, 1985; Ani, 1995). Those models were based more on culturally specific views of mental health and mental illness and are seen as more accurate indicators of normal and/or abnormal behavior in Black people.

In the fourth edition, there is a need to delve more fully into the concept of mental health and illness because our thinking and study has yielded new insights. In defining African-centered psychology, Parham (1995) asserted that it examines processes that allow for the illumination and liberation of the *spirit*. Relying on the principle of harmony within the universe as the natural order of human existence, he argued that African-centered psychology recognizes: *the **spiritness*** that permeates everything, that is the notion that everything in *the universe is **interconnected***; the value that *the **collective*** is the most salient element of existence; and the idea that ***self-knowledge*** is the key to mental health. As we then reviewed the construct of *Ore-Ire* or properly aligned consciousness (introduced earlier in the text), one might conclude that mental health is analogous to aligning one's life space with these values and assumptions. Being in touch with one's spiritual essence, having knowledge of oneself as a cultural being, having favorable impressions of oneself and one's people, being able to develop and successfully navigate the dynamics of relations with others, and accessing the "collective" for one's source of sustenance and support would then define a sense of order and normality.

In other corners of the African-American community, definitions of equal interest have also emerged, some of which emanate from outside of the discipline of psychology. Farrakhan (1996), for example, has suggested that mental health is tantamount to "human beings functioning in accord with the nature, aim, and purpose of their creation." That purpose, according to some texts, is to cultivate the GOD within each of us, such that we use the gifts we are blessed with to master our life circumstances. Fu-Kiau (1991), on the other hand, has suggested that to be healthy, one must be in balance or harmony with oneself, one's environment, and the universe. He contends that each of us is endowed with a power or energy (life force) and that power represents a self-healing potential. When a person acts in opposition to one's nature, he or she loses (moves further away from) his or her self-essence, as well as balance. In essence, this fourth edition seeks to argue that healthy human functioning from an African-centered context is characterized by:

- A sense of self that is collective and extended
- Attitudes wherein one recognizes the sameness in oneself and others
- A clear sense of one's spiritual connection to the CREATOR and the universe
- A positive sense of self that is anchored in an African-centered reality
- A sense of mutual responsibility for African people, and other members of the human family
- The ability to develop and sustain meaningful relationships with others that are characterized by emotional bonds of closeness, intimacy, and love
- A sense of one's spiritual essence and character, and the possession of a self-healing power
- And a conscious understanding that human abnormality or deviance is any act (be it thought, word, or action) that is in opposition to oneself, or proves detrimental to other members of the African community, or the human family.

What implications, then, do these definitions and descriptions have for psychologists and therapists who work with African-American clients in therapy? Personality theory of African Americans especially those articulated by Nobles (1986); Akbar (1981, 2004); Myers (1988, 2009); Baldwin (1984); Parham and Helms (1985); Kambon, (2006), and Parham (2002) stress the necessity of achieving congruence between the "self" one wishes to become and one's true African-American makeup if one is to be a fully functioning and well-adjusted individual. If there is an aspect or factor of personality that does not fit well with, function well with, or contribute constructively to the overall personality organization, then the efficient functioning of the personality is decreased, or perhaps even seriously disrupted. Thus, attitudes and behaviors that devalue one's Africanness, overassimilate White cultural values, isolate one from the source of their spirit and self-healing power, and the like, can be seen as representing degrees incongruent between an African-American's real self and idealized self because they violate the natural order of that person's African makeup.

If one assumes that disordered behavior is related to an absence of spiritual enlightenment, an overreliance on the material versus the spiritual elements of the universe, an inability to develop and sustain close personal relationships with others, or an inability to access that deepest core of our self that illuminates our humanity, then it is likely that therapists and psychologists will see different degrees of psychological maladjustment in the clients that they treat. As such, service providers may need to assist clients with achieving some sense of personal transformation, recognizing who and where they are in time and space while helping them move toward a greater manifestation of what they have the capacity to become. In doing so, therapists will need to deal with the client's past experiences and the stress surrounding such experiences, which have shaped his or her perceptions in a disordered fashion. Service providers may also need to assist clients in analyzing their behaviors that hinder, threaten, or impede their growth as human organisms. Service providers may also want to assist clients in becoming more comfortable with themselves as African-American persons, while helping them to identify their resistance to more positive Black perspectives. Such efforts might include a thorough examination of clients' self-esteem or self-worth. It is also important to recognize here that some attitudes and behaviors African descent people manifest in their daily lives are less about what is "normal," and more about what is "functional" and adaptive in the moment, based upon circumstances and situations individuals have had to cope with. As such, it is important to be understanding, and less critical of these adaptive strategies initially, while helping those in treatment understand that past practices and strategies for "coping" do not have to determine how one responds to life in a more contemporary reality, especially if time has allowed these individual to grow stronger and wiser in their repertoire of available spiritual, mental, emotional, and behavioral coping skills. What we are suggesting here is that therapy can and should be a process of human transformation. As such, spirit, thinking, feelings, and behaviors can each be transformed from their present state to one that is healthier and culturally self-actualizing. But what is the goal? If our desire to facilitate transformation in clients is genuine, then therapists themselves must understand the fundamental nature of the African humanity.

One of the models of human transformation is reflected in the principle of *Ma'at*. *Ma'at* was not simply a principle; it can be more fully understood as a code of conduct and a standard of aspiration. If culture, as we have described earlier in this text, is a person's design for living and his or her patterns for interpreting reality, then conceptual systems like *Ma'at* become the intellectual, emotional, and behavioral template against which our responses to reality and life's challenges should be measured. *Ma'at,* for the ancient Africans and for those who embrace its principles today, is characterized by seven cardinal virtues:

- *Truth*—sincerity in speech, behavior, and character that is in accord with fact
- *Justice*—principle of just dealing and right action where fairness and equity reign
- *Righteousness/Propriety*—acting in accord with divine or moral law such that one is free from guilt or *sin*
- *Harmony*—proper arrangement or alignment of things such that they function together

- *Order*—the natural and harmonious arrangement of things that helps to define one's purpose
- *Balance*—stability produced by an even distribution of elements
- *Reciprocity*—giving of oneself in ways that honor the ways that we have been blessed in our lives.

Beyond these cardinal virtues that described the core principle, *Ma'at* also defines the five dimensions of the African character (Karenga, 1990). Character in this regard speaks to the notable or distinguishable traits that emerge as one responds to life circumstance. In our opinion, they help to define the elements of a healthy personality where spiritual enlightenment and African self-consciousness are present. The dimensions include:

- *Divinity*—the interrelationship between each individual and the divine force (Creator) in the universe
- *Teachability*—the capacity to know, understand, and share knowledge and wisdom
- *Perfectibility*—the transformative process of the human spirit that is always in a state of becoming better
- *Free Will*—the capacity to make conscious, deliberate choices to respond to one's reality in ways each of us chooses
- *Moral and Social Responsibility*—the mandate to have morally and ethically grounded relations with others

If therapists desire to facilitate healing and restore wholeness to clients who are in distress, models like these will help to outline more clearly the personality and character dynamics they seek to understand and treat.

THERAPEUTIC PROGNOSIS: CONTRADICTORY FINDINGS

If one attempts to gain a historical overview of mental illness as it relates to African-American populations, an examination of that literature will readily reveal that African Americans were perceived to be more prone to psychological disorders than Whites and characterized as having higher rates of mental diseases. However, a closer look at the research reveals that although extensive in scope, the literature was often contradictory in its findings. Furthermore, it was clear that many investigations made gross generalizations from their data and/or biased their data with *a priori* assumptions (Thomas & Sillen, 1972). Although the scope of this chapter and this edition limits the time that we can devote to this particular topic, mention should be made of the revised work of Robert Guthrie's *Even the Rat Was White* (1998) and an excellent review article (Fisher, 1969) that, although over 40 years old, has much contemporary relevance.

Fisher reviews the literature on mental illness in Blacks and cites several problems with the research. The first has to do with the conceptualization of the problem, and the fact that service providers employ a different frame of reference than their clients. Ultimately, what emerges as mentally ill or not depends upon how one defines mental illness and his or her frame of reference.

More recent reviews continue to show that Blacks are often stereotyped in the psychiatric literature as not being psychologically minded, and lacking the psychological sophistication and motivation necessary for successful psychotherapy, thus having a primitive character structure, and as being too jovial to be depressed and too impoverished to experience objective loss (Adebimpe, 1981). This tendency to misdiagnose and overdiagnose severe psychopathology has persisted despite the awareness of social-cultural differences between Blacks and Whites brought about by the Civil Rights and Black Power Revolution (King, 1978). Even in more contemporary service delivery, rendered decades later, Adebimpe (1981) was quick to recognize that Black patients run a higher risk of being misdiagnosed as schizophrenics, whereas White patients showing identical behaviors are more likely to receive diagnoses as depressed.

A second issue discussed by Fisher (1969) has to do with the fact that statistically, mental illness was sometimes defined as persons who are admitted to treatment. Fisher then cites research that suggests that in some cases, Blacks are admitted to hospitals faster than Whites. The third issue he addresses is the fact that most research on race or mental illness historically used state facilities for subject pools. Therefore, one would expect an uneven distribution of Black and other low socioeconomic status S.E.S. populations in state versus private facilities. The fourth issue had to do with the fact that assessment of illness rates is also measured by incidence (number of new cases) and prevalence (total number of cases present in a population at a given time). Therefore, since there were and are significantly higher numbers of Blacks in state hospitals, and research samples were taken from state hospitals, obvious biases result when incidence and prevalence data from those institutions were used for assessing mental illness. These biased samples then were used to make generalizations about Black people as a whole.

The contemporary literature appears to be a little more sensitive to race and ethnicity and less biased in the assumptions and conclusions. In fact, although the literature on rates of mental illness is infiltrated with demographic indicators, one is now hard-pressed to find the blatantly biased studies of previous decades where African-descent people were characterized as a more mentally disordered population. Interestingly though, there are still those who cling to the notion that epidemiological as opposed to service utilization studies is the best means available to understand rates of mental illness in a given population like African Americans (Belgrave & Allison, 2010). Certainly, many scholars and researchers have relied on such studies as the National Institute for Mental Health (NIMH) Epidemiological Catchment Area study (Robins & Regier, 1991) and the National Comorbidity Survey (Kessler et al., 1994) to aid in their conclusions about mental disorders among and between certain racial groups. While these are very comprehensive data sets, and both studies show little if any significant difference in major psychological distress across major racial/ethnic groups, we would still invite a measure of caution in interpreting these data, for many of the same reasons Fisher (1969) raised over four decades ago. So, what does the data show?

According to the *Archives of General Psychiatry* (1994), 24 percent of all 18- to 24-year olds will experience some form of mental illness during their lifetime.

Slightly less than 3 percent (2.6 percent) will be afflicted with a severe mental disorder. Although people experience different types of mental illnesses, depression continues to be the most frequently occurring mental disorder in the country, followed by alcoholism and phobias (irrational fears and anxiety). Demographic trends seem to suggest that among children, rates of mental illness appear to be the same until late adolescence. Then, girls tend to experience and manifest more distress. Among the elderly people, rates are increasing with incidence of dementia (impaired intellectual functioning) and Alzheimer's disease on the rise. Mental illness continues to be associated with low socioeconomic status, as data indicate that individuals and families with incomes below $19,000 a year are twice as likely to develop a mental disorder as those earning $70,000 or more.

What data are available on African Americans and mental disorders are interesting and somewhat contradictory. Fabrega, Ulrich, and Mezzich (1993) compared the profiles and charts of 613 African-American adolescents to 1577 of their White counterparts who were treated in a university-based facility. Although Caucasians showed greater clinical morbidity with a higher number of Axis I symptoms (i.e., eating disorders), African Americans showed higher levels of symptoms such as social aggression and conduct disorders. Interestingly, the authors speculated about possible referral bias, because Blacks were referred to psychiatric facilities with lower levels of diagnosed clinical psychopathology, but higher levels of social oppositional behavior.

The trend toward African Americans having fewer clinical symptoms when referred was also echoed by Kendall, Sherman, and Bigelow (1995). In their study of 69 Black and 25 White polysubstance abusers seeking outpatient detoxification, they found White subjects reporting significantly more psychiatric symptoms as rated by the Symptom 90 Checklist (SCL-90). These data, however, were contrasted by the study of Munley, Vacha-Haase, and Busby (1998), who reported a somewhat different outcome. Their sample of 65 Black and 164 White psychiatric inpatients who were administered the Millon Clinical Multiaxial Inventory-Il (MCMI-II) showed scale elevations for Black patients on histrionic, narcissistic, paranoid, drug dependent, and delusional disorder. However, a second analysis (MANOVA) with match samples for primary diagnosis revealed no significant differences. In elderly populations, Hargrove, Stoeklin, Haan, and Reed (1998) compared 207 Black and 1818 White patients with Alzheimer's disease. They reported that African-Americans had: (1) less education and higher rates of hypertension, (2) shorter durations of illness at the time of initial diagnosis of dementia, and (3) more frequently reported insomnia, and less frequently reported anxiety.

These data provide examples of studies conducted prior to the new millennium that report incidence and prevalence of mental disorders in African-American and other populations. Although the reports do show varying rates of clinical symptomatology, it would be inaccurate to assume that any one segment of the population is more prone to mental illness than another. In fact, Adebimpe (1994), in his article entitled "Race, Racism, and Epidemiological Surveys," describes some of the factors that may lead researchers to find higher prevalence rates of mental disorders in particular populations (i.e., Black). They include racial differences in help-seeking behavior, likelihood of involuntary commitment (based on race), representation of research samples, presentation of psychiatric symptoms and resulting diagnosis, accuracy (validity) of psychological tests, and disparities in treatment.

Regardless of the rates of mental disorders in African Americans, there is some evidence to suggest that African Americans cope with the challenges of changing times, as evidenced with the burden of caring for a psychologically impaired loved one. Pickett, Vraniak, Cook, and Cohler (1993) compared Black and White parents on coping mastery ability and self-esteem scores and found Black parents to have higher self-esteem scores and lower levels of depression. However, these data, interestingly enough, stand in sharp contrast to those gathered by Lee, Shen, and Tran (2009) more than a decade later, who found that coping and resilience in distressed African-American Hurricane Katrina survivors was impacted by economic factors influencing health care access, insurance coverage, home destruction, and human loss. Perhaps the nature of the tragedies and the perceptions of the available resources and options account for these discrepant views.

Another interesting analysis related to African-American people in the process of therapy was written by Block (1980), and questions arise as to whether her analysis is still relevant as we move past the new millennium and beyond 2010. Block suggested that the status of Black people in psychotherapy could be understood via several trends. The first trend, which spanned the first half of this century, indicated that Blacks were depicted as persons limited in cognitive, emotional, and social abilities who were, or should be, content with their low status because of their relative immaturity compared to the dominate White culture (Thomas & Sillen, 1972). This emphasis on immaturity and innate limited abilities led White clinicians and other researchers to diagnose higher rates of hysteria and impulse character disorders among Blacks. The second trend discussed by Block began to take shape around the end of World War II when there were large numbers of Black servicemen being treated by White psychiatrists. The psychological literature then began to focus on Blacks' suspicion, hostility, and distrust of White therapists and their preoccupation with discussing racial issues during therapy sessions. These characteristics, according to Block, were interpreted either as resistance or as manifestations of early psychotic processes with diagnosis such as incipient paranoia, uncontrolled aggressive reactions, and chronic schizophrenia being assigned to those Black patients. The third trend began to take shape during and after the Civil Rights/Black Power era when the psychological literature on Blacks shifted to an acceptance of the need for Blacks to develop different defensive coping styles to handle their environmental realities. Racial consciousness, anger, and distrust could now be viewed as appropriate, adaptive behavior (Grier & Cobbs, 1968), particularly since such characteristics were being proposed and validated by Black and other minority psychologists. Regardless of whether or not these characteristics were seen as normal or abnormal, the assignment of these particular descriptors to Black patients made them poor candidates for psychotherapy in the eyes of many White clinicians.

In approaching 2010, the second decade of the twenty-first century, it is clear that the emotional tones expressed in earlier generations some forty years ago will still require attention, even in an age where the United States has seen fit to elect its first African-American President. This is important because despite the air of progress that an Obama Presidency represents, America has much more work to do in managing individual, institutional, and organizational racism and oppression. As of the writing of this text, the U.S. Census Bureau data reports that African Americans continue to be one of the most vulnerable populations in America, representing 40 percent of the homeless, 24.2 percent of those in poverty, 15.1 percent of those unemployed, 34 percent of those being subjected to hate crimes, 46 percent of those incarcerated, despite being slightly less than 13 percent of the U.S. population. And, we are clear that chronic exposure to racism and oppression instigates some very negative consequences for the people victimized by it. These consequences include: higher risks for depression and suicide; feelings of helplessness, fear, hopelessness, and mistrust; damage to one's sense of self; and overall declines in general health because of the chronic exposure to stress. Leary (2005) underscores this point very clearly in her text on the *Post Traumatic Slave Syndrome*. There, she describes in detail the detrimental impact that oppressive conditions have on African Americans, taking particular aim at the assault on the individual psyche of African Americans. She describes such assaults as impacting the power of beliefs, vacant esteem, ever present anger, and racist socialization.

Regarding the POWER OF BELIEFS, individuals are likely to develop a mindset that concludes that the future is bleak, that tragedy and death are just around the corner, and that that individual is incapable or unable to move beyond their own fears and doubts. With VACANT ESTEEM, individuals are likely to experience feelings of worthlessness, feelings of inferiority, a lack of value, and a lack of affirmation that translates into denigrating others in order to affirm themselves. With EVER PRESENT ANGER, a person's anger and rage hover just below the surface, waiting to explode and the least little micro-aggression. They also experience doors to legitimate goal seeking and opportunities blocked, as well as a fear of failure such that some give up trying. With the RACIST SOCIALIZATION, there is a strong urge to identify with the oppressor, and the oppressor's ideology. People also experience a glorification of distorted images, where they identify with caricatures and themes that represent an inaccurate and often grotesque image of themselves and their people. Each of these elements represents a level of psychic debilitation that clinicians and counselors will have to confront. Leary's (2005) analysis further reminds us that because the level of social pathology that exists in our lives and in the lives of African-American people is so pronounced, we can expect these psychological symptoms to manifest themselves in the patients we treat and expect to make whole.

Because we have made a particular point earlier in the text of discussing the importance of spirit in the context of a person's psychological space, we cannot ignore the very real possibility that chronic exposure to the oppressive and unequal conditions that plague people's lives will create an assault of the spirit as well. In this regard, we mean to suggest that clients of African descent may experience a spiritual contamination as a result of these spiritual assaults. These are likely characterized by decreases in energy and motivation to achieve and excel, decreases in the desire to set and complete expectations, relationships with others that are characterized by and "edgy" disposition that is more negative and angry, and the development of dysfunctional neuro-associations that instigate the pairing of two variables (i.e., associating pain with freedom) that should not be aligned.

The challenge here for clinicians to remember is that coping with the vestiges of oppression and oppressive conditions is not just the legacy of those most victimized by it; it is also a challenge of those who identify culturally and racially with those victimizers as well. You begin to see here how a collective, as opposed to an individual orientation to reality and survival, might impact ones' perceptions. No where is this reality more real than examining the context of the Hurricane Katrina disaster, and the aftermath that continues to create nightmare realities for many persons of African descent. The hurricane of record proportion slammed into the U.S. gulf coast in August of 2005. In the immediate aftermath, there were more than 1800 lives lost, two and a half million people displaced, and over 80 billion dollars in property damage (Knabb, Rhome, & Brown, 2006). While many were surprised at the severity of nature's fury, they were more surprised and sickened by the response of the federal, state, and local government to the plight of the people living in the gulf coast area, and especially the City of New Orleans. Clearly, responses with assistance and emergency aid and supplies were slow and often delayed, people were left abandoned in streets, on rooftops, and in public facilities for days, and attempts by the residents most affected by the disaster were met with government red tape, inadequate support, and insufficient resources. Clearly, the emotional and psychological impact of African Americans who were disproportionately impacted by the storm was and continues to be immeasurable (Lee, Shen, & Tran, 2009). And yet, that incident, now some six plus years old, continues to take a toll on the psyche of Black folks principally because of what the response said to all persons of African descent about the value of human life in the Black communities in America. The horror even prompted popular music artists like Kanye West to exclaim, while hosting a national television show, that then President George Bush didn't care about Black people, and many people got that message. And while the conditions in New Orleans and the gulf coast region of the country continue to be what we would consider a national disgrace, the stain on the honor of the United States has not prompted the Congress or the executive branches of government to initiate a more forceful response to the trauma that many continue to feel. Indeed, those African Americans who identify with their brothers and sisters in the New Orleans area have not found any real reassurance that if a similar fate or disaster were to befall them, they would fare any better in a nation as wealthy and prosperous as ours. It is also worth noting that this chronic neglect is contrasted with a 2008 and 2009 reality, where the nation has moved swiftly to shore up and bail out the banking and automobile industry that it believed was in danger of collapse in a time of severe economic recession. Imagine the psychological message that many persons of African descent all across this country take away, when they hear and see that institutions like banks and automotive companies have more priority and attention than the human capital still struggling to reclaim their lives and dignity in the face of what is now both a natural and man-made disaster. This perspective is worth highlighting again, for much of the work with Katrina survivors centered around issues of post-traumatic stress disorder. However, in understanding that this PTSD construct takes on a more complex character when one considers that trauma can be natural (hurricanes, etc.) as well as man-made (a robbery, or government neglect in a time of extreme, life-threatening need). It can also be immediate (acute) or chronic. What studies consistently show is that man-made chronic traumatic incidents are the most difficult to recover from. Clearly, ruptures in the power of beliefs, vacant esteem, ever-present anger, racial socialization, and assaults on the spirit will continue to manifest in the lives of African Americans, even with George Bush now out of office and Barack Obama now seated in the White House as president of the United States.

While these psychic and spiritual debilitations will confront clinicians who work with persons of African descent, it is also important to remember that there are other trends that require attention as well. So, what do we know about mental health trends among African Americans in this new millennium? Reports from the U.S. Surgeon General (2001) indicated that contrary to epidemiological studies of the 1990s, their data and studies indicate that the rates of mental illness overall are slightly higher for African Americans, when compared to other groups. The report also indicates that African Americans are underrepresented in outpatient services, but overrepresented in accessing mental health treatment in hospital emergency rooms. Understand here that by the time services are sought in this way, the level of debilitation is significantly more pronounced than it might otherwise be if care had been rendered in an outpatient clinic or counseling center agency in a more timely and proactive way. The Report of the Surgeon General also concluded that significant disparities continue to exist for African Americans in the area of mental health; and that not surprisingly, poverty and socioeconomic status are related to increases in mental illness. In continuing to discuss trends in mental health research, studies also continue to make between group comparisons, using Whites as a reference group. However, unlike the studies of decades past, where African Americans were seen as manifesting significantly higher rates of mental illness, more recent data reveals that more balance in the distribution and diagnosis of illness is evident. For example, Zhang and Snowden's (1999) work is cited extensively in the Mental health report issued by the surgeon general, and their data indicates the following trends in rates of mental illness diagnoses for African Americans, when they were compared with their White counterparts:

Less Likely	No Significant Difference	More Likely
Major depressive episodes	Manic	Phobia
Major depression	Bipolar	Somatization complaints
Dysthymia	Schizophrenia	
Obsessive compulsive disorder	Schizophreniform disorders	
Antisocial personality disorders		
Drug and alcohol dependence		
Anorexia nervosa		

Their work is supported and reinforced by Williams et al. (2007), who echo these findings in their studies of African American, Caribbean Blacks, and non-Hispanic Whites.

In the third edition of this text, we discussed the explosion of the multicultural counseling literature and how those articles concerned with treating African Americans in therapy have helped to challenge some of the stereotypes about appropriate treatment options (Sue & Sue, 1990; Carter, 1995; Parham & Helms, 1981, 1985; Ponterotto, Casas, Suzuki, & Alexander, 1995). African Americans are exposed to insight-oriented therapies (i.e., psychodynamic, Gestalt), are assessed with supposedly more culturally relevant assessment instruments (i.e., MMPI-II) and diagnostic nosologies (DSM-IV), and are treated by clinicians in public and private treatment facilities. Although these advancements have been applauded by many people, it may be overstating the case to assume that African-American clients in therapy are receiving the best treatment.

One of the challenges for this new millennium, we argued, was to ascertain just how committed the disciplines of counseling and psychology are to effectively treating African-American clients and patients. If the commitment was superficial, then "dressing up" or otherwise disguising traditional approaches to treatment with a few layers of cultural relevance would be the expected outcome. If, however, the commitment was genuine, then we argued that much more work needed to be done on presenting new conceptual paradigms, developing culturally grounded assessment instruments, and utilizing therapeutic approaches that are anchored in an African-centered framework or worldview. In the intervening ten years since the last edition, there have been important advances in assessing and treating African-American clients, and even in the area of cultural competence. To begin, helping to retain African-American clients in therapy and prevent premature termination had always been a concern documented in the literature (Sue, 1978 Takeuchi, Sue, & Yeh, 1998). In addressing that issue, work by psychologists like Sanchez-Huckles (2000) has been instrumental in guiding clinicians through the initial session with Black clients. In 2002, Divisions 17 and 45 of the American Psychological Association (APA) jointly produced a document entitled: *Guidelines on Multicultural Education, Training, Research, Practice, and Organizational Change for Psychologists.* This document serves as a guide for psychologists who are encouraged to both see themselves as racial/ethnic/cultural beings, and develop the skills and competencies necessary to treat, educate, and research persons of African decent, and other cultural groups as well. We have previously discussed the Association of Black Psychologists Certification, Licensure, and Proficiency in Black Psychology program, in which is contained the African Psychology Institute, which is dedicated to training African American psychologists to be more competent in working with their own people. Parham (2007) has also continued his work on helping to guide clinicians through the various phases of therapy treatment, producing another videotape entitled: "Working with African Americans in Therapy," for the APA Multicultural Counseling (Masters of Psychotherapy) Series. In this tape, Parham demonstrates an African-centered, culturally based approach that can augment any therapy with African-American clients.

Parham's approach honors spirituality, interconnectedness, and self-knowledge, and is aimed at treating the client holistically—that is, without dividing a client's issues into affective, cognitive, and behavioral domains and treating them as separate entities. This latest contribution adds to the collection of videotape work previously produced for Microtraining Associates, where Parham (2000) talks about innovative approaches to working with African-American clients; Franklin and Boyd-Franklin (2008) discuss cultural competency issues in treating African-American couples; and Pack-Brown, Whittington-Clark, and Parker (2007) discuss Afrocentric Approaches to Group Work.

Instructional resources have also come in the form of books and articles where various scholars have added important insights to the questions about how to be more competent and effective in working with African-American people. While there are many more resources that could be cited, we want to make special note of resources like *Counseling Persons of African Descent: Raising the Bar of What Passes for Competence* (Parham, 2002), *Akbar Papers in African Psychology* (Akbar, 2004), *African American Psychology: From Africa to America* (Belgrave & Allison, 2006, 2010), and *The Handbook of African American Psychology* (Neville, Tynes, & Utsey, 2009). Each of these texts represents a magnificent contribution to the psychological literature on African-American people, and provides the reader with an intellectual and pragmatic roadmap for better understanding issues in the core of African psychology, personality development in African-descent people, assessment, therapeutic strategies, and community interventions.

HELP-SEEKING BEHAVIORS IN AFRICAN AMERICANS

Contemporary service delivery models in some respect represent a shift away from hospitalization and institutionalization to more outpatient and community mental health center facilities. Unfortunately, even those facilities are in danger of folding, and many have closed under a climate of state and federal government cutbacks and managed care. Despite this shift, African-American patients and clients are still underrepresented and underserved. This suggests that most African-American persons needing some type of psychological care are not receiving such. Historically, of those who began treatment more than 50 percent of them discontinue treatment after the initial session (Sue, 1978. These trends continue into the new millennium, as highlighted by the Surgeon General's report (2001) on Race and Culture in Mental Health. Although several factors were cited for this alarming statistic, diagnosis and treatment by non-Black therapists was and continues to be implicated. Other factors included differential expectations between clients and therapists, service by paraprofessional versus professional workers, and services rendered by professionals who are less sensitive and culturally competent when it comes to clients of African descent. More current research continues to raise a concern about service utilization and continuation, but provides us with a clearer picture of factors that contribute to this trend. Takeuchi, Sue, and Yeh (1998) examined treatment outcomes in a sample derived from the Los Angeles County Department of Mental Health, but compared the influence of "culturally specific" versus "mainstream programs" on utilization and continuation in treatment. Their data reveals that culturally specific programs contributed to more African-American clients having better therapeutic matches, and a greater likelihood to return for treatment in subsequent sessions. In addition, Whaley (2001) found, what Terrell and Terrell (1984) had earlier discovered, that cultural mistrust was also linked to help seeking behaviors in African-American patients.

Examination of literature from 2000 and beyond continues to suggest that, by and large, therapy or counseling has not been adequately utilized by African-American people to deal with their problems. In fact, African-descent people are more likely to rely on traditional support networks (relatives, grandmothers, ministers) during times of stress, anxiety, and tension. The conclusions from the contemporary literature are not much different from those of the past. Remember that Neighbors (1991), in his *National Survey of Black Americans*, reported that decisions to seek help were related to problem severity and type of problem. When the client's presenting problem was rated high on severity, there was a greater likelihood of seeking help for a physical ailment. For other types of personal problems, less than half of the more than 1300 respondents sought assistance from traditional sources (physicians, human services, etc.). Neighbor's data also revealed that women are more likely than men, and younger African-Americans (18(24 years) are less likely than older groups, to seek help.

If, however, a Black person makes a decision to utilize psychotherapeutic services, it is likely that several factors are involved. Block (1980) discussed these issues sufficiently; and based on the clinical experiences of the two senior authors of this text, these issues continue to manifest themselves in the therapy process. The first is an extreme willingness on the part of African-American people to take a risk with the mental health system despite a negative past and recent history of Blacks with respect to the delivery of psychological services. It is also probable that since African Americans may initially utilize traditional support networks in times of stress, these traditional support systems are not functioning effectively for that individual, either because of unavailability or because the person chooses not to use them. Consequently, service providers may see clients who are more debilitated since the amount of time between the presenting problem and therapeutic intervention is apt to be longer. Certainly, the Report of the Surgeon General (2001) reinforces this issue.

There is also the possibility that a Black client may display a greater sense of fear and suspiciousness. These feelings are not only stimulated by the prospect of therapy itself, but also by the possibility and probability of working with a non-Black professional, and having to entrust one's life stories and pain to a non-Black person. This sentiment is borne out in studies like Nickerson, Helms, and Terrell (1994). Their data support the hypothesis that higher levels of cultural mistrust negatively predict help-seeking attitudes in African-American students. In fact, greater mistrust of Whites was associated with more negative general attitudes about help seeking from clinics staffed primarily by Whites and with the expectation that services rendered by White counselors would be less satisfactory. It is also likely that persons seeking therapeutic services may be partially to well-educated since these individuals tend to have a better understanding for and trust in more traditional psychological services. It is also probable that children and adolescents seen in mental health clinics in community facilities may be referrals from two primary sources. Those include the courts and schools. If such is the case, a clinician can expect to encounter a heightened sense of resistance, suspiciousness, and even hostility from the patient related to what may possibly be a mandated participation in therapy.

RECOMMENDATIONS FOR SERVICE DELIVERY

White (1984); White and Parham (1990); and Parham, White, and Ajamu (1999) suggested that in order to increase effectiveness with African-American clients, both African-descent and non African-descent therapists need to be cognizant of four major issues: (1) the impact of oppression on the lives of Blacks, (2) African-American psychological perspectives as a source of strength, (3) African-American language styles (to facilitate communication), and (4) identity concerns that arise as a result of an admixture of African-American and Euro-American influences. Therapists who plan to work with African-American clients would do well to familiarize themselves with these issues.

Cultural confirmation for White's (1984) suggestions can be found in the writings of other Black psychologists. Block (1980), for example, talked about therapist errors, in the same way that Knox, Burkard, Johnson, Suzuki, and Ponterotto (2003) and Constantine, Lewis, Connor, and Sanchez (2000) do now. Each cautions service providers about being influenced by and promoting the illusion of color blindness (e.g., "I don't view you as an African-American client, I see you as a human being."), failing to discuss issues of race unless the client raises the issue, and a general reluctance to explore religious and spiritual issues with clients of African descent. Although the intention of this statement may be admirable, and such exclusions meant to embrace greater levels of sensitivity, such attitudes implicitly deny the authenticity of one's African makeup, negate the value and impact of racial issues in a client's life, and work against the client's moving toward rediscovering and maintaining African-centered values into his or her own life space. This was certainly the case in the work of Thompson and Jenal (1994), who concluded that avoiding topics such as race in the counseling process engendered avoidance and even hostility in the African-American clients being served.

Our observations of Black people lead us to believe that throughout their lives, African Americans will be confronted again and again with the developmental issues of becoming comfortable with one's identity, physical makeup, and ego ideal. These phenomena (issues) are similar to those articulated by developmental psychologists who have discussed many of the developmental crises of the late adulthood era. It is believed that individuals in this society must successfully work through issues of identity, body image, and ego in order to gain a sense of self-satisfaction about their lives. Counselors and other psychological service providers need to recognize that as long as Black people are subjected to racist and oppressive conditions in this society, and are confronted with the question of how much to compromise one's "Blackness" in order to successfully assimilate, they (Blacks) will continue to need therapeutic assistance in struggling with issues of:

1. ***Self-differentiation versus preoccupation with assimilation***— where an individual strives to become comfortable with the recognition that he or she is a worthwhile human being regardless of valuation and validation from Whites.
2. ***Body transcendence versus preoccupations with body image***— where an individual strives to become comfortable with one's physical self, which may be characterized by a continuum of possibilities ranging from African to Afro-European characteristics (i.e., very dark vs. very light skin, very coarse vs. very straight hair, very thick vs. very thin lips).
3. ***Ego-transcendence versus self-absorption***—where a person strives to become secure enough in oneself that they are able to develop personal ego strength by contributing to the uplifting of one's people, rather than oneself exclusively. Such efforts are consistent with the African worldview of *'I* am because *we* are, and because *we* are, therefore, *I* am" (Nobles, 1972; Mbiti, 1970).

In addition to the need for a culturally specific therapeutic knowledge base, psychological service providers in particular, and service delivery agencies in general, need to struggle with the question of how to help African-American clients get the most out of their therapeutic encounter. Earlier in this chapter, we reported that more than 50 percent of ethnic clients terminate therapy after the initial session (Sue, 1978) although more recent studies identify factors like culturally specific treatment venues and cultural mistrust that might be related to trends in this area. And while more contemporary data suggests that those numbers are decreasing, there continues to be too few service providers who have a clue about how to address this dilemma. Unlike their practicing colleagues, however, Fiester and Rudestam (1975) have recognized that lower socioeconomic class patients contributed disproportionately to the dropout rate, with unmet expectations most often being reported as reasons for their dissatisfaction. Yet, some sixteen years later, Neighbors (1991) found that lower income Blacks (presumably low SES) were more likely to utilize mental health services, when compared to their higher socioeconomic counterparts. There was no mention, however, about whether expectations for service delivery were met, and whether those contributed to retentions in treatment. But, this trend of lower SES Blacks utilizing mental health services continues, even as Duncan (2003) found that lower SES African-American college students help favorability ratings about seeking mental health services than their higher SES status counterparts who were younger in age. Admittedly, the impact of SES on the therapeutic process and client's willingness to engage mental health services is an area we still have insufficient knowledge in. However, what is not in contention is the degree to which meeting a client's expectations for treatment facilitates their retention in the therapeutic process. In prior editions (1990, 1999) we have discussed the notion that differential expectations of clients toward therapists may lead clients to expect direct authoritative opinions from therapists, while they (clients) sit passively waiting to be cured. Therapists, on the other hand, often expect their clients to be more active and disclosive, and assume a greater sense of responsibility for their concerns, while they practice a nondirective approach to assessing clients' problems. When the expectations of both therapy participants are not met, clients consider discontinuing treatment believing the therapist himself or herself, or the process of therapy, to be ineffective and irrelevant, whereas the therapist is left with images of an uncommitted or even resistant client.

We believe that one approach that continues to have merit and that might assist service providers in facilitating client commitment to treatment is pre-therapy education. This procedure involves giving the client an orientation to therapy prior to his or her initial session. Although various mediums (audiotape, printed handouts, etc.) have been used, the strongest research support has been demonstrated using videotape film (Dyke, 1983). Surprisingly, many mental health service delivery units have not adopted pre-therapy education in any form; however, we believe that this approach has merit and deserves to be tested further to empirically assess its utility. With the advent of new technologies like CDs and DVDs, WebPages, and the like, the possibilities to employ this strategy as a means of creating more convergence between client-therapist expectations is even more exciting. However, irrespective of how one chooses to connect with clients, that connection and orientation to counseling/clinical services must be made. It is our strong recommendation that such be conducted in a very proactive, outreach oriented, way, along with the strategies that address a client's needs for information once they present for treatment.

The third recommendation centers on the recognition that therapeutic strategies that promote African-centered values are more likely to be effective with an African-American client who also subscribes to that value system. This strategy is reinforced in this fourth edition because of what we now know about African-centered cultural values serving as a source of strength and as protective factors for many clients (Constantine, Alleyne, Wallace, & Franklin-Jackson, 2006). In that study, Constantine et al. (2006) found that higher levels of self-esteem and life satisfaction were related to adherence to cultural values. Consequently, if those values are then incorporated into the delivery of mental health services, then the possibility for clients to use those services and gain from them is further enhanced. Jones (2003) helps to reinforce this point about the need for African-centered cultural values in his proposing of a model he labels T R I O S. The elements of TRIOS, which involve the context of adapting to African-American life in distinctive ways, include: (T) a special notion of *time,* (R) a unique disposition to *rhythm,* (I) a high degree of *improvisation,* (O) a proclivity towards *orality,* and (S) a sense of *spirituality.* Jones argues that coping with racism and life adversities creates the conditions where these elements are employed to detect the occurrence of, protect oneself from, and enhance one's self worth as a defensive posture against societal racism and oppression. Thus, the use of these African-centered cultural patterns is intended to fortify individuals with strategies for resistance, coping, and if necessary, adaptation. In another example where the use of African-centered cultural values can be effectively employed is in the realm of group work. For example, group rather than individual psychotherapy, in some cases, may be a preferred or even more effective mode of treatment for Black clients (Shipp, 1983; Pack-Brown, Whitington-Clark, and Parker, 1998, 2007). Although the notion of using groups is not a new idea (Brayboy, 1971; Yalom, 1975), Shipp, (1983) and Pack-Brown et al. (2007) contend that clinicians fail to recognize how and why group approaches may be effective with their Black clients. Group approaches help to promote the African-centered notion of collective survival, commonality among individuals, mutual cooperation, and shared responsibility, which are traditional values in the Black community. Group approaches also encourage sharing among individual members and facilitate the development of group cohesiveness. Shipp (1983) and Pack-Brown et al. (2007) both believe that studies that imply that the cohesiveness that results from sharing experiences and backgrounds has therapeutic value often overlook the relationship that exists between group work and the client's cultural dispositions. Family systems approaches may also be effective modes of treatment because of the reliance on the group. Hines and Boyd-Franklin (1982) and Boyd-Franklin, (1989), for example, document how the utilization of family kinship networks and bonds during the course of therapy with an African-American client provides an important source of support. McAdoo (1981) also suggests that reliance on natural support systems (extended family) rather than institutional supports may reduce feelings of guilt, defeat, humiliation, and powerlessness some clients feel.

A further recommendation for service providers seriously interested in effectively treating Black clients is to familiarize themselves with a broad-based curriculum of African-American and African psychological principles. Nobles (1986) contends that much of what is meaningful in African psychology has gone unnoticed or unrecognized because of psychologists' and other service providers' inability to understand basic African psychological principles that were revealed to humanity by the ancient Africans through the use of symbolism. If Nobles' contention is accurate (and we suspect it is), it seems possible that suggestions for useful treatment strategies with African-American clients may also become more crystallized if practitioners attempt to understand the symbolism of ancient African teachings.

Nobles (1986) teaches us that in ancient Africa, for example, the symbol of an animal was worshipped as an act of consecration to the vital functions that characterized the animal, "So-called primitive animal worship is not in reality the worship of animals, but a method used to identify and clarify the essential function or law of nature embodied in the particular animal" (p. 34). The jackal, for example, in ancient African thought, was the symbol of judgment and represented the law of digestion. Digestion, in turn, should be viewed as a precise act of innate discrimination and analysis, wherein things ingested into the body, mind, and spirit are transformed into useful energy and separated from that, which is to be discarded as waste. In essence, digestion is a destructive-productive process of transformation wherein that, which contributes to the survival of the organism, is stored by the body and used, and that, which has no usefulness to the organism's survival, is expelled.

Nobles' interpretation of that law of nature through his understanding of symbolism may have some contemporary relevance for clinicians who work with African-American clients. Oppression, discrimination, and racism are unnatural human phenomena. As such, these conditions are often internalized (ingested) and helped to stimulate feelings of confusion, anxiety, anger, guilt, frustration, and self-doubt in Black and African-American people. Sometimes, these factors cause them to become disconnected from self as well as other African Americans in spirit and in physical proximity. However, the traditional African-centered view of self is contingent upon the existence of an interconnectedness with other Black people. As such, therapists might need to assist clients in reconnecting themselves in body and spirit to other African-American people or at least help them to realize that their personal sense of discomfort (anxiety, guilt, confusion, etc.) may be related to being disconnected from those Black experiences.

It might even be necessary for therapists to assist Black and African-American clients in having a culturally corrected experience whereby the client is assisted in: (1) promoting thoughts, feelings, and behaviors that affirm his or her humanity as a Black person of African descent; and (2) purging from one's mind, body, and spirit those ideas, feelings, and behaviors that prove destructive to oneself as an organism and do nothing to affirm one's humanity as an African American.

Assisting an African-American client with a culturally corrective experience may also force the therapist to question his or her role within the therapy process itself. Some theoretical orientations assume that the most important role of the clinician working with the client is to be an objective outsider who supports the client in working through his or her issues in ways only important to the client. Counseling is assumed to be an interactive process in which the therapist attempts to facilitate the client's personal awareness and movement toward self-actualization. Seldom is a therapist expected to align himself or herself with the client or confront the client in ways that might violate the unwritten rule of remaining neutral, anonymous, objective, and a passive listener or observer. However, Basch (1980) reminds us that there is nothing wrong with influencing the client, and there is no ideal way for a therapist to behave. Certainly, nonpsychodynamically oriented theories practice alternate approaches.

Indeed, we would contend that a theoretical orientation that encourages a therapist to be a subjective companion rather than just an objective outsider may be an effective approach with African-American clients. Therapists adopting a subjective companion role attempt to become interpersonally connected to the client (development of a kinship bond), and may be guided by personal biases about what is ultimately best for the client's mental health. The therapist's attitudes are influenced by the recognition that confronting a client about his or her self-destructive attitudes and beliefs may be the catalyst that stimulates a client's movement toward becoming a self-actualizing Black or African-American. Therapists should be cautious, however, about interpreting the client's self-actualization efforts as a process of simply becoming a better individual for self sake. In the African ethos (Nobles, 1972, 1986; Mbiti, 1970), the self one seeks to become is related to and influenced by a more collective consciousness defined by the community or group. Unlike Western philosophical systems, the African tradition does not place heavy emphasis on the individual;

it is recognized that only in terms of other people does one become conscious of his or her own being. Only through others does one learn his or her responsibilities toward himself or herself and others (Nobles, 1980, p. 29).

THE INFLUENCE OF IDENTITY STATES ON THE THERAPEUTIC RELATIONSHIP

Regardless of which theoretical orientation a psychologist chooses to adopt, one factor seems to remain constant. That is, the *relationship* between the therapist and the client is a vital and necessary part of the therapeutic process (Highlen & Hill, 1984).

Parham (1989, 2002) has recommended that service providers look beyond the skin color of a client, or the client's racial self-designation (i.e., Black, Negro, African American) in trying to determine an appropriate therapeutic match. Furthermore, he asserts that recognizing the within-group variability that exists among African-American clients may assist a therapist in understanding how the racial identity attitudes of a client discussed in Chapter 6 may influence the ability to establish a qualitative (workable) relationship with that client (Parham, 1989). Figure 8-1 illustrates how racial identity attitudes impact the ability of the service provider to break down the social distance between himself or herself and the client.

For example, a Caucasian therapist who begins treatment with a Black person possessing pro-White/anti-Black attitudes will have little difficulty breaking down the social distance between himself or herself and the client where ethnicity is concerned. However, one might expect ethnicity to be an obstacle if the client treated by the Caucasian therapist were more immersed in his or her racial identity.

Racial Identity Stages and Counseling Relationships

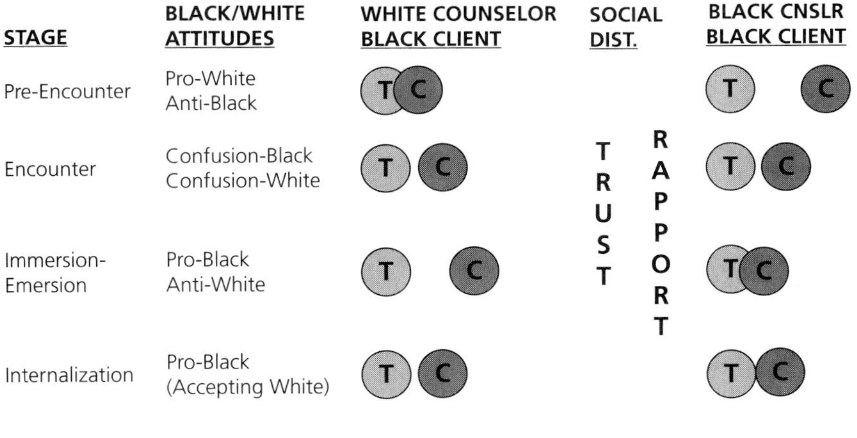

Parham(1989)

Relationship Between Social Distance and Racial Identity Attitudes

FIGURE 8.1

Given this latter scenario, readers should be cautioned against inferring that a relationship between White therapists and Black clients with strong ethnic identification is impossible. Indeed, positive therapeutic work can occur if these issues of the client's perception of the therapist are worked through in the *initial* stages of therapy.

Service providers should also be cautious about assuming that an inability of the client to become "hooked" on the therapy process is indicative of client resistance, and/or factors beyond the therapist's control. Although this may be the case in some instances, it is also possible that the service provider has not spent sufficient time exploring trust issues related to cross-ethnic interactions and relationships.

Figure 8-1 also provides a prediction of the ability of a Black therapist to work with Black clients at various attitudinal stages. This issue is particularly important, since many service providers and even entire agencies assume that a Black staff member is a better therapeutic match for a Black client with strong pre-encounter attitudes. One consequence of such an interaction might be premature termination by the client who believes that the therapist is an "affirmative-action psychologist" who is less qualified than his or her White counterpart, and thus less capable of delivering effective treatment.

In the same context, it is also inappropriate to assume that ethnicity alone and not training is a necessary and sufficient criterion to work with a client. This assumption is also questionable, since most Black service providers receive similar training and degrees as their White counterparts, with little if any ethnic content as part of their core curriculum (Franklin, 1975). Arguably, similarity in ethnic background *may* provide one with a common life experience, but such is not always the case. Certainly, courses in African-American psychology are essential and are considered by us to be a minimum prerequisite for anyone working with Black clients.

TRAINING SERVICE PROVIDERS

Although the disciplines of psychology and counseling struggle with the desire to better serve African-American populations, perhaps no other issue is more important than the training of mental health professionals. After all, serving culturally different clients generally, and African-Americans in particular, does require some requisite knowledge in how to provide the most effective interventions. In response to this demand for better training, and a recognition of the ethical responsibility to provide culturally sensitive services, training programs have begun to slowly address the issue (Rogers, Ponterotto, Conoley, & Wiese, 1992). We mention "slowly" since Rogers et al. (1992) report that although 90 percent of training directors in college and university psychology programs and counseling centers agree that multicultural training is essential, 40 percent of their programs incorporate little, if any, ethnic content into core courses of the curriculum. Despite this alarming trend, Rogers, Hoffman, and Wade (1998) provide other evidence that the APA-approved counseling psychology programs may be faring somewhat better. In citing Hill and Strozier's (1992) survey of faculty in such programs, 87 percent reported offering one multicultural issues course in their curriculum.

Although we applaud the strides that have been made in providing some training over the last decade, we are generally appalled at what passes as acceptable training. Furthermore, we are concerned that the "bar" (standard of excellence or acceptability) is so low that any addition to the curriculum or the faculty is seen as acceptable. In this regard, it is interesting to note that most psychology programs that train therapists/clinicians require an average of five years of study to achieve a doctorate degree and two years for a master's. Included in the standard training curriculum are courses (i.e., personality theory, testing and assessment, psychopathology, counseling/ clinical interviewing skills), research training (statistics, measurement, research design, thesis, dissertation), and practicum (hundreds of hours of counseling/clinical training in mental health agencies), little, if any, of which is culturally specific. Yet, it is expected that trainees and professionals alike will develop genuine competence in working with African Americans in one course on "multicultural counseling," where ethnicity is but one of several demographic dimensions (i.e., gender, sexual orientation) covered during a single semester. Is it any wonder that clinicians are ill-equipped to treat African-Americans effectively?

One of the more promising movements to emerge in the counseling field in particular is the focus on the development of competency in specific areas (Sue, Arredondo, & McDavis, 1992). In their presentation of cultural competence requirements, Sue, Arredondo, and McDavis (1992) suggested that the domains of competence should include awareness, knowledge, and skills. The promise of this effort lies in the ability to identify specific areas of expertise and training needed to consider oneself skilled enough to work with culturally different populations. Despite this promising practice and the revisions it has undergone, a limitation of this approach is its reliance on generic principles of multicultural theory and practice to treat what may be very unique cultural groups. Certainly, similar critique was leveled at Sue, Ivey, and Pedersen (1996 by Parham (1997) as he evaluated the efficacy of their Multicultural Counseling and Therapy (MCT) model. Parham (1997) advocates for, and we support, the development of a more culturally specific set of competencies from which to train clinicians.

Although space and the focus of this fourth edition text do not allow for a thorough and comprehensive detailing of the components of a counseling competency model for African Americans, we do want to again provide a framework for this. In doing so, we continue to embrace the structure of the model originally provided by Sue, Arredondo, and McDavis (1992, and since reiterated and highlighted in the works by Pope-Davis, Coleman, Liu, and Toporek (2003); Constantine and Sue (2005); and White and Henderson (2008), in highlighting the awareness, knowledge, and skill dimensions of cultural competency for African-centered psychology and therapy. We believe these attributes are essential for anyone working with African-American populations, and we highlight here the work done by Parham (2005) in stylizing the competencies for clinicians' and counselors' specific use with African-American clients.

AFRICAN-AMERICAN PSYCHOLOGY PROPOSED PRACTICE COMPETENCIES (PARHAM, 2005)

Awareness

- Therapists must be cognizant of his or her own personal biases and assumptions about African-descent people.
- Therapist must be aware of how they have been impacted by the MAAFA, a great disaster of death and destruction beyond human comprehension and convention. The chief feature is the denial of the humanity of African people (Ani, 1994) and how the residuals from those experiences impact their lives.
- Therapist must be aware of his or her own role as "healers."
- Therapist must have access to his or her own historical memories about the majesty of African life and culture as well as the pain and tragedy of historical and contemporary Black suffering.
- Therapist must be aware of how people and elements in the universe are interconnected.
- Therapist must have a sense of his or her own essence as spirit and be in touch with his or her own spirituality.
- Therapist must have a relationship with the divine force in the universe.
- Therapist must have strong knowledge of himself or herself and provide answers to the three critical questions: Who am I?; Am I who I say I am?; Am I all I ought to be? (Fanon, 1966).
- Therapist must have a sense of his or her own ethnic consciousness, which is not simply anchored in race (biology), but in the shared struggle and collective heritage of African people.
- Therapist must have a vision for African-descent people that embraces the transformative possibilities of the human spirit.
- Therapist must be aware of how to move from possessing intellect to dispensing wisdom.

Knowledge

- Knowledge of African psychology and history in ancient Kemetic, historical African, and contemporary African-American societies.
- Knowledge of the essential components of an African-centered worldview.
- Knowledge of the principle of *Ma 'at*.
- Knowledge of the limitations of traditional Euro-American psychological perspectives when applied to African-descent people.
- Knowledge of how science has been used as a tool of oppression.
  - Knowledge of the limitations of traditional approaches to therapy.
- Knowledge of the characteristics and dynamics of personality development.
  - Models of African self-consciousness (Kambon, 1992).
  - Dimensions of the soul (Akbar, 1994; Nobles, 1986).
  - Dimensions of African character (i.e., *Ma'at*).
  - Models of nigrescence (i.e., Cross, 1971,1991; Thomas, 1971; Parham & Helms, 1981, 1985).

- Knowledge of assessment instruments appropriate for use with African-descent adults, youth, and children.
- Knowledge of the limitations of traditional assessment instruments when used with African Americans.
- Knowledge of therapeutic rituals.
- Knowledge of the diagnostic nosologies used to classify disordered behaviors in African Americans.
- Knowledge of the ethical principles germane to treating African-descent people.
- Knowledge of how traditional ethical standards of some psychological and counseling associations may be culturally inappropriate for African-descent people.
- Knowledge of a geopolitical view of African people and their condition in America and throughout the world.
- Knowledge of what racism and White supremacy are and how individual, institutional, and cultural racism impact the lives of African-descent people.
- Knowledge of traditional help-seeking behaviors in African Americans.
- Knowledge of communities, institutions, and resources that provide both tangible and intangible support to the African-American community.
- Knowledge of the dynamics of family in the African-American community.

Skills

- Ability to maximize congruence between healing messages and proper conduct.
- Ability to connect with, bond with, or otherwise establish rapport with African-American clients.
- Ability to conduct and participate in rituals.
- Ability to hear both the surface structure and deep structure messages as client communicates.
- Ability to administer and interpret culturally appropriate assessment instruments.
- Ability to advocate on behalf of clients to social agencies and institutions.
- Ability to utilize theories and constructs in forming diagnostic impressions.

9

■ ■ ■

Applications of an African-Centered Psychology: The Juvenile Offender

By Roslyn Caldwell
California Polytechnic University San Luis Obispo

Thus far in our text, we have discussed the need for a world view that centers on African ideology, the needs and function of the Black family, critical issues related to identity development and congruence, the educational profile of African-American people, the need to cope with the continuing vestiges of oppression, and mental health issues affecting African Americans. While all of these topics have been a focus of interest throughout the general discipline of psychology, an emerging problem that has arisen over the last several years, which has impacted African-American people as a whole, and has contributed to the concerns previously discussed in our text, has been the growing number of young African-American males engaging in delinquency, violence, and criminality. In each edition of *The Psychology of Blacks*, we have devoted a chapter related to contemporary issues. We believe that one of the biggest issues plaguing African Americans, particularly youth, is related to the level of violence and criminal involvement, and the impact that the criminal justice system has on our young people. The importance of understanding the issues faced by this population is significant given the high prevalence and incidence of exposure to violence, including both being victimized by and witnesses of specific events. Moreover, not only has the level of violence against African-American youth increased, so has their perpetration of violence and criminal activity. Despite the level of violence and criminal involvement occurring among African-American youth, the ways in which such activities occur, and the factors associated with them, are not well studied or well understood. Therefore, the purpose of this chapter is to shed light on such issues in an effort to more effectively intervene with these youth.

INTRODUCTION

Although African-American youth are overrepresented in the criminal justice systems, the majority of our youth are doing well. According to the National Center of Education Statistics (2003), African-American youths' performance in mathematics and reading has improved since 1999 as compared to the years 1973-1982 (Hoffman & Llagas, 2003). The dropout rate for African-American students has declined by 8 percent between the years 1972 and 2000, with an average high school completion rate of approximately 84 percent in 2000; a significant increase since 1982. A higher proportion of African-American high school graduates are also attending college as compared to more than 20 years ago (Hoffman & Llagas, 2003). Most recent educational statistics from 2000 reveal: 31 percent of 18- to 24-year olds were enrolled in colleges and universities, up from 19 percent in 1980; nearly two-thirds or 63 percent of college enrollment by African Americans comprised females, the highest level of enrollment than any other racial/ethnic group; African-American college students earned degrees in the fields of business, social sciences/history psychology, health professions, and related sciences at rates higher than the national average; and the proportion of African Americans completing college has increased between 1975 and 2000 (Hoffman & Llagas, 2003).

In spite of the educational gains African-American youth have achieved in the past 20 years, one cannot ignore their overrepresentation in the context of the criminal justice system as compared to the general population. What is even more surprising is the pervasive lack of attention that exists throughout the psychological literature in regards to understanding the unique challenges faced by this population and the factors that place them at risk for criminal involvement. The latest textbooks representing the fields of forensic psychology, law, and criminal justice (i.e., Bartol & Bartol, 2008; Huss, 2008) often make reference to the large number of African Americans represented within every phase of the justice system (arrest, detention, parole, and probation); however, little concern is given to the unique challenges particularly faced by our youth and young adults who exhibit a vicious cycle of intersecting and remaining involved in these systems. More times than not, these youth spend the majority of their lives maintaining this relationship at some level, ultimately impacting his or her ability to live as productive citizens and contributing to the success of Black people. Given this current state of affair, it is important to bring to light these issues in order to effectively intervene and provide services to a population with special needs.

AFRICAN AMERICANS AND THE CRIMINAL JUSTICE SYSTEM: POLICING, COURTS, AND CORRECTIONS

Current statistics reveal that African Americans make up approximately 13 percent of the total U.S. population with 4.5 percent being African-American males (United Census Bureau, 2007); however, given this small percentage of the general population and as previously mentioned, they are overly represented within all sectors of the criminal justice systems. In fact, African-American males have a one-in-three chance of going to prison, which is eight times the rate for Caucasians and two times the rate for Hispanics (Bureau of Justice Statistics, 2006). Currently, African Americans represent 44 percent of the total prison population, and 92 percent encompass African-American adult males (U.S. Census Bureau, 2007; Bureau of Justice Statistics, 2006). Some estimates report that by 2015, the number of African-American adult males involved in the criminal justice system is expected to increase by approximately 19 percent (Bureau of Justice Statistics, 2007, 2006).

Parallel to the alarming statistics regarding African-American adult males and their relationship with the justice systems, an even bleaker picture emerges when it comes to our African-American youth (individuals under the age of 18 years), who are disproportionately targeted by and represented in the juvenile and adult justice systems and encompassing 44 percent of all juvenile offenders, with more than 50 percent being African-American males (Caldwell, Silverman, Lefforge, & Silver, 2004; Office of Juvenile Justice and Delinquency Prevention [OJJDP], 2006). These rates are astounding given that African-American youth constitute approximately 15 percent of the juvenile population nationwide; however, they represent 26 percent of all juveniles arrested, 45 percent of those who are detained, and 40 percent of those in residential placements with significant increases in the last fifteen years (OJJDP, 2004). Given the disproportionate confinement of African-American youth, governmental agencies throughout the United States have acknowledged a number of factors that contribute to these statistics: racial stereotyping and cultural insensitivity, lack of alternatives to detention and incarceration, harsher punishments and treatment for African-American youth, and a lack of culturally relevant and sensitive services aimed at intervening with this population (OJJDP, 2004). The disproportionate number of African-American youth in the criminal justice systems has far-reaching consequences not only for the youth themselves, but also for society at large. However, the challenges are complex and appear multidimensional in nature.

As a result of the relationship between African-American youth and the juvenile and adult criminal justice systems, the limited research that has emerged and which focuses on violence among African Americans has historically been related to the social, political, and economical constraints imposed on this population. However in more recent years, research has examined other potential factors that have been related to increased delinquency and violence given the ever-increasing surge of African-American adolescent males becoming entangled in the criminal justice systems; African-American adolescents are two times more likely than Caucasians and three times more likely than any other race to engage in delinquent and/or violent behavior, ultimately resulting in incarceration (Puzzanchera, Stahl, Finnegan, Tierney, & Snyder, 2004). Moreover, over 50 percent of our adolescent African-American males who are incarcerated are serving time in adult prisons with lengthy sentences, including life imprisonment (Puzzanchera et al., 2004). Despite the fact that psychology in general has identified risk factors that increase one's likelihood of engaging in violence and delinquency from a broad developmental perspective, little attention has been given on identifying the effects of this behavior as it relates to the culture of African Americans; consequently, several questions still remain unanswered: How does criminality among African Americans as a group effect the family structure? What is the future of our young Black males involved in the juvenile and adult criminal justice systems? How does criminogenic behavior influence one's sense of internal identity? How can society effectively intervene with this population, given the triple jeopardy of poverty, racism, and stigma associated with being an ex-offender?

While the focus of this chapter pertains to African-American juvenile males, one cannot ignore the relationship that African-American females have with the criminal justice systems. As of 2006, the Bureau of Justice Statistics revealed that the majority of imprisoned females were African Americans. In fact between 2000 and 2007, African-American females on average have been three to seven times more likely compared to Caucasians to be incarcerated (Bureau of Justice Statistics, 2007; Freudenberg, 2002). Similar statistics hold true for African-American adolescent females who make up approximately 35 percent of the U.S. juvenile and adult justice systems. Studies have also revealed that African-American females as a whole compared to Caucasian and Hispanic females are committing more violent and drug-related offenses and that the criminality imposed by this population has more to do with different experiences and/or different ways of responding to experiences associated with social, economic, and educational deprivations (Koons-Whitt & Schram, 2003). Furthermore, the incarceration experiences faced by African-American females presents a downward cycle of economic dependence, social isolation, substance abuse, and mental health issues, especially given the unique challenges they face not only as females but also as an ex-offender as compared with African-American males. It is also important to note that the relationship that African-American females have with the justice system has a direct impact on the future of African-American adolescent males, thus a significant reason for such discussion.

Because of the significant relationship that African-American adolescent males have with the juvenile and adult criminal justice systems, especially their increasing overrepresentation at all levels, it is imperative that attention is brought to this population given that these youth represent the future, thus impacting the potential success of Black people as a whole. The purpose of this chapter is to discuss the relationship between African-American male youth and the criminal justice systems, including historical origins, dynamics that lead them to have such contact, and how these issues contribute to their mental health and well-being. We close this chapter with a discussion that focuses on the implementation of practical strategies and our role as educators, clinicians, and mental health professionals in effectively intervening and treating our youth.

HISTORICAL ORIGINS OF AFRICAN-AMERICAN MALES AND THE CRIMINAL JUSTICE SYSTEM

The 1960s through 1990s saw African-American males caught in the vortex of two life span trajectories, as the collapse of the most intrusive forms of racism helped open pathways toward a college education, while the disappearance of good-paying factory jobs and the rise of the drug trade pushed others toward street life and the underground economy. Between the years 1970 and 2000, the number of African Americans going to college nearly doubled and the African-American middle class expanded threefold (Caldwell & Cross, 2006). However, for the same time period, the supposed African-American underclass increased at an alarming rate, and the number of African-American males entangled in some aspect of the judicial system (i.e., under arrest and awaiting trial, incarcerated, or on probation or parole) nearly equaled the number of African-American males in college (Bureau of Justice Statistics, 2007).

The lingering effects of historical racism, oppression, and discrimination and the subsequent deepening of inner-city poverty pushed many African-American males toward street life and the underground economy, which in turn has made eventual incarceration highly probable. In many ways, the situation surrounding African-American males is similar to the urban poor from the 1920s to 1930s, during which the forces of the Depression Era stirred low-income males from the Irish, Italian, and Jewish communities to form gangs for loan sharking, prostitution, and the distribution of the "illegal" substance of its time—alcohol. However, today, the underground economy that entangles African-American males is built around the sale and distribution of illegal drugs, particularly marijuana, crack cocaine, and heroin, as well as engaging in drug-related violent behavior that appears to be related to gang affiliation and involvement, as well as territorial issues. This "lure" and draw of street life and the underground economy is so strong that in recent studies of African-American urban street life, poor African-American males have stated that in light of the negative conditions and struggles faced by their individual families and the plight of their immediate communities, the decision to turn toward street life and crime seems "natural," "normal," or "routine" as a means of survival (Dance, 2002; Ginwright, 2004). Some research illustrates that this normalcy to engage in violence and delinquency may be attributed to cultural factors that are either understudied or misunderstood about African Americans.

Although the source of criminality can be traced back to economical issues and drug cartels and the influences of such developments on many African-American male youth presently, on the other hand, a host of other confounding variables exist that seem to be related and include factors such as transgenerational oppression and troubled consciousness tracing back to slavery and continuing to haunt and traumatize our youth today, ultimately impeding their abilities to form a sense of self-identity and definition. An example of this relationship can be seen when looking at the history of the 1954 landmark Supreme Court case of Brown v. Board of Education, which resulted in the desegregation of American schools. Prior to the Supreme Court's decision of desegregating schools due to unconstitutionality in 1950, Drs. Kenneth and Mamie Clark, psychologists during that time who intervened with African-American children, interviewed and recorded their responses related to an activity centered around the preference of black vs. white dolls (Clark & Clark, 1950, 1940, 1939a). Overwhelmingly, youth preferred the white dolls over the black dolls and ascribed negative and deviant characteristics toward the black dolls.

Community organizations such as the National Association for the Advancement of Colored People (NAACP) attributed youth's responses to poor self-image caused by the segregated and inferior school systems (Clark & Clark, 1950). While the findings may not have been surprising for those times, more than fifty years later, this experiment was repeated in 2005 by a 17-year old student Kiri Davis in a film entitled "A Girl Like Me" who found the same results (Davis, 2005). From a bigger picture, this example is not only an illustration of the impact of the injustices that African Americans have historically encountered and overcome, but also the transgenerational psychological impact of such experiences and the relationship that continues to shape our youth's way of thinking and behaving, which may be related to behavior characteristic of criminal activity. The adoption of having a negative self-image by youth and a lack of identity congruence pushes youth toward venues that put them at risk for engaging in delinquent behavior partly due to a lack of or search for a sense of self and the way in which they feel about themselves. This notion that is centered on the basic need of developing a sense of self appears to be the psychology behind young Black males engaging in delinquency and violence, whereby they instead develop a sense of inferiority and self-hatred.

An example that seems to illustrate this notion is written by the noteworthy author, Michael Eric Dyson, *Holler If You Hear Me* (2001), a book pertaining to the life of the late rap artist, Tupac Shakur, the son of a Black Panther who happened to be his mother. Dyson (2001) makes mention of the phenomena that Shakur encountered at a very young age and references that the choices he made, including the lifestyle of violence he often engaged in or was associated with, was influenced by the forces of mainstream society that classified and stereotyped "nobodies" as poor, black, hopeless, thugs who were part of a ghetto life or part of a society that viewed African Americans as inferior. One might argue that Shakur glorified violence, thuggery, and engaged in misogyny, but examining his life more closely reveals that Shakur experienced a lack of ethical clarity and identity, something very familiar among young African-American males. On the surface, one could easily say that Shakur chose his circumstances; however, in reality he was "forced" to live and promote a life that was representative of a personality that was to be portrayed to society (i.e., thug life) that in essence conflicted with the principles (i.e., Black Nationalism) by which he wanted to live by. In order to obtain the wealth and success that was needed to ultimately achieve his goal of advancing his principles, Shakur abided by the rules of the game (i.e., the entertainment industry), which prohibited him from expressing himself as who he was and the principles by which he desired to live by, ultimately leading to his demise. Like many of our young African-American males, Shakur exhibited a deep level of social consciousness but was not able to control his own life. That is, he did not have the right positive opportunities and, for survival purposes, was forced to continue portraying behavior that promotes the downfall of Black males rather than the educational and survival of Black males, a common form of institutionalized racism.

Utilizing Shakur as an iconic example of the effects of the negative expectations placed on young Black men, we can also apply his situation to many of our African-American male youth in present society. Although youth today who are involved in the legal system may at some conscious or unconscious level know the difference between right and wrong, their struggle between morality and survival is so great and oftentimes overshadowed by the persistent and negative imagery portrayed in our society. Through such venues as the media (i.e., music videos, television shows, etc.), the definition of success is often portrayed as living a lifestyle that is characteristic of "thuggery," degradation of females, and the importance of promoting and maintaining a behavioral style of being "hard" or "gangsta" on the street. It is these characteristics that make youth more prone to engage in activities and behavior consistent with criminality. Once a relationship between youth and the legal system has been established, it is oftentimes difficult for them to be provided opportunities that would aid in successful navigation of behaving and living life in prosocial ways. As a result of this type of deprivation, youth instead continuously develop a personality or social consciousness that emulates negative behavior, including violence and delinquency—behavior that conflicts with the true principles and standards consistent with African-centered values and ideologies, ultimately leading to the cyclical tragedies that plague our youth in the present day. The challenge for psychologists and academicians is to understand this dynamic in order to instill in youth the notion that despite having been involved in the criminal justice system, they are divine possibilities of success and that the difficult situation(s) they may have encountered does not mean they need to be a product of their circumstance.

Another illustration of the cycle of violence and criminality is illustrated in a book by Sayika Shakur, as known as a Monster Kody Scott (2004) and entitled, *Monster: The Autobiography of an L.A. Gang Member.* In this life story, Shakur discusses his experience of becoming a prominent gang member (being initiated at the age of 11) and how his involvement, both the process and representation, fulfilled needs in his life (a sense of family, belonging, and admiration), while also serving as a "rites of passage" of transitioning from childhood to manhood or adulthood. Moreover, Shakur's perpetuation of engaging in violence and criminal behavior was due to a conscious and unconscious notion that "I am already dead" lessening the effects of fear of mortality from such behavior (Shakur, 2004). Although Shakur is able to use the human spirit to triumph over insurmountable odds of the daily battles for survival, both Dyson (2001) and Shakur (2004) illustrate the incessant relationship and vulnerabilities of the streets.

Although it is difficult to generalize these two real life stories to all African-American male youth, these situations are indicative of what many young males experience and the decisions they make that lead them down a path of self-destruction. As we examine these stories and apply such experiences to general child and adolescent development, we know that all children have needs: cognitive, emotional, behavioral, mental, and social, just to name a few. However, when such needs are lacking in a youth's life, a strong desire to obtain such fulfillment occurs by youth behaving in socially inappropriate ways that are usually associated with street life. For instance, Parham (2007) identifies internal and external factors that contribute to the epidemic of violence and criminality among African-American youth. Examining the chart below, one can observe the various internal factors or needs that are a result of external factors that plague the lives of our young people. Likewise, the needs that youth receive from the streets are the same *unfulfilled* needs that are in the home, school, and/or community environment. For instance, in both biographies mentioned previously, association and involvement with gang life represented a sense of belonging, power, respect, love, validation, and attachment; all of which should be available through a youth's family, school, and community. However, when these three entities of a youth's life are disconnected, vulnerability to go outside of this "triangle of success" increases in proportion to the degree of disconnect (Caldwell et al., 2004; Parham, 2007). We as clinicians and educators need to understand the internal and external factors that play a role in risk to antisocial behavior and what needs this involvement meets in a youth's life, and how can we create ways that reconnect this "triangle for success," which will allow youth to get these needs met in ways that are more nurturing and affirming (Parham, 2007).

Internal Factors	External Factors
Unfulfilled Emotional Needs:	History (Family, Friends)
Need for Love	Peer Pressure/Negative Peer Influence
Need for Validation (Humanness)	
Need for Respect	**Family Neglect:**
	Absent Fathers (Physical/Psychological)
Unfulfilled Cognitive Needs:	Lack of Accountability
Worry too Much about Others' Opinions	Abusive Mothers
Low Frustration Tolerance/Poor Coping	Hostile Environment/Neighborhood
Externalize Blame	Poverty/Economic Hardship
	Lack of Legitimate Career Options
Social Roles:	Negative Images Portrayed in the Media
Need for Power	Lack of Positive Community Activities
Need for Achievement	Media Socialization
Need for Affiliation	Hostile School Environments
Need for Responsibility	Exposure to Violence
Need for Defense/Safety	
Displaced Aggression	
Distorted Information:	
Lack of Self-Knowledge	
Distorted Definitions of Manhood	
Lack of Spirituality	

THE RELATIONSHIPS BETWEEN FAMILY DYNAMICS, DELINQUENCY, AND VIOLENCE

One way to examine the relationship between vulnerability for a young Black male to engage in delinquency and violence is to understand the structure of the Black family, which is a system that is unique and complex with varying combinations that include: female- or male-headed single and intact; extended; and reconstituted (i.e., a biological and nonbiological parent residing in the home) families. The family is an extremely important entity in the lives of young Black males and can represent a risk factor for those involved in the criminal justice system. Irrespective of the Black family structure, it is also noteworthy to understand the importance and significance of elements or essential ingredients familial characteristics, including attachment, culture, values, and legacy that increase youth's risk to delinquency and violence. Nevertheless, the social influences that plague our young Black males are also dependent upon these family factors that include the role of the family, and its structure and function, which can significantly impact positive emotional and behavioral development (Bruce, 2004). Historically, the American family has been defined as having a two-structure system: male-headed families and female-headed families with the latter being characterized as unstable and more often seen in African-American households (Billinglsey, 1968; Staples & Boulin-Johnson, 1993). Nevertheless, the family is generally the support system in the lives of youth that assists in helping them to successfully avoid the negative risk and propensity toward violence and delinquent related activities (Bryant & Zimmerman, 2003), and instead, serves as a buffer in terms of providing prosocial beliefs, values, and also modeling appropriate behavior. However, the structure, function, and resources of the family can also have a negative impact on youth and increase their likelihood to engage in violence and delinquency via other mechanisms such as the quality of the family-child relationship (Caldwell et al., 2004).

As previously discussed in our text, the structure of the African-American family has not always resembled the traditional or conventional intact family (i.e., encompassing both biological parents within the same household) seen in the general U.S. population. More often than not, the African-American family is often composed of single-parents and/or extended family members (i.e., grandmother) who serve as the youth's parent and/or guardian, providing supervision, monitoring, nurturance, and care. Some research shows that single-parent family structures have been found to increase the vulnerability of youth to engage in violent and delinquent behavior (Bruce, 2004; Sampson & Laub, 2003) because the family may lack the resources and support (i.e., monitoring, supervision, role modeling) that youth need in order to foster positive identity development and resilience. This type of family structure is often seen among African-American male youth intersecting with the juvenile justice system, with over 50 percent of incarcerated African-American adults being parents, and a vast majority being males (Bureau of Justice Statistics, 2008) —a significant hardship for young Black males who need mentoring that would facilitate positive life transitions, opportunities, and resources.

Although extended family members and/or nonbiological relatives may offset the issues related to an absent father in the youth's household to some degree, it is clear that young African-American males have greater difficulty with this adjustment. This notion is further supported by research that illustrates adolescent males in general have more intimate relationships with fathers and that they play a central role in their lives (Bryant & Zimmerman, 2003). The opportunity to develop this type of relationship presents difficulty for African-American youth whose fathers are incarcerated for long periods of time, including life imprisonment. Research also points out that families characterized by single parents who have less economic support oftentimes have less contact with their child(ren), which presents challenges in terms of monitoring the child's activities and his or her associates or peer relationships. Consequently, parent-adolescent bonding that is characterized by emotional support, attachment, supervision, and monitoring and that is needed from a developmental perspective may be lacking, thus resulting in youth seeking out other venues by associating with peers (usually delinquent), thereby increasing the likelihood of engaging in criminal behavior. Some scholars believe that the single parenthood is a major contributor to the high incidence of delinquent and violent behavior among African-American male adolescents (Bruce, 2004; Sampson & Laub, 2003). For instance, between 1990 and 2000, not only were the number of incarcerated African-American parents at an all time high, the percentage of African-American youth living with only their mothers was about 55 percent. During this same time period, assault and murder among African-American youth increased by 89 percent and 145 percent, respectively (OJJDP, 2006). Although these statistics cannot be attributed to a single factor, the notion of single parenthood and father absences are often heard as explanations for interpersonal violence among young African-American males and Black on Black violence with statistics revealing: African-American youth accounting for almost 50 percent of American murder victims, with African-American males between the ages of 14 and17 years old eight times more likely to be murdered than their Caucasian counterparts, and homicide being the leading cause of death among our youth (Bureau of Justice Statistics, 2006; Caldwell, Kohn-Wood, Schmeelk-Cone, Chavous, & Zimmerman, 2004; Caldwell et al., 2004; OJJDP, 2006).

Although research and statistics regarding the African-American family structure and the impact on Black youth has been illustrated, this information underestimates or ignores the importance of instrumental and expressive strengths associated with the different and varying levels of family structure. While the research has provided significant information pertaining to the relationship between the composition of the family and vulnerabilities for youth to engage in delinquency and violence, the literature that exists has overlooked the confounding variables impacting this relationship, including the function of the Black family including the historical resilience associated. For instance, Billinglsey (1968) outlines three types of family functioning or roles: instrumental, expressive, and instrumental-expressive according to our society. The instrumental functions are twofold: that the family is self-sustaining and is able to maintain consistent physical and social boundaries. However, these functions become problematic when African-American families, particularly those with youth who have intersected with the justice systems, have other issues impacting these functions such as the need for pubic assistance or those families whose justice-involved youth have legal obligations to fulfill that ultimately impact their instrumental and expressive needs.

Billingsley (1968) theorizes that while functioning is essential to the survival of the family in general, when attention is placed on the functioning of the African-American family, little attention is placed on the resiliency of this family and instead presents a distorted picture and negative characterization of Black family life. He argues that the functioning of the Black family and the issues characterized within this function can oftentimes be attributed as a reflection of the issues surrounding our society. In other words, Billingsley (1968) argues that the variation and dynamics associated with the African-American family (i.e., instrumental, expressive, and instrumental-expressive functions) and the ability to meet the needs of the members, particularly African-American male youth, can also be interpreted as forces related to the intricacies of our society. Moreover, the assumption that American families are defined by the father being the provider and the emphasis placed on male youths' needs for a male role model in order to have healthy mental and emotional development, and social achievement, ignores the expressive roles of the father and the impact on positive development among female youth. Similarly, the mother's role as being nurturing ignores the significant involvement they play in the social, educational, and occupational attainment of youth as a whole. Given the cross-gender parent-child relationships in terms of the changing expressive and physical roles of parents within the African-American family is an important phenomenon to understand regarding kinship bonds (Staples & Boulin-Johnson, 1993).

An example of the relationship between instrumental roles as being more of an influence in a youth's vulnerability to engage in delinquency and violence is illustrated in an autobiography by John Edgar Wideman (1984) entitled *Brothers and Keepers: A Memoir*, which pertains to the life of Wideman and his brother. Wideman (1984) provides an excellent illustration that risk to delinquency and violence and the relationship to violence and delinquency is more complex than family structure and functioning. He further asserts that other extraneous forces including personal choice are also important to note. In this memoir, Wideman discusses the environmental and social factors and pressures of the "quick-get-over" street life mentality and an individual's psychological responses that led his brother to life imprisonment for murder and him to a life as a reputable professor of English, two divergent paths taken by biological brothers (Wideman, 1984). Another example is illustrated in a true story written by Sylvester Monroe and Peter Goldman (1988) about twelve men who grew up together and who are not biologically related but rather related by life circumstances and none of whom were aiming for the wrong direction but most of the individuals were victims of environmental or individual circumstance related to the street life rather than familial issues alone. The authors also illustrate how each of the brothers' circumstance imposes a narrow view of the world and how they learn the dangers of reaching beyond what they know, ultimately resulting results in being confined to their circumstance with only a few of the "brothers" overcoming their situation (Monroe & Goldman, 1988).

Both of the aforementioned true stories give a good depiction of young Black males who come from a negative familial environment and can lead positive and productive lives, while others engage and involve themselves with criminal behavior. However, what happens to youth who have positive environments that are noncharacteristic of street life with intact and supportive family functioning and structure? What factors are involved when youth have consistent positive life experiences and still connect with the criminal justice systems? What characterizes these youth to make them vulnerable to antisocial behavior? Thus, we must make a conscious effort in solidifying and assuring that our family structure is functional in order for youth to get their needs met.

THE RELATIONSHIP BETWEEN IDENTITY DEVELOPMENT, DELINQUENCY, AND VIOLENCE

In Chapter 6, we have examined and explored the notion of *Ore-Ire*, a sense of balance between one's ideas and actions; in other words one's sense of self-identity and congruence, which among African-American adolescent males, is an important area to be explored in terms of how such a concept relates to violence and delinquency among these youth.

Because of the relationship between familial and environmental dynamics and issues, theorists have explored the linkage between the process of identity development and delinquency and violence among African-American male youth. As a result of the lack of positive male role models, or having a family that lacks instrumental and/or expressive needs, many youth have a tendency to seek support and guidance outside of the family by associating with peers. In many cases involving African-American delinquent youth, it is often found that individuals with marginal status in peer groups have committed delinquent or violent behavior to gain and maintain acceptance and respect. As a result, young Black males tend to tailor their behaviors to reflect the attitudes of the designated group (Bynum & Weiner, 2004) due to a negative self-concept or sense of self that is related to a negative parent-child relationship, which in turn strengthens delinquency involvement, representing a balance in the youth's deficiencies in identity congruence. However, a positive and stable sense of self-identity tends to insulate and protect youth from engaging in delinquency, especially violence (Bynum & Weiner, 2002). Theorists have hypothesized that with every delinquent and/or violent act, the youth is reinforced of his behavior through delinquent peer association. The self-concept of the individual becomes increasingly favorable to himself as he begins to internalize perceived approval of others of his violent and delinquent behavior. This internalization becomes highly regarded as a way of effectively dealing with the outside world and also ensures survival. That is, successful and supported self-presentation of violence and delinquency boosts youths' self-concept and allows the person to endure the pressures within the environment. Furthermore, which are related to historical inequities and continuing racism and discrimination, result in a tendency for African-American male adolescents to discount future consequences in lieu of present gratification by pursuing self-interests in the absence of self-control that leads to criminal behaviors (Burt, Simons & Simons, 2006; Gottfredson & Hirschi, 1990; Ogbu, 1988).

THE RELATIONSHIP BETWEEN ACADEMIC ACHIEVEMENT, DELINQUENCY, AND VIOLENCE

Historically, school achievement among African-American male adolescents has been a social concern, particularly because African-American adolescents as a whole have achieved at substantially lower levels in comparison to many other racial/ethnic groups despite significant strides in academic performance in the past several years (U.S. Census Bureau, 2005). As a result, academic under-achievement has limited this population from economic and occupational at-tainment and, in turn, has been linked to delinquency and other maladaptive behaviors including adult criminality (Dornsbusch, Erickson, Laird, & Wong, 2001). In addition, studies have also found that African-American adolescents, particularly males, are much less likely to form an attachment with teachers and tend to anticipate rejection by school staff more than other racial/ethnic groups (Gnaulati & Heine, 2001). Such perceptions by African-American adolescents may be reality based given that research studies have found school personnel, particularly teachers, tend to have lower expectations of African-American ado-lescents and, in turn, the adolescent places less value on their academic achievement and performance (Griffin, 2001).

Furthermore, research has discovered a relationship between specific as-pects of an adolescent's school environment to delinquent and violent behaviors (Acock & Demo, 1999) including negative peer influences, lack of attachment with school personnel (i.e., teachers), boredom, and stereotypes or biases by teachers and school staff (Liu, 2004; Taylor & Lopez, 2005). As a result of these factors, stud-ies have revealed a relationship between poor academic achievement (i.e., poor academic preparation, truancy, etc.) by adolescents and their perception of nega-tive support by teachers, lack of motivation on the part of the adolescent, and feelings of isolation (Catterall, 1998; Dimmitt, 2003). Moreover, a reciprocal relationship has also been found between an adolescent's home and school envi-ronment. For instance, when an adolescent experiences a negative home environ-ment (negative parental involvement), the school environment may actually serve as a buffer against delinquency if an adolescent can connect with prosocial peers and supportive school staff, which in turn can promote academic achievement (Desimone, 2001; Kenny, Gallagher, Alvarez-Salvat, & Silsby, 2002).

An example of this has been argued by Parham and Howard (1999). As Chair of the Education Committee for the National 100 Black Men of America, Inc. organization, Parham discusses in his *State of Education for African American Youth* address the tendency for our society to hold African-American youth and their families 100 percent accountable for their educational deficits or underachievement. However, it seems evident from the research regarding the factors involved with this epidemic that the educational underachievement by African-American youth is only partly to blame for the problems that our youth face and the school environment should also be held accountable for the con-tributions to these issues. In fact, Parham and Howard (1999) have proposed and *Institutional Report Card*, which would provide an evaluation method to assess school systems and their contributions to the personal and intellectual growth and development of young people. One of the objectives of the report card is partnering with schools to evaluate them in key areas to determine whether or not a school is successful in educating African-American youth. These areas are comprehensive and include: faculty/staff composition, curriculum, instructional methodologies, special education placements, gifted education placements, counseling resources, administration, parental involvement, academic achievement rates, social climate, and influence on learning environment (Parham & Howard, 1999).

These areas are essential elements to achieving a successful teaching and learning environment for African-American youth. In addition, such a framework can be used as a guide to evaluate schools to become more accountable on how they can partner with the community and the youth's family in an effort to meet their academic, social, and cultural needs.

IMPLEMENTATION AND PRACTICAL STRATEGIES

As it has been frequently mentioned in our text, the success of African-American male youth is dependent upon a cooperative relationship between the home, school, and community and has been termed by Parham (1999) as the "triangle for success." Our goal is that we reconnect these domains in an effort to better assist our youth in successfully navigating their way through life and buffering the vulnerabilities to engage in delinquency and violence. This next section outlines ways in which to implement such activities in all three domains.

Home Environment

In terms of the home environment, it is important to recognize and assess the instrumental and expressive roles of the family, including parental dispositions, expectations, accountability of the parent or guardian *and* youth, and disciplining techniques. Along with these roles, the level of involvement (including physical and emotional) should also be taken into account. Understanding these issues will guide one to recognize the needs of our African-American male youth and more consistently achieve mechanisms to develop and sustain these needs in prosocial ways. In addition, creating parenting classes that assist and train parents on how to develop positive elements of a parent-child or parent-adolescent relationship is essential. In this manner, psychologists can assist in helping parents identify, understand, and raise awareness as to the "red flags" characteristic of delinquency involvement by African-American youth.

School Environment

As mentioned by Parham and Howard (1999), an institutional report card is one method for assessing ways in which the school environment can be more appropriately tailored to promote successful educational experiences in a youth's life. Other examples are to implement culturally specific curricula into the existing school curriculum. Such action would aid in the issues involving a lack of cultural awareness and pride on the part of youth, which is oftentimes found in gang affiliation and involvement. In addition, school programs that infuse anti-gang and antidrug messages into curriculum are also useful and effective tools to assist with deterring violence and criminality, which has shown to be related. Also, identifying youth who are at risk of delinquency and/or gang involvement and implementing a prevention program about gang awareness is also essential. Reaching youth before they have developed a relationship with the justice system has proven to be effective in terms of prevention for future involvement in criminal behavior.

Community Environment

The community is an essential element in the lives of our young people, and if utilized appropriately can serve as a buffer in one's life if other areas are lacking. Mentoring programs that can be utilized in the community as a resource for assisting young African-American males includes 100 Black Men of America, Inc., an organization that specialize in the development and implementation of youth programs. Involvement in mentoring programs previously mentioned in our text such as the *Passport to the Future Program or The Bakari Project, taught out of Orange County, California,* are examples of effective programs for reconnecting the "triangle for success." In addition to mentoring programs, reconnecting youth in local community churches and activities is also important given the lack of identity congruence and a sense of spirituality evident among justice-involved youth, particularly African-American males. It is also important that psychologists become involved in the community by partnering with such organizations by offering their support as a service that will supplement what the designated organization has developed in terms of their education and mentoring initiative. More often than not, community organizations need and desire the psychological foundation to complement their programs to increase effectiveness.

PRACTICAL STRATEGIES

Along with implementation, the following is a list of strategies that researchers, academicians, and clinicians should consider:

Education- and Training-Related Strategies

- Psychologists, educators, and mental health professionals must continuously educate themselves in order to be informed and understand the specific issues and risk factors faced by African-American youth, particularly those aspects that are related to social (family, peers, and school) environments and that shape youth development.
- Understanding the mechanisms by which the juvenile and adult criminal justice systems function and the subsequent effects on African-American youth is also key, particularly with regards to understanding criminogenic behavior. Being aware of the effects of this relationship on Black youth will not only assist in developing prevention and intervention programs

but will also provide useful information in order to understand the social world of African-American youth, particularly juvenile offenders.

- Importance should also be focused on obtaining knowledge and understanding at the local level that can help with program development at the national level. Becoming involved with organizations that have a sincere investment in developing programs that assist young African-American males is crucial in countering the problems at a national level.

Prevention and Intervention Program Strategies

- Given the relationship between the home, school, and community to the lives of our young people, it is important that programs incorporate these entities at all levels of programming.
- Programs that are developed should incorporate skill development that is culturally sensitive that help African-American youth develop improved ways of coping and social competencies in order to better address the unique stressors that they face in their lives.
- Most of the previous work related to justice-involved youth has focused on changes solely with the family; however, programs should also incorporate and focus on changes with peers given the interconnected relationship to risk to delinquency involvement. Programs that focus on improved instrumental and expressive roles and functioning (i.e., quality of family functioning, family cohesion, and parent monitoring) have generally decreased delinquent peer affiliation and delinquent behavior. Understanding this relationship is essential.
- Programs should be structured such that multiple risky behaviors, such as violence, school delinquency, substance use, and sexual behavior, are targeted in order to facilitate the process of change. From a public health and education perspective, focusing on reducing these risk behaviors can also decrease morbidity and mortality related to these behaviors and that plague our community. For example, a reduction in the use or carrying of weapons not only can prevent homicides, the leading cause of death among young African-American males, but also can help decrease other crimes that impact the Black community.
- Along the same lines, given that a high number of Black youth engage in violence, more times than not, a connection exists that is highly related to gang involvement that tends to not only increase the overall level of violence among this population but also continue beyond adolescence and into adulthood. Given the social organizations of gangs and the dominance over the lives of our youth, interventions *must* specifically emphasize helping lessen youth susceptibility to gang recruitment. It is also important to consider the role and the need that the gang may play in the lives of youth in order for a program to be successful.
- In addition, program development should focus on being culturally and ethnically sensitive as it relates to understanding issues related to African-American cultural values, family structure, communication, and learning

styles that are tailored to youths' needs and strengths. Although general or generic interventions may provide some level of reducing risk to delinquency and/or violence among African-American male youth, African-centered programs may be more advantageous over such programs in terms of participant satisfaction and reception by the community.

- Program development should also identify the unique stressors confronted by African-American youth in order to weave such issues into the intervention such that prevention and intervention programs can be more meaningful and relevant to the lives of our youth.
- Similarly, understanding the need, level and intensity of the intervention and/or prevention programs is also important in terms of whether the program is acceptable by youth and their families. Understanding and designing interventions that are relevant to the everyday experiences of African-American youth and their families increases acceptability.
- Moreover, programs that are developed should be designed to move beyond crisis intervention, but rather long-term intervention that includes fundamental change within the individual youth, family, school, and community.
- Also, programs should incorporate an evaluative component that examines not only the process and outcome of youth participants, but also the primary caregiver(s) and school staff in terms of perceptions of change of the youth.
- Facilitating strong partnerships with community organizations including community-based mental health organizations is also essential. Programs should involve stakeholders, including academia, schools, and other organizations in order to work in a cohesive manner and have a greater impact on changing the lives of African-American male youth.
- Most important, developing prevention and intervention programs that assist in making changes among African-American male youth must begin with programs that can work to recognize the specific goals of the community. Programs that are developed must recognize the strengths and resources of the African-American community, promote the sharing of skills and knowledge, and work to break down social barriers.

Consultation and Training Strategies

- As social change agents, we can have the biggest impact on policymakers. Therefore, it is important to know what the trends and how legislation affects the African-American community, thereby allowing us to serve as consultants with local, state, and national policymakers.
- Designing and facilitating neighborhood forums in an effort to educate the community at large about the African-American community and the effects of current legislation on African-American youth involved in the criminal justice system will undoubtedly inform not only our community but also policy decision makers, thereby making efforts to create a better way of life for our youth.

Research Strategies

- As mentioned previously, an evaluative component should be incorporated into prevention and intervention programs. In addition, research should include assessing change in the neighborhood and community, particularly those characteristics beyond the assessment of youth participants and their families.
- Similarly, capturing peer and other developmental influences such as violence exposure, support available to the family, and social functioning of youth prior to adolescence might provide greater explanatory power and optimize positive outcomes.

Summary

As noted earlier, African-American youth who engage in violence and delinquency face a host of issues that are multidimensional and which increase their vulnerability to such behavior. Mental health professionals, educators, and clinicians can and should intervene to serve as social change agents who can provide the most optimal intervention and prevention strategies that will maximize youths' ability to be successful and lead productive lives. Effective mental health intervention for young Black males is dependent upon understanding mechanisms through which Black youth and their families experience change. There are several steps that can be taken in order to promote such change.

10

■ ■ ■

African-Centered Psychology: A Look Beyond 2010 to 2020

In writing this Fourth edition of *The Psychology of Blacks,* we have once again attempted to capture the essence of the African-centered perspective in each chapter. We have also been deliberate in our intent to expose you the reader to perspectives grounded in African deep thought, which extend back to the reservoirs of ancient Kemetic civilization. After all, if African psychology is going to be successful in "building for eternity," then it must take some of its cues from that family of ancient Africans, whose genius we admire, respect, and celebrate to this day. It is our hope that the information contained within this text will be both informative and challenging as you navigate the waters of culturally specific psychological theories and practices.

THE VALUE OF PRAXIS IN AFRICAN-AMERICAN PSYCHOLOGY

In the third edition of *The Psychology of Blacks,* we argued that from its inception, African-American psychology has been concerned with the notion of praxis in African-centered psychology. But what is this construct we call praxis, and why do we focus on that here? In referring to Roget's II *New Thesaurus,* sixth edition (Kipfer & Chapman, 2003), praxis is defined as a habitual way of behaving, or a habitual pattern of practice. Within the context of African psychology, we believe that the concept of praxis is the self-conscious attempt to ensure that maximum congruence is achieved between thought and practice. Thus, praxis as a conceptual tool allows both for reflection on the state of the field and a representation in the form of future directions the field might pursue in maximizing that intellectual and pragmatic congruence.

EMERGING PERSPECTIVES IN PURSUIT OF A CONSENSUS

Achieving the paradigmatic coherence, theoretical consistency, and method-ological conciseness necessary to fashion a discipline can be an arduous and protracted process that often involves extended periods of discourse and debate before a tenuous agreement (i.e., consensus of compromise) can be made about the philosophic foundations upon which the discipline should be grounded. When this precarious agreement about the nature of reality (ontol-ogy), the relationship of that reality to the larger world and the divine CREATOR (cosmology), the implications of that knowledge for human interactions (axiol-ogy), and the parameters of that knowledge (epistemology) are arrived at by critical mass of well-trained thinkers, then the conditions of possibility for the creation of a discipline can be said to exist.

However, in order for this tenuous agreement to be achieved and, more important, maintained, most of the thinkers engaged in this process must share or at least agree upon the same set of deep structure cultural assumptions (i.e., ontology, cosmology, epistemology, etc.). The resultant worldview such para-digms, theories, and methodological conventions in turn generate governs the pursuit of knowledge and gives rise to the subsequent epistemological assump-tions (evidence), all of which defer to and are consistent with the worldview that brought the discipline into being in the first place. The results are para-digms upon which the construction of theories and methods that verify, vali-date, authenticate, and exclude particular types of knowledge production rest. This, then, renders these paradigms immune to, or at least insulates them from critiques that operate under a different set of cultural assumptions by generating rules for refutation and critique that rely on the internal cultural logic that spawned the paradigms in the first place (Carruthers, 1972; Banks, 1992; Semaj, 1981 However, when that tenuous consensus about the dimensions and propor-tions of the field is in turmoil or nonexistent, then the state of the field is said to be pre-paradigmatic (Kuhn, 1970; Banks, 1992).

As is the case with any emerging discipline, the great difficulty in achiev-ing paradigmatic coherence and methodological consistency speaks to, in no small measure, the lack of fragile consensus about the parameters of knowl-edge construction and the subsequent evaluation of various approaches to knowledge configuration. That is to say, up to the third edition of this text (1999), there had yet to be a tenuous agreement by a critical mass of well-trained African/African-American psychologist about the philosophic founda-tions upon which the field of Black psychology should be grounded. In the intervening eleven plus years since that body of work, there has been some movement within the discipline that gives rise to the promise of achieving a more coherent consensus about what we mean by this movement and disci-pline called African psychology. This consensus has appeared and can now be found in primarily three domains: literature of African psychology, the practice and employing of treatment interventions, and the conduct of research. We hope that this text has provided you the reader with some perspective on con-sensus on the first two; although for us, we see the most convergence of ideas coming from the theoretical constructs that now serve as conceptual anchors for the discipline of African psychology in the psychological literature.

African Psychological Literature

Some forty years ago, the field of psychology was introduced to what was then called the area of Black psychology. While the rallying cry for the movement was sounded by Dr. Joseph White (1972), in his seminal article "Toward a Black Psychology" (which first appeared in Ebony Magazine in 1970), it was quickly bolstered by a series of first, second, and third edition books entitled *Black Psychology*, authored by Reginald Jones in 1972, 1980, and 1991. While Jones himself contributed to the volumes, by and large, the texts were edited contributions with some of the best and brightest minds in Black psychology at that time contributing their thoughts on theory, issues in testing and assessment, identity development, the Black family, clinical/counseling interventions, the need for social advocacy, and even the role of Black psychologists in their communities. While the list of contributors was a "who's who" of Black psychology, there was no attempt to achieve any consensus on how to specifically define the discipline, and what were the guiding principles that characterized Black psychologists work in academic instruction, research endeavors, counseling interventions, or even social advocacy that everyone could agree on. The challenge of achieving some semblance of consensus was further exacerbated by the fact that the posture many writers and authors assumed when contributing to the discourse on African psychology was necessarily one of critique, mixed with occasional confrontation. This stylistic adherence could certainly be understood given the tremendous time and energy these pioneers of a new discipline had invested in reacting to the racist and distorted perceptions of African-American life and culture that emerged from the halls of traditional psychology's Euro-American base. And yet, even in that necessity to defend the honor of a new emerging discipline, there might have been some efforts to synthesize what seemed to be differing viewpoints into some workable theory about the psychology of Black people. That outcome may have been achieved in the selected volumes of work represented in the Jones' texts on *Black Psychology* (1972, 1980, 1991), in individual contributions like *the Psychology of the Black Experience* or *the Psychology of the Afro-American*, authored by Pugh (1972) or Jenkins (1982) respectively, or perhaps at an annual convention or regional meeting of the Association of Black Psychologists where scholars and students alike present their work, discuss their theories, and propose their methods for clinical/counseling interventions. However, what emerged from those domains was a bounty of knowledge and opinion centered more in a desire for laying out divergent views of each author/presenter, which seemed to be compounded by an air of competition about which theory or perspective was best-suited to conceptualize the psychological life space of African-American peoples. This seemed to have occurred primarily in the debates between the more traditional Black psychologists and their more orthodox African-centered counterparts, whose voices of militancy and cultural nationalism seemed to be loud and confrontational. Interestingly, this intellectual exchange of ideas and opinions in the literature seems to parallel some energy that general African-American society itself has wrestled with for decades. That being the tension that exists between the more integrationists versus nationalist ideologies in trying to wrestle with the best way for African people living in an oppressive America to achieve some sense of liberation and social progress. Certainly, the debates by W.E.B DuBois and Booker T. Washington are reminiscent of that struggle, as are the discourse and rhetoric of Dr. Martin Luther King and Malcolm X, and even the social advocacy highlighted by a Reverend Jesse Jackson and Minister Louis Farrakhan. Ultimately, while writing this fourth edition, we have come to recognize that age-old truth Parham (1993, 2002) is fond of quoting: *that life at its best is a creative synthesis of opposites in fruitful harmony*. In essence, it is important to recognize that truth is rarely anchored at any extreme, and usually resides somewhere between two apparent opposites. Once scholars, authors, and others recognize that, and incorporate this perspective into their work, we then begin to see a more synthesized body of work where themes of convergence and congruence begin to outweigh the needs for divergence and unnecessary competition. This trend is what we began to witness and are continuing to see within the discipline of African psychology, and it allows us to more comfortably argue in this fourth edition that there is a new air of emerging consensus about what this field of African psychology really is, which is reflected in the literature.

Aláánú: African-Centered Psychology and Spirituality—Toward an Inclusive Epistemology

In the forty-plus years since the founding of the Association of Black Psychologists, African-American psychology has matured as discipline, that growth process and the achievements that have come along with given the obstacles that confront African-American psychologists is nothing short of astounding. But as we look forward, the focus must also be on the challenges that lie ahead and the possible roads that can lead to continued growth and maturation. In this regard, it's important to reflect on where the discipline is, and where it must go if it is to remain a relevant and viable contributor to the African-American experience. And while the successes have been noteworthy, there are some distinct limitations that must be addressed if the discipline is to continue to mature. One limitation that must be addressed is the imbalance that exists in African-American psychological research between description and prescription, which is largely an inheritance from mainstream psychology. Many of the efforts in African-American psychology begin and end with the description of problems that exists in the African America, but there is a paucity of literature that focuses to ameliorative prescriptions. Without a balance, we run the risk of pathologizing African Americans by simply adding to the extant literature that already problematizes the African-American experience.

Another limitation is the shift in focus on understanding African Americans solely within the contours and context of racism and oppression and not as self-determining agents of their own liberation. That is to say that there needs to be an increased shift away from racial identity vis-a-vis in relation to European Americans, to a focus on ethnicity and cultural diversity as expressed among and between African Americans. With the influx of African immigrants, Afri-latino populations and Afri-Carribean populations, the ways in which we think about and understand the notion of African Americaness will necessarily have to expand to respond to the cultural variations within and between those groups. This will have profound implications for our understanding and development of African-American psychology.

Another limitation is the need to develop of models of spirituality that embrace the broad range of spirituality as expressed by African Americans. In Chapter 3, we addressed the spiritual core of African-centered psychology; we looked at traditional Western religions as well as traditional African spiritual systems such as Ifa and the Akan systems both of which have an increasing following among African-American communities.

And the last challenge will be to develop models and methods that not only reflect the aforementioned challenges but also seek to actively engage them in ways that lead to measureable outcomes. The place that may offer the most fertile promise for addressing all of these challenges through a "creative synthesis" may be in the arena of African-centered psychology.

African-centered scholars (Akbar, 1991, 2004; Ajamu, 1998; Myers, 1988; Parham, White, & Ajamu, 1999; Ani, 1994; Nobles, 1998, 2008; Azibo, 1996; Wilson, 1978; Grills, 2002, 2004; Kambon, 1992; Kambon & Bowen-Reid, 2009; among others) have asserted that the core of the African-American reality is spiritual, believing that from an African worldview, everything that exists is first and foremost spirit. They assert that any deep understanding of African-American psychology must also begin with an understanding of spirit and spirituality and the role it plays in the lives of African Americans.

African-centered psychologists have been advancing the notion of a spiritual epistemology for nearly three decades (cf. Akbar, 2004; Nobles, 1980, 1986, 2008 Azibo, 1989; Kambon, 1992; Myers, 1988; Grills, 2004;). More recently Cheryl Grills (2004) has called for the utilization of an *inclusive epistemology* that incorporates spirituality not merely as a form of knowing, but also as the mode of inquiry and understanding, as well as a means of effective treatment. This perspective in seizing the power to define reality also represents an epistemological break from the prevailing Western order of knowledge that has been the bedrock of much of African-American psychology.

While Christianity to a large extent and Islam to a lesser extent have been a part of the African-American vernacular experience, it has also been a part their psychological experience and has found its way into the literature as faith, religion, and spirituality are critical to the African-American experience. However, increasingly there has been a rise in African-American involvement in traditional African spiritual systems such as Ifa—its derivative Santeria—of Nigeria and the Akan system of Ghana. Not surprisingly, a number of African-centered psychologists who also participate in these traditions have begun exploring African spiritual systems as a mode of inquiry that speaks to the existential realities of African Americans, asserting that it is a form of knowing and knowledge rooted in the African worldview, one which offers its own methodologies and modes of verification, which are entirely relevant to the question of African human beingness and functioning. These modes of inquiry include but are not limited to divination as legitimate means of knowing, understanding, and problem solving (Peek, 1997) and can serve as a valuable heuristic in the psychotherapeutic process (cf, Zea, Quezada, & Belgrave, 1997. This is critical at three important levels of concern: power, paradigm, and praxis. At the level of power, African-centered psychology has always seen itself as moving along a different power axis than African-American psychology—in fact its very existence was also a form of praxis—but increasingly the shift has become more pronounced (Kambon, 2006; Grills, 2002, 2004; Nobles 2008). Nobles' emerging idea of Sakhu Sheti—illumination of the spirit—represents simultaneously an advance in African psychology and a break from it, and is emblematic of the focus on spirit and spirituality as guiding the praxis in African-centered psychology. This suggests that the Western (materialist) and African (spirit centered) epistemologies may be in diametric opposition, as some have suggested (e.g., Kambon, 1999; 2006). However, what is less clear are the implications this shift will have on the field of African-American psychology more broadly. Will African-centered psychology with its inclusive epistemology be merely one school of thought among other schools of thought in the overall discipline of psychology? Will its connection to African spiritual traditions prove to be a stumbling block for psychologists from different faith traditions? Will this inclusive epistemology have to find vitality outside of the normal reward power centers? Will African-centered psychology have an influential role in shaping other schools of thought in terms of its power-paradigm framework? What is clear is that it will likely be judged by the same standards that African-American psychology will be judged by, and that is its ability to clearly impact and improve the quality of African-American lives through its praxis and its performance.

ASPIRATIONS OF RELEVANCE

Although we take some measure of pride in offering the ideas in this text of an African-centered psychology to the discipline of psychology and various African-American communities across America and the diaspora, we are nonetheless cognizant of the fact that the knowledge we present is but a sampling of what one must know to develop a deep understanding, sincere appreciation for, and working knowledge of the culture of African-descent people. In this fourth edition, we have attempted to capture the vibrancy, vitality, and continuity of the African ethos in each chapter. One of the challenges in dealing with the psychology of people whose history and culture is so complex, nuanced, varied, and textured is that it is not possible to cover every aspect of their psychological lives. Choices have to be made: choices about what topics to cover, choices about the vantage point from which those topics are viewed and discussed, choices about the literature to consult, and choices about how much of that literature survives to the bibliography. And those choices, like most choices, are based on one's cultural orientation and perspective. Ours is decidedly African-centered; we understand that our perspective, like all perspectives, has the potential to offer both sunlight and shade. We also understand that all human perspectives are cultured. And as such, all psychological perspectives are offered from a cultural perspective. We simply have chosen, in the spirit of intellectual honesty and openness, to make our perspective explicit. It is our hope that the information contained within this text will be both informative and challenging as you navigate the waters of culturally specific psychological theories and practices.

The most difficult challenge in advancing these theories and constructs is not what to present. The plethora of written resources in the field of Black psychology leaves one with sufficient material to substantiate, and in some cases augment, our thinking. In fact, this fourth edition is replete with a host of new information on steps for "building for eternity," spirituality, the challenges of identity development, education concerns, issues in African-American families, coping with oppression, working with youth in the criminal justice system, and managing issues related to mental health. The most challenging aspect of our work remains one of relevance. We believe that the authenticity of these principles of African-centered psychology must be measured against our ability to apply them to people's lives in meaningful ways. If that can be done, if people's lives are better or somehow transformed, if academic instruction is more informative and inspiring, or service providers are more effective by using our work, then the question of authenticity will have been answered.

The strength and resolve of our determination to produce this book have been fortified by a belief that one should be cautious about criticizing what exists unless one is able to put something more constructive in its place. We are clear that the principles and practices of Euro-American psychology have severe limitations when applied to African-descent people. In contrast, we believe that anchoring one's analysis in an African-centered worldview is a more enlightened approach in seeking to understand the spiritual, cognitive, affective, and behavioral dimensions of African-American people's lives and experiences. However, those who accept the challenge of integrating African-centered perspectives into their work with African-American people must come to grips with several issues. The first of these centers around the necessity to develop a personal comfort level and commitment with the worldview itself.

The socialization each of us receives through society's institutions often conditions us to be uncomfortable with our unique cultural heritage. In some cases, our thinking is so contaminated that we accept society's notions that to be in support of African-centered principles and practices, one must by necessity be in opposition to Euro-American people and ideas. Clearly, the notion of denigrating others in order to affirm oneself is contrary to African ways of being, and to believe otherwise is a distortion of that cultural heritage and ideology. As a consequence of this discomfort and confusion, people sometimes, at worst, distance themselves from ideas and people that are African-centered, and at best, only tangentially commit themselves to embracing the personalities and principles of those who are considered important in the field. Neither of these perspectives is acceptable if you expect to be successful in working with African-American people. Those who are serious about effectively intervening with African-American population must be: (1) less focused on "personalities" in psychology, (2) more focused on the "principles" our scholars advance, and (3) more committed to achieving greater congruence between what we profess in principle and what actually occurs within the institutions that serve the mental health needs of African-descent people.

Avoid Becoming Secondary Scholars

The second issue involves identification and study of the original sources of knowledge and truth, and not just the citation of authors who cite other people's work. Throughout this fourth edition text, we have deliberately looked back to the past for the information that will assist us in the future. The reclamation of African-centered principles that emerged from ancient Kemetic and historical African times provides all of us with the conceptual anchors necessary to embrace the original human psychology. Once reclaimed, this knowledge can be used to assist African-descent people, and those who serve them, with promoting greater levels of order, harmony, mental health, family integration and stability, educational achievement, spiritual uplift, and general wellness in their lives. The challenge, of course, becomes how to translate and adapt this ancient and historical knowledge and truth into strategies for intervention. Each of you readers must play a part in this as well.

Social Engineering

The third issue we would like to re-emphasize is social engineering. Let us discuss this in some depth. In 1990 when Drs White and Parham authored the second edition of *The Psychology of Blacks*, they boldly pronounced that the key to the next phase of African (Black) psychology would be applied psychology and social engineering. There was first a recognition that often, the issues clients present with in treatment, or people just struggle with generally, are not simply intra-psychic phenomenon. These presenting issues really represent reactions to the socio-cultural environment that is seen and experienced by many as oppressive and destructive. Thus, when clients come in seeking support and/or treatment, and are angry, anxious, guilty, or depressed as a result of exposure to critical incidents or life circumstances, one could conclude that those are "normal" or "ordered" reactions to a disordered world. Beyond this recognition, there was an invitation extended to mental health service providers recommending that some of their intervention energies needed to be directed at addressing some of the social ills that plagued the lives of the clients they treat. This posture, out of necessity, would require a level of social advocacy and community intervention that previously might have been viewed as beyond a clinician's or academician's role and responsibility. Nevertheless, that invitation was brokered. In the intervening twenty-plus years since that publication, it is our opinion that the social ills that contaminate the lives of African-descent people continue to do so. This fourth edition text has been clear in illustrating this issue. Furthermore, the level of advocacy and hard core engagement in confronting these issues has been weak, or in some cases, nonexistent. Concluding notes from the text by Belgrave and Allison (2010), for example, aspire to help those readers develop a richer and more complex understanding of the African-American condition and the diversity that exists among this population as a whole. These authors argue for the inclusion of more within group analysis, without sacrificing the collective commonalities that capture the emotional and psychological tone of a people. They also argue for a broader set of research methodologies that inform people's understanding of the African-American condition. Similarly, the text by Neville, Tynes, and Utsey (2009) concludes by highlighting the new and enhanced theories, more sophisticated research methodologies, and relevant counseling/clinical interventions that make the field of African psychology so dynamic and vibrant. They even acknowledge that since the work of the modern African-American psychology movement grew out of struggle, there was a need to remain committed to a movement toward social justice. Neville et al. highlight the fact that several authors writing chapters in their book encourage "society" to sustain some semblance of momentum in achieving those ends. Each of these magnificent contributions to the African psychology literature argues that the application of their body of knowledge should inform public policy that addresses disparities in mental health, education, economic viability, and health care. We absolutely agree with their individual and collective stance. However, wishing that "society" would promote greater social justice exudes a tone of externality, without the requisite admonition that African-American psychology must engage in a more self-determined and internally focused effort to address the disparities, and create the social justice they so desperately seek. In short, African-American psychology, as a field of study, a discipline of training, and an organization of members, must be the change they wish to see in the world. African-American psychologists and those who treat our people cannot simply wish and advise that men and women develop more loving and trusting attitudes about each other that serve as a more stable foundation to future relationships. They must make themselves available in communities, churches, and even household living rooms if necessary, in order to provide deliberate training, instruction, and facilitation on the development of healthy male-female and appropriate parent-child relationships. African-American psychologists and those "others" cannot wait on schools to modify and/or change teacher expectation, modify curriculum, or improve instructional methodologies that might foster greater achievement levels among African-American children. They must present themselves before local school boards and neighborhood primary and secondary school leadership, volunteering if asked, and demanding if not, that they be included in the discourse on improving public education for Black children. African-American psychologist and "others" cannot wait on law enforcement personnel and the justice department to address the myriad of criminal activity that plagues our communities, especially the violence perpetrated by our youth. They must proactively reach out to community groups, neighborhood centers, and even young people who occupy the streets and the corners in various neighborhoods, offering to help them develop greater levels of self-esteem and efficacy, navigate conflicts, and broker peace between neighborhood factions that have a history of bad blood and violent conflict between them. African-American psychologists and "others" cannot wait on educational institutions, county mental health facilities, or mental health hospitals that treat our people to vacillate on the question of whether their service providers need to develop more cultural competencies in understanding and working with African-American client and patient populations. They must proactively approach these facilities and the leadership that manage them and offer to provide the instruction we expect their personnel to have. If the resistance is too great, then their efforts should be directed at the public policy arena. Efforts in this regard cannot wait on politicians to propose legislation, or for funding arms of the universities, or local, state, or federal government to magically manipulate the resources these agencies receive. African-American psychologists must make specific recommendations and demands to political and civic leaders that these agencies be required to conform to new standards of culturally specific (i.e., African-centered) professional and ethical practice that to date has been conspicuous by their absence. This is the level of advocacy and social engineering that African-American people require if the conditions that negatively impact their life circumstances are going to change. In this regard, we agree with Akbar (2004), who argued that while the prophetic thinkers and scholars have helped to usher in the new paradigms, methodologies, and models that can help achieve liberation for African-descent people, they may not have the energy or the longevity to implement the structures that must stand on the foundations they spent a professional lifetime building. That task must fall to the new generation of professionals and students who should now be more confident in the repertoire of awareness, knowledge, and skills necessary to effect much needed change.

Pharmacotherapy

A fourth issue we would like to emphasize is the use of pharmacological agents in the treatment of severe mental disorders. Within the context of mental health treatment, we are painfully aware of the myriad of issues that continue to negatively impact the life space of too many in the African-American community. Admittedly, there are those who struggle with severe mental illness. And yet, with all of our culturally specific theoretical orientations and therapeutic interventions that help to frame the work of African-centered psychologists, there are those in African-American communities that could benefit from psychiatric services, including medication. Psychiatry is that branch of medicine that is concerned with the assessment, diagnosis, treatment, prevention, and rehabilitation of mental health and illness. And just like their psychologist counterparts, there is a national association of Black psychiatrists that is headquartered in Washington, D.C., representing an autonomous body of African Americans distinct from the American Psychiatric Association. Because psychiatry is a medical specialty and professional training includes medical school and psychiatry residency, these professionals are able to prescribe and dispense psychotropic medications to patients they believe might benefit from those pharmacological interventions. Clearly, psychiatry can be an important adjunct to treatment by a psychologist. Despite the benefits that psychiatry can offer, however, there are those in African-American communities that hesitate to utilize these services or resist them all together. Perhaps the fact the African-American psychiatrists are so few in number, it is difficult for many in the African-American community to identify with them. It is also quite possible that given the negative history between Black people and psychiatric facilities, that is so beautifully outlined in the classic books *Black Rage* (Grier & Cobbs, 1968) and *Racism in Psychiatry* (Thomas & Sillen, 1972), Black folks have a profound distrust of psychiatrist and psychiatry as a discipline. It is also possible that many individuals in the African-American community associate the discipline and treatment services with something "White people do," assuming the very activity itself is a "White thing." However, irrespective of the reason for the underutilization, the fact that African Americans struggle with severe mental disorders that include major depression, bipolar disorder, and even schizophrenia demands that consideration be given to this specialty of services.

   Why do we make a point in this fourth edition to underscore this issue? Because severe mental illness and disorders impact people's psyches, negatively influence their economic livelihood, and interfere with their ability to lead more productive and rewarding lives. In addition, data from the National Center for Health Statistics (2007) indicate that significantly smaller percentages of African Americans take antidepressant medications when compared with their White counterparts (3.8 percent vs. 9.5 percent, respectively). Take for example the issue of major depressive disorders (MDD). Williams et al. (2007) report that data on MDD and African Americans indicate that only 50 percent of those with the illness (1 in 2 people) received treatment for the disorder. This is a troubling trend because as Newton (2009) reminds us: MDD can be chronic, recurrent, and progressive; it is associated with functional and structural changes in the brain; and MDD, along with stress and pain, are associated with similar suppression of neurotropic factors and compromised neuroplasticity. Newton further asserts that it is important to treat illnesses like MDD because (a) the rates of recovery diminish with the duration of each MDD episode, (b) each successive occurrence is likely to be more severe and of longer duration, (c) inadequate treatment has a progressive course, and (d) rapid remission of depressive symptoms is the most important predictor in hoping for a favorable long-term outcome. Newton's work, and that of other conscious African- centered psychiatrists, reminds us that if left undiagnosed or untreated, major psychological disorders can and will deteriorate into more chronic and debilitating illness in the future. Her perspective also informs us about the existing and new classes of drugs that have shown to be effective in treating illnesses like major depression. These include MAOs (manoamine oxidase inhibitors), tricyclics, heterocyclics, and SSRIs (seretonin re-uptake inhibitors), where depending on a host of factors including whether the patient/client's issue is related to decreased energy, irritation or impulse, or drive, mood, or emotion, one of these medications might serve as an important adjunct to treatment. A look beyond 2010 into 2020 must involve a greater consideration in using pharmacotherapy as a legitimate treatment option.

Personal Congruence

The fifth and final issue involves the necessity for helpers to integrate African-centered principles into their own life space. We continue to believe that it will be difficult to effect meaningful change in the lives of African-American clients, students, and others unless service providers are themselves culturally grounded and conscious. The power to become a healing presence in some-one's life or a contributor to someone's growth and nurturing can never be achieved by the superficial application of African-centered knowledge and truth (Parham, 2002). These principles are not something that can be pulled down off a shelf and accessed when it is convenient. African-centered psychology is about the life-affirming principles that bring order and harmony to the life space of both client and healer. Consequently, the healer cannot facilitate spiritual enlightenment and illumination, or any other health state, unless and until he or she is in a state of health and enlightenment himself or herself. Hopefully, this text will aid each reader in the processes of knowledge acquisition and self-discovery. Once achieved, we grow in confidence in knowing that our sensitivity, awareness, and understanding are congruent with the principles of human psychology and mental and spiritual liberation.

11

■ ■ ■

African-American Psychology: Evolution of an Idea—A Selected Annotated Bibliography

In this text, we have advanced the position that the core of the African cultural and psychological universe is rooted in an African worldview as transmitted through various cultural retentions that remain vibrant and vital at the deep structure level of culture. Our task as scholars has been to simply allow the evidence to guide us. The evidence marshaled in support of African cultural retentions, not just in African-descended populations in the United States but throughout the Caribbean and Latin America, has not just been compelling—it has been overwhelming (Gomez, 1998; Midlo Hall, 1995; 2007 Stuckey, 1988 Holloway, 2005 Walker, 2001, etc.). In recent years aided by a veritable explosion of multidisciplinary scholarship not just in the social sciences, but across numerous disciplines like African-American studies, African studies; African art and African history; African philosophy, African literature, as well as other disciplines like religion and geology. Now, we know more about people of African ancestry than at any other time in history. Consequently, we conclude this fourth edition, as we have in the past, with an invitation to solidify your exposure to African-centered perspectives in psychology by reading and studying other resources that inform this important perspective. The recommendations of reading materials are not meant to be exhaustive. They are considered essential reading for anyone wanting to engage in serious study and deep thought and acquire a greater mastery of the knowledge required to understand and facilitate mental health with African Americans.

A SELECTED ANNOTATED BIBLIOGRAPHY

African Ontological Narratives (History)

Armah, A.K. (2000) Two Thousand Seasons. Popenguine, Senegal: Per Ankh Books. Armah's novel is a pan-African epic, which covers one thousand years of African history.

Ba, H. (1981). The living tradition. In J. Ki-Zerbo (Ed.) UNESCO General History of Africa I: Methodology and African prehistory (pp. 197–199). Paris: UNESCO. This is a brilliant exposition on the interconnection between African deep thought, spirituality, and interconnectivity of African cultures.

Barry, B. (1997) Senegambia and the Atlantic Slave Trade. Cambridge University Press. Originally published in French in 1988 by this exile from Guinea living in Senegal, Barry's account of the "geopolitical dismemberment" of the West African region that encompasses six contemporary states is encyclopedic in its details of the political history of the communities involved.

Carruthers, J. H. III (1995) MDW NTR Divine Speech: A Historiographical Reflection of African Deep Thought from the time of the Pharaohs to the Present. An in-depth exploration of African deep thought across the ages by a master scholar at the height of his scholarly powers.

Carruthers, J. H. III and Leon Harris (Eds.) (1998) Association for the Study of Classical African Civilizations World History Project: Preliminary Challenges. An important overview concerning the creation of an African-centered general history of Africa by some of the pre-eminent thinkers in the African-centered movement.

Chinweizu. (1975) The West and the Rest of Us: White Predators, Black Slavers, and the African Elite. Random House. An in-depth exploration of the impact of the maafa on pre- and postcolonial Africa.

Clarke, John H. (1993) Africans at the Crossroad: Notes on an African World Revolution. New York: African World Press. It is a collection of essays that have been broadly amassed in five thematic sections. Clarke begins with the roots of the African and African-American freedom struggle in the African world.

Diop, C.A. (1959) The Cultural Unity of Black Africa. Chicago: Third World Press. One of the most important books ever written on Africa's cultural unity. Diop explores and makes a cogent argument for the social, cultural, and linguistic unity of African peoples.

Jackson, J.G. (1980) Introduction to African Civilization. New Jersey: Citadel Press. A classic introduction to the vast history of Africa and her peoples, from ancient Kemet (Egypt) to the nation states of Ghana, Mali, and Songhay.

James, G.G.M. (1976) Stolen Legacy. San Francisco: Julian Richardson Associates. Professor James suggests that what is currently known as Greek philosophy was in fact stolen from the ancient Africans.

Moses, W.J. (1988) The Golden Age of Black Nationalism, 1850–1925. Cambridge: Oxford University Press. Moses thesis asserts that by adopting European and American nationalist and separatist doctrines, Black nationalism became a vehicle for the assimilationist values among Black American intellectuals. Moses explores the specific manifestations of this tradition in the intellectual and institutional history of African Americans.

Williams, C. (1974) The Destruction of Black Civilization: Great Issues of a Race 4500 B.C> to 2000 A.D. Chicago: Third World Press. One of the most important historical studies of African history and culture to date. Essential reading for anyone interested in an easy-to-read study of African history.

Wobogo, V. (1976, Winter) "Diop's Two Cradle Theory and the Origin of White Racism." Black Books Bulletin, 4 (4), 20–29, 72. One of the most important early writings on the history of European cultural chauvinism.

Africanisms and Diasporan African World

Ani, M. (1989/1997) Let the Circle Be Unbroken: Implications of African Spirituality in the Diaspora. Trenton: Red Sea Press. An excellent primer for anyone interested in understanding the African worldview.

Carney, J. (2002) Black Rice: The African Origins of Rice Cultivation in the Americas. Cambridge: Harvard University Press. Judith Carney's text dispels a common belief that rice was brought by Europeans to the Americas by way of Asia. Instead she demonstrates that, in fact, rice cultivation was introduced to the Americas by enslaved Africans and cultivated by enslaved Africans slaves, particularly in South Carolina, where rice crops proved to be one of the most profitable plantation-based economies.

Gomez, M. A. (1998) Exchanging Our Country Marks. Chapel Hill: The University of North Carolina Press. Based on his research, Michael A. Gomez suggests that Africans, upon arriving in America, were dispersed much more closely along ethnic and cultural lines than previously acknowledged, and that they retained much of their original cultures far longer than was originally suspected.

Hall, G.M. (2007) Slavery and African Ethnicities in the Americas: Restoring the Links. Chapel Hill: The University of North Carolina Press. Drawing on a wide range of materials in four languages as well as on a lifetime of study of slave groups in the New World, Gwendolyn Midlo Hall explores the persistence of African ethnic identities among the enslaved over four hundred years of the Atlantic slave trade.

Herskovits, M. (1941/1990) The Myth of the Negro Past. Boston: Beacon Press. Almost fifty years ago, Melville Herskovits set out to debunk the myth that Black Americans have no cultural past. Originally published in 1941, his unprecedented study of Black history and culture recovered a rich African heritage in religious and secular life, the language and arts of the Americas.

Heywood, L. (2010) Central Africans and Cultural Transformations in the American Diaspora. Cambridge: Cambridge University Press. This volume sets out a new paradigm that increases our understanding of African culture and the forces that led to its transformation during the period of the Atlantic slave trade and beyond, putting long due emphasis on the importance of Central African culture to the cultures of the United States, Brazil, and the Caribbean. Focusing on the Kongo/Angola culture zone, the book illustrates how African peoples re-shaped their cultural institutions as they interacted with Portuguese slave traders up to 1800, then follows Central Africans through all the regions where they were taken as slaves and captives.

Holloway, J. E. (2005). Africanisms in American Culture (Blacks in the Diaspora). Bloomington: Indiana University Press. An important work in the field of African diaspora studies for the past decade, this collection has inspired scholars and others to explore a trail blazed originally by Melville J. Herskovits, the father of New World African studies.

Stuckey, S. (1988). Slave Culture: Nationalist Theory and the Foundations of Black America. Oxford: Oxford University Press. Stuckey examines the ways in which the culture of enslaved Africans emerged from an independent value system that utilized the ancestral African past central to construct a usable identity in America, and how enslaved Africans achieved a common culture, despite coming from diverse ethnic groups.

Thompson, R.F. (1984) Flash of the Spirit: African & Afro-American Art & Philosophy. New York: Random House. This groundbreaking book explores the ways in which five African civilizations—Yoruba, Kongo, Ejagham, Mande, and Cross River—have informed and transformed the aesthetic, social, and metaphysical traditions of African peoples in the United States, Cuba, Haiti, Trinidad, Mexico, Brazil and other places in the diaspora.

Walker, S. (2001) African Roots/American Cultures: Africa in the Creation of the Americas. Lanham: Rowman & Littlefield Publishers, Inc. This multidisciplinary volume of essays illuminates the African cultural presence throughout the Americas and African Diaspora.

The History and Evolution af African (Black) Psychology

Akbar, N. (2004) The Akbar Papers. Tallahassee: Mind Productions. A reader that cover thirty years of thinking and doing around the question of African psychology by one of the founders of the African psychology movement.

Akbar, N. (1985) Nile Valley Origins of the Science of the Mind. In Ivan Van Sertima (Ed.) Nile Valley Civilizations, New York: Journal of African Civilizations. A historical and philosophical discussion of the ancient African foundations of Western psychology.

Akbar, N. (1986) "Africentric Social Sciences for Human Liberation." Journal of Black Studies, 14 (4), 395–414. An important discussion of the ways in which worldviews inform psychology and the role that an Africentric worldview can play in helping to humanize psychology.

Bynum, E.B. (1999) The African Unconscious: Roots of Ancient Mysticism and Modern Psychology. New York: Teachers College Press. An interesting thesis, which attempts to unify the strands of human development with the origins of the human species on the African continent. A well-written and thought-provoking treatise.

Clark, C.X., Nobles, W., McGee, D.P., and Weems, X.L. (1975) "Voodoo or I.Q.: An Introduction to African Psychology." The Journal of Black Psychology, 1 (2). Voodoo or I.Q. is the article that launched a movement. This is the seminal article that literally changed the face of Black psychology. In many ways, this article was ahead of its time in its dealing with the importance of African culture as a means of psychological order.

Guthrie, R.V. (1998) Even the Rat Was White (2nd Ed). Needham Heights, MA: Allyn and Bacon. A much updated sequel to the first edition, with stories and perspectives from a more contemporary generation of Black psychologists.

Guthrie, R. (1976) Even the Rat Was White. New York: Harper & Row. A historical analysis of the racist use of Western psychology and the African-American pioneers in Western psychology.

Jenkins, A. (1982) The Psychology of the Afro-American: A Humanistic Approach. New York: Pergamon Press. A very well-done text on the psychological experiences of Black folks in America, written from the perspective of a humanistic personality theoretical base, by one of that generation's leading scholars.

Jones, R. (Ed.) (2004) Black Psychology (4th ed.). Hampton, VA: Cobb and Henry. This hook is the culmination of nearly thirty years of theory, research, and practice in the area of Black psychology. This is a must-have book for anyone seriously interested in the writings of some of the seminal thinkers in the field.

Jones, R.L. (1991) Black Psychology (3rd ed.) Hampton, VA: Cobb and Henry. A very good synthesis of articles published in the first and second editions of the *Black Psychology* series, with some new articles by emerging authors.

Kambon, K.K. (1998) African-Black Psychology in the American Context: An African-Centered Approach. Tallahassee: Nubian Nation Publications. Explores the historical and philosophical foundations of African Psychology, while laying out its theoretical and paradigmatic parameters for and African-centered psychology.

Myers, L.J. (1988) Understanding the Africentric Worldview: Introduction to an Optimal Psychology. Dubuque, IA: Kendall/ Hunt. A theoretical discussion of the humanizing potential that an Afrocentric psychology can have on the continued development of psychology.

Nobles, W.W. (2006). Seeking the Sakhu: Foundational Writings for an African Psychology. Chicago: Third World Press. This critical collection of essays follows the earliest articulations of Black philosophy as the foundation of Black psychology to the development of African psychology to the beginning of Sakhu Sheti—the ancient Kemetic notion of illuminating the spirit.

Nobles, W.W. (1972) African Philosophy: Foundation for a Black Psychology. In R. Jones (Ed.), Black Psychology. New York: Harper Row. Nobles posits that there exists a core African philosophy that should be the basis for a Black psychology. In many ways, this article helped to launch the African-centered psychology movement.

Nobles, W.W. (1986) African Psychology: Toward Its Reclamation, Reascension and Revitalization. Oakland: Institute for the Advanced Study of Black Family Life and Culture. The first text to explore in detail the basis for an African psychology.

Pugh, R. (1972) The Psychology of the Black Experience. Monterey, CA: Brooks/Cole. This text provides some in-dept analysis on the psychological challenges African-descent people confront while living in and growing up in America.

Thomas, A. and Sillen, S. (1972) Racism in Psychiatry. Secaucus, NJ: Citadel Press. A classic text by two Black psychiatrist who detail how the discipline of psychiatry was not only biased, but subjectively brutal in its treatment and classification of Black people within the mental health system.

White, J.L. (1972) Toward a Black Psychology. In R.L. Jones (Ed.) Black Psychology. New York: Harper and Row. The seminal article that served as a call to the profession of Black Psychology by an individual considered by many to be one of the contemporary godfathers of the Black Psychology movement.

Williams, R.L. (2008) (Ed.) History of the Association of Black Psychologists. Bloomington, IN: Author House. The text presents a full volume of profiles of African-American psychologists, many of whom were presidents of the national Association of Black Psychologists.

African-American Psychology: General Studies

African American Psychology: From Africa to America (2010) Beverly Hills: Sage Publications. Faye Z. Belgrave and Kevin W. Allison (Editors). This textbook follows the evolutionary development of African-American psychology as a field. Each chapter explores the integration and synthesis African and American influences on the psychology of African Americans.

Handbook of African American Psychology (2009) Thousand Oaks, CA: Sage Publications. Helen A Neville, Brendesha M. Tynes, and Shawn O Utsey (Editors). This book provides a comprehensive overview of the contemporary theoretical, empirical, and practical developments in African-American psychology.

Personality and Identity Development

Akbar, N. (1976) "Rhythmic Patterns in African Personality." African Philosophical: Assumption and Paradigm for Research of Black Persons, In L.M. King, V.J. Dixon, and W.W. Nobles (Eds.), Los Angeles: Fanon Center Publications. A unique look at the interconnectedness of African culture and its implications for the development of a theory of African-American personality.

Cross, W.E. (1991) Shades of Black. Philadelphia. Philadelphia: Temple University Press. Cross offers a meta-study of racial identity research.

Cross, W.E. (1971) "The Negro to Black Conversion Experience: Towards the Psychology of Black Liberation." Black World, 20, 13–27. Foundational reading for any one interested in Black identity development. This invaluable work gave rise to two generations of scholarship on Black identity.

Dubois, W.E.B. (1903/1996) The Souls of Black Folks. Penguin Books. Penned in 1903, it remains his most studied and popular work; its insights into African-American life at the turn of the twentieth century still ring true.

Jones, R.L. (1998) (Ed.) African American Identity Development. Hampton, VA: Cobb and Henry. A wonderful mix of established and emerging scholars who present chapters on issues of racial, ethnic, and cultural identity development.

Kambon, K. (1992) The African Personality in America: An African Centered Framework. Tallahassee, FL: Nubian Nation Publications. An African-centered theory of personality in an American context.

Mama, A. (1995) Beyond the Masks: Race, Gender and Subjectivity. London: Routledge. This text is an account of Black psychology, exploring key theoretical issues in race and gender. It examines the history of racist psychology and implicit racism throughout the discipline.

Nobles, W.W. (1998) To Be African or Not to Be: The Question of Identity or Authenticity-Some Preliminary Thoughts. In R.L. Jones, (Ed.) African American Identity Development. Hampton, VA: Cobb & Henry Publishers. A look at the importance and value of asserting an African agency based on a notion of human authenticity.

Parham, T.A. (1989) "Cycles of Psychological Nigrescence." The Counseling Psychologist, 17, 226. Building on the Cross nigrescence model, Parham offers a seminal examination of the Black identity development as a lifespan phenomenon.

Thomas, C. (1971) Boys No More. Beverly Hills: Glencoe Press. Articulates the concept of Negromachy, which is a confusion of self-worth, where the individual in appropriately depends on White society for self-definition.

Assessment and Appraisal

Ajamu, A. A. (2004) Rekh: Prelude to an Intergenerational Conversation about African psychological Thought. In Jones, R. (Ed.) Black Psychology (4th ed.). Hampton, VA: Cobb and Henry. The author explores the theoretical and methodological conditions surrounding the question of an African psychology.

Banks, W.C. (1982) Deconstructive Falsification: Foundations of Critical Method in Black Psychology. In E. Jones and S. Korchin (Eds.), Minority Mental Health. New York: Praeger. Banks advances a notion of a self-reflective critical method in Black psychology that seeks to interrogate and expand knowledge production in Black psychology.

Banks, W.C. (1992) "The Theoretical and Methodological Crisis of the Africentric Conception." Journal of Negro Education, 61 (3). An in-depth discussion of the current theoretical and methodological state of the field in Black psychology.

Banks, W.C. (1976) "White Preference in Blacks: A Paradigm in Search of a Phenomenon." Psychological Bulletin, 83. A groundbreaking discussion of the ways in which method in psychology has been used as a tool to maintain and perpetuate oppression.

Hilliard, A.G. III. (1981) "I.Q. as Catechism: Ethnic and Cultural Bias or Invalid Science." Black Books Bulletin, 7 (2). A deconstructionist examination of ways in which intelligence testing has been used to assert, maintain, and justify racism.

Hilliard, A.G. III. (1994) "What Is This Thing Called Intelligence and Why Bother to Measure It?" Journal of Black Psychology, 20 (4), 430–444. An examination of the limitations of intelligence as a construct.

Nobles, W.W. (1978) African Consciousness and Liberation Struggles: Implications for the Development and Construction of Scientific Paradigms. Presented at the Fanon Research and Development Institute, Port of Spain, Trinidad. An examination of the relationship between culture, worldview, and the development and use of science.

Smith, L.T. (1999) Decolonizing Methodologies: Research and Indigenous Peoples. Tuhiwai Smith's masterpiece is a must-read for any discipline. Her work questions the most basic assumptions upon which academic research lies; her influence is widely felt in fields as diverse as anthropology, social work, women studies, film studies, indigenous studies, psychology, history, sociology, and ethnic studies.

African-Centered Education

Akoto, K.G. (1992) Nation-Building: Theory and Practice in Afrikan Centered Education. Washington, D.C.: Pan Afrikan World Institute. A look at the theory and practical application of an African-centered educational model.

Anderson, J.D. (1988) The Education of Blacks in the South, 1860–1935. University of North Carolina Press. A critical reinterpretation from reconstruction to the Great Depression. Places Black schooling within a political, cultural, and economic context; considers Black commitment to education; the peculiar significance of Tuskegee Institute; conflicting goals of various philanthropic groups.

Erny, P. (1973) Childhood and Cosmos: The Social Psychology of the Black African Child, New York: New Perspectives. An early study on the African conception of childhood development.

Hilliard, A.G. III. (1997) SBA: The Reawakening of the African Minds Gainesville: Makare Publishing. Professor Hilliard explores the ancient African foundations of wisdom, and their implications for contemporary education and teacher training.

Shujaa, M. (Ed.) (1994) Too Much Schooling, Too Little Education: A Paradox of Black Life in White Society. Trenton: Africa World Press. A compilation of 17 Afrocentric essays exploring the contours and complexities of education in African America.

Tedla, E. (1995) Sankofa: African Thought and Education. New York: Peter Lang. A look at the basis for a model of education that is rooted in African thought and wisdom.

Woodson, C.G. (1990) The Miseducation of the Negro, Trenton: Africa World Press. A classic exposition on the psychological effects of oppression and dependency.

Counseling/Clinical Therapeutic Interventions

Akbar, N. (1981) "Mental Disorders Among African Americans." Black Books Bulletin. Naim Akbar challenges some of the prevailing traditional conventions regarding mental disorder, while introducing the reader to an African-centered conception of mental order and disorder.

Azibo, D.A. (1989) "African Centered Theses on Mental Health and a Nosology of Black/African Personality Disorder." The Journal of Black Psychology, 15(2), 173–214. Azibo discusses the implications for an African-centered conception of personality disorder while offering a nosology that attempts to categorize eighteen personality disorders not found in the DSMIV and endemic to African Americans.

Parham, T.A. (Ed.) (2002) Counseling Persons of African Descent. In a provocative series of essays the authors argue that attempts to effectively treat African-American clients cannot be successful if these attempts rely solely on seasoning traditional Eurocentric theories and constructs with the cultural flavor of an African worldview. Contributors look at the ancient Kemetic worldview and the more historical Akan and Yoruba systems of belief in an effort to understand the personality dynamics of African Americans. In recognizing that the literature is scarce with respect to operationalizing an African-centered worldview in therapeutic practice, this text concludes with a model in intervention strategies that can be followed when working with African-American clients.

Parham, T.A. and Helms, J.E. (1981) "Influences of Black Students Racial Identity Attitudes on Preference for Counselor Race." Journal of Counseling Psychiatry, 28 (3), 250–256. Parham and Helms explore the ways in which the nigresence model might he used to understand counselor race influences on Black students' racial identity and attitudes on preference.

African-American Family

Billingley, A. (1968) Black Families in White America. Englewood Cliffs, NJ: Prentice-Hall. A psychosocial study of the Black family in America. It remains a classic study of the African-American family.

Boyd-Franklin, N. (1989) Black Families in Therapy. New York: Guilford Press. A theoretically sound and practically relevant guide to working with African-American families in a Family Systems approach.

Clark, R. (1983) Family Life and School Achievement. Chicago: University of Chicago Press. An ethnographic study out of Chicago that makes the essential point that it is not family composition but parental disposition that makes the biggest difference in facilitating educational achievement in Black children.

McAdoo, H.P. (Ed.) (2006) Black Families. Beverly Hills: Sage. A comprehensive cross-disciplinary look at the multidimensionality of the African-American family.

Nobles, W.W. (1974) "African Root American Fruit: The Black Family." Journal of Social and Behavioral Sciences, 20, 66–75. A look at African cultural retention's as a source of strength and vitality for African Americans; and the implications for the study of the African-American family.

Nobles, W.W. (1985) Africanity and the Black Family: Toward a Theoretical Model. Oakland: Black Family Institute. In many ways, this text represents the amplification of his earlier work on African cultural retentions as a source of strength and vitality for African Americans.

Staples, R. (1994, 1998) The Black Family: Essays and Studies. Belmont, CA: Wadsworth Publishing. A collections of essays from noted social scientists who provide a comprehensive overview of the dynamics of Black family life.

Culture, Worldview, and Philosophy

Ajamu, A. A. (1998) From Tef Tef to Medew Nefer: The Importance of Utilizing African Terminologies and Concepts in the Rescue, Restoration, Reconstruction, and Reconnection of African Ancestral Memory. In ASCAC: The African World History Project. Carruthers, J.H.III and Harris, L. (Eds.). Explores the importance of utilizing African languages in fully apprehending contour and complexities of African phenomena and their explicative import.

Ani, M. (1996) Let the Circle Be Unbroken. Trenton: Red Sea Press. An excellent and user-friendly book for anyone interested in understanding the African worldview.

Ani, M. (1994) Yurugu: An African Centered Critique of European Cultural Thought and Behavior. Trenton: African World Press. Ani offers an African-centered examination and analysis of Greek thought and its impact on European culture and behavior, and the ways in which European cultural thought and behavior have created a system of global domination and oppression.

Bulhan, H.A. (1985) Frantz Fanon and the Psychology of Oppression. New York: Plenum. Perhaps the most comprehensive review and distillation of Frantz Fanon's thinking to date.

Cress-Welsing, F. (1991) The Isis Papers: Keys to the Colors. Chicago: Third World Press. A penetrating and provocative thesis about the European psyche and the perpetuation of global white supremacy.

Fanon, F. (1967) Black Skin, White Mask. New York: Grove Press. Fanon's classic study of the impact of oppression on the development of identity.

Gbadegesin, S (1990) African Philosophy: Traditional Yoruba Philosophy and Contemporary African Realities (American University Studies, Series V, Philosophy, Vol 134). Explores the Yoruba concepts of spirituality and ultimate reality.

Gomez, M.A. (1998) Exchanging Our Country Marks: The Transformation of African Identities in the Colonial and Antebellum South. Chapel Hill: University of North Carolina Press. Michael A. Gomez suggests that Africans, upon arriving in America, were dispersed much more closely along ethnic and cultural lines than previously acknowledged. The underlying theme of his provocative work, *Exchanging Our Country Marks*, is that while Blacks eventually replaced their African ethnic identities with new racial ones after arriving in the American South, they retained much of their original cultures far longer than was originally suspected.

Gordon, L.R. (2000) Existentia Africana: Understanding Africana Existential Thought (Africana Thought). *Existentia Africana* is an engaging and highly readable introduction to the field of Africana philosophy and will help to define this rapidly growing field.

Gilroy, P. (1995) The Black Atlantic: Modernity and Double Consciousness. Cambridge: Harvard University Press. Paul Gilroy brings a fresh eye and mind to the challenging task of examining Black cultural and political manifestations as they affect the transglobal community.

Gyekye, K (1995) An Essay on African Philosophical Thought: The Akan Conceptual Scheme. Philadelphia: Temple University Press. In this sustained and nuanced attempt to define a genuinely African philosophy, Kwame Gyekye rejects the idea that an African philosophy consists simply of the work of Africans writing on philosophy. It must, Gyekye argues, arise from African thought itself, relate to the culture out of which it grows, and provide the possibility of a continuation of a philosophy linked to culture.

Jones, J. (1997) Prejudice and Racism (2nd ed.). New York: McGraw-Hill. A compelling analysis of racism and prejudice and how they impact the lives of all people.

Mudimbe, V.Y. (1988) The Invention of Africa: Gnosis, Philosophy and the Order of Knowledge. A studied meditation on African philosophy and the epistemic foundations for an African order of knowledge.

Nobles, W.W. (1974) "Black People in White Insanity: An Issue for Black Community Mental Health." Journal of Afro American Issues, 4, 21–27. A look at the negative psychological effects of Western culture on the psychosocial well-being of African Americans.

Outlaw, L. (1996). On Race and Philosophy. New York: Routledge Press. It is a collection of essays written and published across the last twenty years, which focus on matters of race, philosophy, and social and political life in the West, in particular in the United States.

Wilson, A. (1993) The Falsification of Consciousness: Eurocentric History, Psychiatry and the Politics of White Supremacy. New York: Afrikan World Infosystems. A look at the colonization of African history by Europeans and its negative impact on the psychological functioning of African peoples.

African Spiritual Traditions

Armah, A.K. (2000) The Healers. Popenguine, Senegal: Per Ankh Books. A historical novel set in nineteenth-century Africa during the Ashanti-British Wars of 1873–1874. The story pivots on a group of healers who see their work as restoring unity where the disease of division has paved the way for European rulers, aided by African collaborators, has laid the groundwork for the systematic pillaging of Africa.

Appiah-Kubi, K. (1981) Man Cures, God heals: Religion and Medical Practice among the Akan of Ghana. New York: Friendship Press. Explores the healing arts from an Akan cosmology.

Austin, A.D. (1997) African Muslims in Antebellum America: Transatlantic Stories and Spiritual Struggles. New York: Routledge. A condensation and updating of the author's *African Muslims in Antebellum America: A Sourcebook,* this book features the stories of nearly eighty Africans brought to America as slaves between 1730 and 1860. What was unusual about these slaves is that they were Muslims and that they left some sort of documentary record of their presence. Many came from elite classes—one was a military officer, several were schoolteachers, and another was studying to become a religious leader.

Diouf, S.A. (1998) Servants of Allah: African Muslims Enslaved in the Americas. New York: New York University Press. This book presents a history of African Muslims following them from West Africa to the Americas. It details how, even while enslaved, many Muslims managed to follow most of the precepts of Islam. Literate in Arabic, urbane and well-traveled, they drew on their organization and the strength of their faith to maintain successful, cohesive communities and to play a major role in the most well-known slave uprisings.

Fu-Kiau, K.K.B. (1993) Self-Healing Power and Therapy: Old Teachings from Africa. Explores the healing arts based on the Kongolese cosmology.

Mbiti, J.S. (1992) African Religions & Philosophy. London: Heinenman. Discusses the philosophies, rituals, and ceremonies of various African religions and their influence in the lives of the people.

Neimark, P. (1993) The Way of Orisa: Empowering Your Life through the Ancient African Religion of Ifa. San Francisco: Harpers Collins. A very accessible introduction to the religious practice of Ifa, which includes ancestor and Orisa worship and divination. .

Some, M. P. (1995) Of Water and the Spirit: Ritual, Magic, and Initiation in the Life of an African Shaman. New York: Penguin Group USA, Inc. Malidoma Some's autobiography illustrates the profound culture clashes between Western civilization and indigenous cultures.

S, Some. (2000). The Spirit of Intimacy: Ancient African Teachings in the Ways of Relationships. In *The Spirit of Intimacy,* Some distills the ancient wisdom of Dagara of Burkina Faso to offer insights into the role of spirit in every marriage, friendship, relationship, and community, sharing ancient ways to make our intimate relationships more rewarding.

J, Awolalu. (1996) Yoruba Beliefs and Sacrificial Rites. New York: Athelia Henrietta Press. This serious study provides an in-depth understanding of Ifa, the spiritual system of the Yoruba through the skillful use comparative religious, scientific, and theological perspectives from the West.

E, Idowu. (1994) Olodumare: God in Yoruba Belief. New York: A & B Book Dist Inc. An in-depth exploration of the Yoruba cosmology and their conception of God. A great text for anyone interested in understanding African spiritual traditions.

GENERAL READINGS

Connor, M.E. & White, J.L. (2006) BLACK FATHERS: AN INVISIBLE PRESENCE IN AMERICA. Mahwah, N.J.: Lawrence Erlbaum and Associates.

Dr.'s Michael Connor and Joe White provide an insightful edited volume of manuscripts highlighting and celebrating the triumphs of Black fathers, who are so maliciously attacked in the mainstream media.

Brown, E.M., Haygood, M., & McLean, R.J. (2010) THE LITTLE BLACK BOOK OF SUCCESS: LAWS OF LEADERSHIP FOR BLACK WOMEN. New York: Random House. A beautifully written and very concise book of life lessons and experiences offered to African American females by three very accomplished and high powered African American women.

Smiley, T. (2009) ACCOUNTABLE: MAKING AMERICA AS GOOD AS ITS PROMISE. New York: Atria Books. The companion piece and follow-up to the COVENANT WITH BLACK AMERICA, this volume is the blueprint for how African Americans and others can hold themselves and their elected officials accountable for the changes we wish to see in all walks of life in America.

West, C. (2010) BROTHER WEST: LIVING AND LOVING OUT LOUD, A MEMOIR. New York: Smiley Books. Brilliant Scholar and public intellectual Cornel West teaches many lessons in growth, development, family, friendship, love, relationships, academic success, personal pitfalls and challenges, and speaking truth to power. This book is a must read for its keen insights that mirror so much of what Black folks struggle with, mixed with a down home conversational style that is the essence of Cornel West' authenticity.

White, J.L. & Cones, J. (1999) BLACK MAN EMERGING: FACING THE PAST AND SEIZING THE FUTURE IN AMERICA. Dr.'s White and Cones do a masterful job of weaving the reader through the developmental and social challenges that African American males must face within the context of this American Society.

Williams, R.L. (2008) HISTORY OF THE ASSOCIATION OF BLACK PSYCHOLOGISTS: PROFILES OF OUTSTANDING BLACK PSYCHOLOGISTS. Bloomington, In.: Author House. Dr. Robert L. Williams, a giant in the field of Black Psychology, compiles an impressive volume of biographical profiles on some of the most important and distinguished psychologists of African descent this nation has ever produced.

Wyatt, G.E. (1997) STOLEN WOMEN: RECLAIMING OUR SEXUALITY, TAKING BACK OUR LIVES. New York: John Wiley and Sons. Dr. Wyatt, one of America's best experts on sex and sexuality, provides a portrait of Black female sexuality, and the impact it has on African American women's lives, from the habitual habits they develop, the men they engage in relationships with, to the choices they make in living out their dreams and aspirations.

Wyatt, G.E. & Wyatt, L. (2003) NO MORE CLUELESS SEX: 10 SECRETS TO A SEX LIFE THAT WORKS FOR BOTH OF YOU. NEW YORK: JOHN WILEY AND SONS. Dr. Gail Wyatt teams with her husband Dr. Lewis Wyatt, MD. to share advice and counsel about physical intimacy in relationships. Because of the discomfort many people feel in even approaching the subject of sex, this book is an important resource and guide to that conversation.

AFTERWORD

A Note to the Minds of My Generation

By
Kenya Taylor Parham
Undergraduate Student
California State University, Northridge

Dr. Cornel West reminds us that there is a qualitative difference between a voice and an echo. A voice is an individual creation based on other voices that came before. An echo is about imitation, which is suicide, and emulation, which is of an adolescent mind.

I consider myself a conscious student, endeavoring to stay in touch with and informed about the discourse of historical and contemporary Black thought. Consequently, I'd like to think we've simply gotten our acronyms mixed up, perhaps, a harmless "slip of the memory gone wrong?" Maybe we've incorrectly assigned our categories and unconsciously bought into this notion of personality worship. After all, we are the generation behind this new movement of . . . wait—What's the movement called again? I know I'm not the only person who notices this absence of accountability lurking above the heads of the Millennial's. In addition to our "cloud cover," I've become increasingly concerned with the outlets we derive our information and culture from. We are starved, malnourished for substance, and in desperate need of something to mobilize and lubricate our hinges and joints. Oil can—Oil can, anybody?

Have you ever sat back and realized that we may not be the writers of our own story? Instead, I believe it is fair to argue that we young people of the Millennial Generation are simply blindfolded co-signers. We are fiscally and emotionally invested into trade marking our fingerprint, too lazy to patent it ourselves, reliant on the outsourcing and revival of past coined ideology. Newsflash kids: That "new new" ain't so new after all . . . We are regurgitating the messages of generations past, thus encapsulating us into an "echo." So what do we have to say for ourselves?

While the power of pop culture should not be underestimated, I do believe it is fatally dangerous and detrimental to subsidize the debate of psychological and political rhetoric and intellectual discourse with a lyrical battle between two recording artists. A dear friend of mine once shared with me, "Good scholars read source material as read and interpreted by someone else. Great scholars read source material for themselves."

In the pursuit of becoming the scholars of our time and fulfilling the legacy generations before handed to us, I believe it vital and necessary to take control of our genius. It is time for us to become critical consumers of information like that contained in the pages of this text. We need not rely on getting rallied up by semi-political lyrics in a song, or a controversial statement repeated on Access Granted, or limit our defiance against status quo to a mass-produced bumper sticker or T-shirt logo. While pop culture headlines might have incited a political fire beneath you, don't allow that to be the only source of your heat. Instead, research the theory behind the message; I'm sure you'll find all droppings trace back to the purist forms of African psychology, Black political literature, race theory, cultural ideology, and thought. It is to our advantage to become less consumed with personality worship of the great thinkers of our day, and more concerned with principles they each articulate in texts like the pages of this book. Let's absorb the responsibility of becoming more versed in the principle, in the message behind the movement. There is plenty of time remaining for us to reverse the stigma attributed to us as "The most aggressively inarticulate generation." After all, the blood of some of the "baddest" Brotha's and Sista's to ever walk this planet flows through our veins. We are of Kings and Queens, heirs of dynasties, and the inheritors of, excusing my bias, the richest culture created by God. . . . How dare we allow our legacy to drag, or even grace, the rough, unfinished paths of today! So my question is, what is your vibration contribution?

Trust that, much like throwbacks, samples, and remixes, most psychological and political messages spewing from our generation today are echoes, as well. So when are we going to find our voice? I challenge you to step out and speak up! But please don't censor your booming outbursts. After all, who can predict how the layers of vibrating echoes, stemming from your voice, will affect generations to come?

SPEAK UP & BE HEARD, DAMN IT!

—**Kenya Taylor Parham**

REFERENCES

Acock, A.C., & Demo, D.H. (1999). Dimensions of family conflict and their influence on child and adolescent adjustment. *Sociological Inquiry, 69,* 641–658.

Adebimpe V.R. (1994). Race, racism, and epidemiological surveys. *Hospital and Community Psychiatry, 45,* 27–31.

Adebimpe, V. (1981). Overview: White norms in psychiatric diagnosis of Black patients. *American Journal of Psychiatry, 138*(3), 275–285.

Aikens, N.L., & Barbarin, O.A. (2008). Socioeconomic differences in reading trajectories: The contribution of family, neighborhood, and school contexts. *Journal of Educational Psychology, 100*(2), 235–251.

Ajamu, A.A. (2004). Rekh: Prelude to an intergenerational conversation about African Psychological Thought. In R. Jones (Ed.) *Black Psychology* (4th ed.). Hampton: Cobb and Henry.

Ajamu, A.A. (1998). Ubunye Umuzi: Distinguishing Essence from Expression—The African American Contribution. San Francisco, CA: *San Francisco State Journal of Black Studies.*

Akbar, N. (2004). *The Akbar Papers in African Psychology.* Tallahassee, FL: Mind Productions.

Akbar, N. (1992). *Chains and Images of Psychological Slavery.* Tallahassee, FL: Mind Productions.

Akbar, N. (1991). Mental disorders among African Americans. In R.L. Jones (Ed.) *Black Psychology* (3rd ed., pp. 339–352). Berkeley, CA: Cobb & Henry.

Akbar, N. (1994). *Light from Ancient Africa.* Tallahassee, FL: Mind Productions.

Akbar, N. (1989). Nigrescence and identity: Some limitations. *The Counseling Psychologist, 17,* 258–263.

Ames, R. (1950). Protest and Irony in Negro Folksong. *Social Sciences, 14,* 193–213.

Ani, M. (1980). *Let the Circle Be Unbroken.* New York, NY: Nkonimfo Publications.

Ani, M. (1994). *Yurugu: An African Centered Critique of European Cultural Thought and Behavior.* Trenton, NJ: African World Press.

Ani, M. (1989/1997). *Let the Circle Be Unbroken: Implications of African Spirituality in the Diaspora.* Trenton: Red Sea Press.

Armstrong, T.D., & Crowther, M.R. (2002). Spirituality among elder African Americans. *Journal of Adult Development, 9,* 3–12.

Arnez, N.L. (1972). Enhancing Black self-concept through literature. In J. Banks and J. Grambs (Eds.) *Black Self-Concept.* New York: McGraw-Hill.

Asante, M. (2002). *The Egyptian Philosophers: Ancient African Voices from Imhotep to Akhenaten.* Chicago: African American Images.

Asante, M. (2003). *Erasing Racism.* Amherst, NY: Prometheus Books.

Azibo, D. (1996). Personality, clinical, and social psychological research on blacks: Appropriate and inappropriate frameworks. In D. Azibo (Ed.) *African Psychology in Historical Perspectives and Related Commentary.* Trenton, NJ: African World Press.

Azibo, D. (1989). *Advances in Black/African Personality Theory.* Unpublished manuscript.

Azibo, D., & Robinson, J. (2004). An empirically supported reconceptualization of African-U.S. racial identity development as an abnormal process. *Review of General Psychology, 8*, 249–264.

Baldwin, J. (1963). *The Fire Next Time*. New York: Dell Publishing Company.

Baldwin, J.A. (1985). African self-consciousness scale: An Afrocentric questionaire. *Western Journal of Black Studies, 2*(9), 61–68.

Baldwin, J.A. (1986). Black psychology: Issues and synthesis. *Journal of Black Studies, 16*(3), 235–249

Banks, W.C. (1992). The theoretical and methodological crisis of the Africentric conception. *Journal of Negro Education, 6*(3).

Banks, J.A., & Grambs, J.D. (1972). *Black Self Concept*. New York, NY: McGraw-Hill.

Barbarin, O., Mc Candies, T., Early, D., Clifford, R., Bryant, D., Burchinal, M., et al. (in Press). Parental perceptions of school readiness: Relation to ethnicity, socio-economic status, and children's academic skills. *Early Education and Development*.

Barnes, E.J. (1972). The Black community as the source of positive self-concept for Black children: A theoretical perspective. In R.L. Jones (Ed.), *Black Psychology*. New York: Harper & Row.

Bartol, C.M., & Bartol, A.M. (2008). *Current Perspectives in Forensic Psychology and Criminal Behavior*. Thousand Oaks, CA: Sage Publications.

Basch, M.F. (1980). *Doing Psychotherapy*. New York: Basic Books.

Bashir, M. (2003). *Living with Michael Jackson*. Documentary film/report produced for television. Granada Television Limited/ITV.

Bayton, J.A., McAlister, L.B., & Hamer, J. (1956). Race-class stereotypes. *Journal of Negro Education, 25*, 75–78.

Beale-Spencer, M. (1997). A phenomenological variant of ecological systems theory (PVEST): A Self organization perspective in context. *Development and Psychopathology, 9*, 817–833.

Beez, W.V. (1969). Influence of biased psychological reports on teacher behavior and pupil performance. *Proceedings of the 76th Annual Conventions of the American Psychological Association, No. 3, 605–606*.

Belgrave, F.Z., & Allison, K.W. (2006). *African American Psychology: From Africa to America*. Thousand Oaks, CA: Sage Publications.

Belgrave, F.Z., & Allison, K.W. (2010). *African American Psychology: From Africa to America (2nd Ed.)*. Thousand Oaks, CA: Sage Publications.

Bennett, Jr., L. (1966). *Before the Mayflower: History of Black America*. Chicago: Johnson Publishing Co.

Berkel, L.A., Armstrong, T.D., & Copley, K.O. (2004). Similarity and differences between spirituality and religiosity in African American college students: A preliminary investigation. *Counseling and Values, 49*(1), 2–26.

Berry, G. (1982). Television, self-esteem and the Afro-American child: Some implications for mental health professionals. In B.A. Bass, G.E. Wyatt, and Gj. Powell (Eds.), *The Afro-American Family: Assessment Treatment and Research Issues*. New York: Grune & Stratton.

Blassingame, John W. (1979/1972). *The slave community: Plantation life in the Antebellum South* (1972; rev. ed., New York: Oxford University Press).

Brofenbrener, U. (1979). *The Ecology of Human Development: Experiments by Nature and Design*. Cambridge: Harvard University Press.

Billingsley, A. (1968). *Black Families in White America*. New York, NY: Prentice Hall.

Billingsley, A. (1986). *Black families in White America*. Englewood Cliffs, NJ: Prentice Hall.

Block, C. (1980). Black Americans and the cross-cultural counseling experience. In A.J. Marsella and P.B. Pederson (Eds.), *Cross-Cultural Counseling and Psychotherapy*. New York: Pergamon.

Blyden, E.W. (1908/1997). *African Life and Customs*. Baltimore: Black Classic Press.

Boyd-Franklin, N. (1989). *Black Families in Therapy*. New York: Guilford Press.

Brayboy, T. (1971). The Black patient in group therapy. *International Journal of Group Psychotherapy, 2*(3), 288–293.

Brawer, P.A., Handall, P.J., Fabricatore, A.N., Roberts, R., & Wajda-Johnston, V.A. (2002). Training and education in religion/spirituality within APA accredited clinical psychology programs. *Professional Psychology: Research, and Practice, 33*(2), 203–206.

Brigham, J.C. (1974). Views of Black and White children concerning the distribution of personality characteristics. *Journal of Personality, 42,* 144–158.

Brofenbrenner, U. (1979). *The Ecology of Human Development*. Cambridge, MA: Harvard University Press.

Bruce, M. (2004). Contextual complexity and violent delinquency among Black and White males. *Journal of Black Studies, 35*(1), 65–98.

Brussat, F., and Brussat, M. (1996). *Spiritual Literacy*. New York: Simon & Schuster.

Bryant, A.L, & Zimmerman, M.A. (2003). Role models and psychosocial outcomes among African American adolescents. *Journal of Adolescent Research, 18*(1), 36–67.

Bureau of Justice Statistics (2006). *Prison Population Statistics*. Retrieved March 14, 2006, from http://ojp.usdoj.gov/bjs/.

Bureau of Justice Statistics (2007). *Prison Inmates at Midyear 2007*. Retrieved November 20, 2008, from http://www.ojp.usdoj.gov/bjs/pub/pdf/pim07.pdf.

Bureau of Justice Statistics (2008). *Parents in Prison and Their Minor Children*. Retrieved November 20, 2008, from http://www.ojp.usdoj.gov/bjs/pub/pdf/pptmc.pdf

Burkhardt, M. (1989). Spirituality: An analysis of the concept. *Journal of Holistic Nursing Practice, 3*(3), 69–77.

Burt, C.H., Simons, R.L., & Simons, L.G. (2006). A longitudinal test of the effects of parenting and the stability of self-control: Negative evidence for the general theory of crime. *Criminology: An Interdisciplinary Journal, 44*(2), 353–396.

Bynum, E.G., & Weiner, R.I (2002). Self-concept and violent delinquency in urban African-American adolescent males. *Psychological Reports, 90*(2), 477–486.

Bynum, E.B. (1999). *The African Unconscious: Roots of Ancient Mysticism and Modern Psychology*. New York, NY: Teachers College Press.

Caldwell, R.M., & Cross, W.E. (2006). *The Collective Group Identity Project: An examination and comparison of identity development, cultural mistrust, and mental health issues among Black male college students and Black male first time offenders*. Grant funded by the CUNY Collaborative Incentive Research Grants Program.

Caldwell, C.H, Kohn-Wood, L.P, Schmeelk-Cone, K.H, Chavous, T.M., & Zimmerman, M.A. (2004). Racial discrimination and racial identity as risk or protective factors for violent behaviors in African American young males. *American Journal of Community Psychology, 33*(1–2), 91–105.

Caldwell, R.M., Silverman, J., Lefforge, N., & Silver, N.C. (2004). Familial emotional support, self-esteem, and emotional well-being as predictors of delinquency among adjudicated Mexican American adolescents. *American Journal of Family Therapy, 32*(1), 55–69.

California Postsecondary Education Commission (1988). Eligibility of California's 1986 High School Graduates for Admission to Its Public Universities: A Report of the 1986 High School Eligibility Study (3/1988) Sacramento, CA: CPEC

Campbell, D.T. (1976). Stereotypes and the perception of group difference. *American Psychologist, 22,* 817–829.

Carney, J. (2002). *Black Rice: The African Origins of Rice Cultivation in the Americas.* Cambridge: Harvard University Press.

Carter, R. (1995). *The Influence of Race and Racial Identity in Psychotherapy.* New York: John Wiley and Sons.

Carter, R.T., & Helms, J.E. (1987). Relationship of Black values orientations to racial identity attitudes. *Measurement and Evaluation In Counseling and Development, 19*(4), 185–195.

Carruther, J.H., Jr. (1972). *Science and Oppression.* Chicago: Northeastern Illinois University, Center for Inner City Studies.

Catterall, J.S. (1998). Risk and resilience in student transitions to high school. *American Journal of Education, 106*(2), 302–333.

Cervantes, J.M., & Parham, T.A. (2005). Toward a meaningful spirituality for people of color: Lessons for the counseling practitioner. *Cultural Diversity & Ethnic Minority Psychology, 11,* 69–81.

Clark, C. (1972). Black studies or the study of Black people. In R.L. Jones (Ed.) *Black Psychology.* New York: Harper & Rowe.

Clark, R. (1983*). Family Life and School Achievement: Why Poor Black Children Succeed or Fail.* Chicago: University of Chicago Press.

Clark, K.B., & Clark, M.K. (1950). Emotional factors in racial identification and preference in Negro children. Journal of Negro Education, 19, 341–350.

Clark, K.B., & Clark, M.K. (1940). Skin color as a factor in racial identification of Negro preschool children. *The Journal of Social Psychology, 11,* 159–169.

Clark, K.B., & Clark, M.K. (1939a). The development of consciousness of self and the emergence of racial identification in Negro preschool children. *Journal of Social Psychology, 10,* 591–599.

Clark, K.B., & Clark, M.K. (1939b). Segregation as a factor in the racial identification of Negro pre-school children: A preliminary report. *Journal of Experimental Education, 8,* 161–163.

Clarke, J.H. (2005). *John Henrik Clarke: A Great and Mighty Walk.* (Documentary Film) New York, NY: The Cinema Guild, Inc.

Claiborn, W.L. (1969). Expectancy effects in the classroom: A failure to replicate. *Journal of Educational Psychology, 60,* 377–383.

Cokley, K.O. (2007). Critical issues in the measurement of racial and ethnic identity: A referendum on the state of the field. *Journal of Counseling Psychology, 54,* 224–234.

Cokley, K.O., & Chapman, C. (2009). Racial identity theory-adults. In H. Neville, B. Tynes, and S. Utsey (deeds.), *Handbook of African American Psychology*. Thousand Oaks, CA: Sage Publications.

Collins, C.A., & Williams, D.R. (1999). Segregation and mortality: The deadly effects of racism? *Sociological Forum, 14*(3).

Collins, C.A., & Williams, D.R. (1995). U.S Socioeconomic and Racial Differences in Health: Patterns and Explanations. *Annual Review of Sociology, 21*, 349–386.

Connor, M.E., & White, J.L. (2006). *Black Fathers: An Invisible Presence in America*. Mahwah, NJ: Lawrence Erlbaum Associates.

Constantine, M.G., Redington, R.M., & Graham, S.V. (2009). Counseling and Psychotherapy with African Americans. In H. Neville, B.Tynes, and S. Utsey (Eds.) *Handbook of African American Psychology*. Thousand Oaks, CA: Sage Publications.

Constantine, M.G., Alleyne, V.L., Wallace, B.C., & Franklin-Jackson, D.C. (2006). Africentric cultural values: Their relation to positive mental health in African American adolescent girls. *Journal of Black Psychology, 32*(2), 141–154.

Constantine, M.G., Lewis, E.L., Connor, L.C., & Sanchez, D. (2000). Addressing spiritual and religious issues in counseling African Americans: Implications for counselor training and practice. *Counseling and Values, 45*, 1, 28–38.

Constantine, M., & Sue, D.W. (2005). *Strategies for Building Multicultural Competence in Mental Health and Educational Settings*. Hoboken, NJ: John Wiley and Sons.

Cooper. A.J. (1998). *The Voice of Anna Julia Cooper: Including a Voice from the South and Other Important Essays, Papers, and Letters*. Lanham, MD: Rowman and Littlefield.

Cress-Welsing, F. (1991). *The Isis Papers*. Chicago, IL: Third World Press.

Cross, W.E. (1971). The Negro to Black conversion experience. *Black World, 209*, 13–27.

Cross, W.E. (1980). Models of psychological nigrescence: A literature review. In R.L. Jones (Ed.) *Black Psychology* (2nd ed., pp. 81–98). New York: Harper & Row.

Cross, W.E. (1991). *Shades of Black: Diversity in African American Identity*. Philadelphia, PA: Temple University Press.

Cross, W.E. (2001). Encountering Nigrescence. In J.G. Ponterotto, J.M. Casas, L.A. Suzuki, and C. M. Alexander (Eds.) *Handbook of Multicultural Counseling (2nd ed.)*. Thousand Oaks, CA.: Sage Publications.

Cross, W.E., Parham, T.A., & Helms, J.E. (1998). Nigrescence revisited: Theory and re-search. In R.L. Jones (Ed.) *African American Identity Development*. Hampton, VA: Cobb & Henry Publishers.

Cross, W.E., & Vandiver, B.J. (2001). Nigrescence theory and measurement: Introducing the Cross Racial Identity Attitude Scale (CRIS). In Ponterotto, J.G., Casas, J.M., Suzuki, L.A., and Alexander, C.M. (2001). *Handbook of Multicultural Counseling* (pp. 371–393). Thousand Oaks, CA. Sage Publications.

Culp, A., Hubbs-Tait, L., Cuilp, R., & Starost, H. (2001). Maternal parenting characteris-tics and school involvement: Predictors of kindergarten cognitive competence among head start children. *Journal of Research in Childhood Education, 15*, 5–17.

Dance, L.J. (2002). *Tough Fronts: The Impact of Street Culture on Schooling*. New York: Routledge.

Davis, K. (2005). *A Girl Like Me*. Podcast retrieved from http://www.kiridavis.com/index.php?option=com_content&task=view&id=17&Itemid=99999999

214   References

Delaney, M. (1852/1993). *The Condition, Elevation, Emigration and Destiny of the Colored People of the United States, Politically Considered.* Baltimore: Black Classic Press.

Dent, H. (2008). *The Association of Black Psychologist: Past, Present, and Future.* Presentation delivered at the annual meeting of the American Psychological Association, San Francisco, CA., August

Desimone, L. (2001). Linking parent involvement with student achievement: Do race and income matter? *The Journal of Educational Research, 93,* 11–30.

Dimmit, C. (2003). Transforming school counseling practice through collaboration and the use of data: A study of academic failure in high school. *Professional School Counseling, 6*(5), 340–349.

Diop, C.A. (1974). *The African Origins of Civilization: Myth or Reality.* Westport: Lawrence, Hill & Company.

Diop, C.A. (1959). *The Cultural Unity of Black Africa.* Chicago: Third World Press.

Dornbusch, S.M, Erickson, K.G., Laird, J., & Wong, C. (2001). The relation of family and school attachment to adolescent deviance in diverse groups and communities. *Journal of Adolescent Research, 16*(4), 369–422.

Du Bois, W.E.B. (1965). *The World and Africa, an Inquiry into the Part Which Africa Has Played in World History.* New York: The Viking Press.

Du Bois, W.E.B. (1903). *The Souls of Black Folk.* New York: Bantam.

Du Bois, W.E.B. (1935/1998). *Black Reconstruction in America, 1860–1880.* New York: The Free Press.

Du Bois, W.E.B. (1896). *Suppression of the African Slave Trade to the United States: 1638–1870.* New York: Longman, Green, & Co.

Du Bois, W.E.B. (1903). *The Souls of Black Folks.* New York: Signet Classic.

Du Bois, W.E.B. (1899). *The Philadelphia Negro.* Philadelphia: University of Pennsylvania Press.

Duncan, L.E. (2003). Black male college students' attitudes toward seeking psychological help. *Journal of Black Psychology, 29,* 68–86.

Dyke, B. (1983). *"Pre-Therapy Education Techniques for Black Families: Expectancies and Cognitions."* Unpublished Doctoral Dissertation, University of Pennsylvania.

Dyson, M.E. (2004). *The Michael Eric Dyson Reader.* New York: Basic Cervitas Books.

Dyson, M.E. (2001). *Holler If You Hear Me.* New York: Basic Cervitas Books.

Ellison, R. (1952). *The Invisible Man.* New York: Random House.

Elkins, Stanley M. *Slavery: A Problem in American Institutional and Intellectual Life* (Chicago: University of Chicago Press, 1969)

Fabrega H. Jr., *Ulrich* R., & Mezzich J.E. (1993). Do Caucasian and Black adolescents differ at psychiatric intake? *Journal of the American Academy of Child and Adolescent Psychiatry, 32*(2):407–413.

Fanon, F. (1967). *Black Skin, White Masks.* New York: Grove Press.

Fanon, F. (1966). *Wretched of the Earth.* New York: Grove Press, Inc.

Farrakhan, L. (1996). Mental Health in the African American Community. Invited Address delivered at the annual convention of the Association of Black Psychologists, Chicago, August.

Fernald, L.D., & Fernald, P.S. *Introduction to Psychology* (4th Ed.). Boston, MA: Houghton Mifflin Company.

Fields, J. (2003). *Children's Living Arrangements and Characteristics: March 2002. U.S. Bureau of Census, current population reports*, pp. 20–547. Washington, DC: U.S. Printing Office.

Fisher, J. (1969). Negroes and Whites and rates of mental illness: Reconsideration of a Myth. *Psychiatry, 32,* 428–446.

Fiester, A.R., & Rudestam, K.E. (1975). A multivariate analysis of the early drop-out process. *Journal of Consulting and Clinical Psychology, 43*(4), 528–535.

Fleming, E.S., & Anttonen, R.G. (1971). Teacher expectancy or my fair Lady. *Aera Journal, 8,* 241.

Franklin, A.J. (1971). To be young, gifted, and Black, with inappropriate professional training. *The Counseling Psychologist, 2*(4), 107–112.

Franklin, A.J. (1999). Invisibility syndrome and racial identity development in psychotherapy and counseling African American men. *The Counseling Psychologists, 29*(6), 761–793.

Franklin, A.J. (2006). *From Brotherhood to Manhood: How Black Men Rescue Their Relationships and Dreams from the Invisibility Syndrome.* Hoboken, NJ: John Wiley & Son.

Franklin, A.J., & Boyd-Franklin, N. (2008). Cultural Competency in the Treatment of African Couples (DVD). Hanover, MA: Microtraining.

Franklin, J.H. (1974). *From Slavery to Freedom.* New York, NY: Alfred Knopf Publishers.

Frazier, E. Franklin. (1948). *The Negro Family in the United States (1939).* Chicago: University of Chicago Press.

Freudenberg, N. (2002). Adverse effects of US jail and prison policies on the health and well-being of women of color. *American Journal of Public Health, 92*(12), 1895–1899.

Fu-Kiau, K.K. (1991). *Self Healing Power and Therapy: Old Teachings from Africa.* New York, NY: Vantage Press.

Fu-Kiau, K.K. (2001). *African Cosmology of the Bantu-Kongo.* Brooklyn, NY: Althelia Henrietta Press.

Fuller, N. (1969). *United Independent Compensatory Code System Concept.* Washington, DC: Library of Congress.

Gates, H.L. (1994). *Colored People.* New York, NY: Alfred Knopf.

Genovese, Eugene D. (1974). *Roll, Jordan, Roll; the World the Slaves Made.* New York: Random House.

Gilmore, M. (2009). *A Tribute to Michael Jackson.* Rolling Stone Magazine, July, Special Edition.

Ginwright, S.A. (2004). *Black in School: Afrocentric Reform, Urban Youth, and the Promise of Hip-Hop Culture.* New York: College Press.

Gnaulati, E., & Heine, B.J. (2001). Separation-individuation in late adolescence: An investigation of gender and ethnic differences. *Journal of Psychology: Interdisciplinary and Applied, 135*(1), 59–70.

Goddard, L., & Nobles, W.W. (2008). *To Be African: From the Beginning to Now: 40 Years of Meeting the Challenges of Black Mental Health.* Fortieth Anniversary Convention Prospectus, Unpublished document.

Gomez, M.A. (1998). *Exchanging Our Country Marks.* Chapel Hill: The University of North Carolina Press.

Goodlad. (1984). *A Place Called School*. New York: McGraw-Hill.

Goodman, M.E. (1952). *Racial Awareness in Young Children*. Cambridge: Addison Wesley.

Gottfredson, M.R., & Hirschi, T. (1990). *A General Theory of Crime*. Stanford, CA: Stanford University Press.

Greenberg, B. & Dervin, B. (1970). Mass communication among the urban poor. *Public Opinion Quarterly, 34*, 224–235.

Griffin, B.W. (2001). Academic disidentification, race, and high school dropouts. *The High School Journal, 85*(4), 71–81.

Graham, S. (1994). Motivation in African Americans. *Review of Educational Research, 64*, 55–117.

Grier, W.H., & Cobbs, P.M. (1968). *Black rage*. New York: Basic Books.

Grills, C. (2002). African centered psychology: Basic principles. In T.A. Parham (Ed.) *Counseling Persons of African Descent: Raising the Bar of Practitioner Competence*. Thousand Oaks, CA: Sage Publications.

Grills, C. (2004). African psychology. In R.L. Jones (4th Ed.) *Black Psychology*. Hampton, VA: Cobb & Henry.

Grills, C., & Ajei, M. (2002). African centered conceptualizations of self and consciousness: The Akan Model. In T.A. Parham (Ed.) *Counseling Persons of African Descent: Raising the Bar Of Practitioner Competence*. Thousand Oaks, CA: Sage Publications

Grills, C., & Rowe, D. (1998). African traditional medicine: Implications for African-centered approaches to healing. In R. Jones (Ed.) *African American Mental Health*. Hampton, VA: Cobb & Henry.

Guthrie, R.V. (1976). *Even the Rat Was White: A Historical View of Psychology*. New York: Harper & Row.

Guthrie, R.V. (1998). *Even the rat was white: a Historical View of Psychology* (2nd ed). Needham Heights, MA: Allyn & Bacon.

Gutman, Herbert G. (1976). *The Black Family in Slavery and Freedom, 1750–1925*. New York: Vintage Books.

Guttman, L.M., & Midgley, C. (2000). The role of protective factors in supporting the academic achievement of poor African American students during middle school transition. *Journal of Youth and Adolescence, 29*, 233–248.

Hall, G.C.N. (2010). *Multicultural Psychology* (2nd ed.). New York: Prentice Hall.

Hall, G.M. (2007). *Slavery and African Ethnicities in the Americas: Restoring the Links*. Chapel Hill: The University of North Carolina Press.

Hargrove, R., Stoeklin, M., Haan, M., & Reed, B. (1998). Clinical aspects of Alzheimer's disease in black and white patients. *Journal of the National Medical Association, 90*(2), 78–84.

Herskovits, M.J. (1941/1958). *The Myth of the Negro Past*. Boston: Beacon Press.

Heywood. L. (2010). *Central Africans and Cultural Transformations in the American Diaspora*. Cambridge: University Press.

Hines, P., & Boyd-Franklin, N. (1982). Black families, In M.Mc Goldrick, V. Pearce, and J. Giodane (Eds.) *Ethnicity in Family Therapy*. New York: Guilford Press.

Holloway, J.E. (2005). *Africanisms in American Culture (Blacks in the Diaspora)*. Bloomington: Indiana University Press.

Harley, D.A., & Dillard, J.M. (2005). *Contemporary Mental Health Issues among African Americans*. Alexandria, VA. American Counseling Association.

Helms, J.E. (2007). Some better practices in measuring racial and ethnic identity constructs. *Journal of Counseling Psychology, 54*, 235–246.

Herndon, M.K. (2003). Expressions of spirituality among African Americans. *Journal of Men's Studies, 12*(1), 75–84.

Highlen, P.S. & Hill, C.E. (1984). Factors affecting client change in individual counseling: Current status of theoretical speculations. In S.D. Brown and R.W. Lent (Eds.) *The Handbook of Counseling Psychology*. New York: John Wiley & Sons.

Hill, R. (1971). *Strengths of the Black Family*. New York: National Urban League.

Hill, H.I., and Strozier, A.L. (1992). Multicultural training in APA approved counseling psychology training programs: A survey. *Professional Psychology: Research and Practice, 23*, 41–43.

Hillburn, R. (2009). His fragile lonely heart had broken long ago. Los Angeles Times, Sunday July 12, pp. S18–19.

Hilliard, A.G. (1997). *SBA: The Reawakening of the African Mind*. Gainesville, FL: Marare Press.

Hoffman, K., and Llagas, C. (2003). *Status and Trends in the Education of Blacks* (NCES 2003–034). U.S. Department of Education, Washington, DC: National Center for Education Statistics.

Holloway, J.E. (2005). *Africanisms in American Culture*. J.E. Holloway (Ed.). Bloomington: Indiana University Press.

Holt, C.L., Lewellyn, L.A., & Rathweg, M.J. (2005). Exploring religious health mediators among African American pasishioners. *Journal of Health Psychology, 10*(4), 511–527.

Hudley, C. (2009). Academic motivation and achievement of African American youth. In H. Neville, B.Tynes, & S. Utsey (Eds.) *Handbook of African American Psychology*. Thousand Oaks, CA: Sage Publications.

Huss, M.T. (2008). *Forensic Psychology*. Hoboken, NJ: Wily-Blackwell.

Ivey, A., D'Andrea, M., Bradford-Ivey, M., & Simek-Morgan, L. (2002). *Theories of Counseling and Psychotherapy: A Multicultural Perspective* (5th Ed.). Boston, MA: Allyn and Bacon.

Jackson, L., Gregory, H., & Davis, M. (2004). Ntu Psychotherapy and African American Youth. In J.R. Ancis (Ed.) *Culturally Responsive Interventions: Innovative Approaches to Working with Diverse Populations*. 49–70. New York, NY: Brunner-Routledge.

Jahoda, M. (1958). *Current Concepts of Positive Mental Health*. New York: Basic Books.

James, A.D. (1998). What's love got to do with it: Economic viability and the likelihood of marriage in African American men. *Journal of Comparative Family Studies, 29*(2), 373–386.

Jenkins, A.H. (1982). *The Psychology of the Afro-American: A Humanistic Approach*. New York, NY: Pergamon Press.

Jensen, A. (1969). How much can we boost IQ and scholastic achievement? *Harvard Educational Review, 39*, 1–23.

Johnson, L.B., and Staples, R. (2004). *Black Families at the Crossroads*. New York: John Wiley and Sons.

Jones, F. (1972). The Black Psychologist As Consultant and Therapist. In R.L. Jones (Ed.) *Black psychology*. New York, NY: Harper & Row.

Jones, R.L. (1972). *Black Psychology*. New York: Harper and Rowe.

Jones, R.L. (1980). *Black Psychology* (2nd ed.) New York: Harper and Rowe.

Jones, R.L. (1991). *Black Psychology* (3rd ed). Hampton, VA: Cobb & Henry.

Jones, J.M. (2003). TRIOS: A psychological theory of the African legacy in American culture. *Journal of Social Issues, 59,* 217–242

Jones, N., & Jackson, J.S. (2005). *Black Collegiate Magazine*. New Orleans, LA: IM Diversity Publishers.

Jones, C., Wainwright, G., & Yarnold, E. (1986). *The Study of Spirituality*. New York: Oxford University Press.

June, L., & Parker, R. (1991). *The Black Family: Past, Present, and Future*. Michigan: Zondervan Publishers.

Kambon, K. (2006). *Kambon's Reader in Liberation Psychology: Selected Works, Volume 1*. Tallahassee, FL: Nubian Nation.

Kambon, K.K. (1992). *The African Personality in America: An African Centered Framework*. Tallahassee, FL: Nubian Nation Publications.

Kambon, K.K., & Bowen-Reid, T. (2009). Africentric theories of African American personality. In H. Neville, B. Tynes, and S. Utsey (Eds.) *Handbook of African American Psychology* (pp. 61–74). Thousand Oaks, CA: Sage Publications.

Kardiner, A., & Ovessey, L. (1951). *The Mark of Oppression*. New York: Norton.

Kardiner, A., & Ovessey, S. (1968). The psychological dynamics of the negro personality. In C. Gordon and Gregen, K. (Eds.) *The Self in Social Interaction*. New York: John Wiley.

Karenga, M. (1976). *Kwanzaa, Origin, Concepts, Practice*. Los Angeles: Kawaida Publications.

Karenga, M. (1990). *The Book of Coming Forth by Day: The Ethics of the Declaration of Innocence*. Los Angeles, CA: University of Sankore Press.

Karoly, L. (1993). The trend in inequality among families, individuals, and workers in the United States: A twenty-five year perspective. In S. Danziger and P. Gottschalk (Eds.) *Uneven Tides: Rising Inequality in America* (pp. 19–97). New York: Russell Sage Foundation.

Kendall J.C., Sherman M.F., and Bigelow G.E. (1995). Psychiatric symptoms in polysubstance abusers: Relationship to race, sex, and age. *Addictive Behaviors, 20*(5), 685–690.

Kenny, M.E., Gallagher, L.A., Alvarez-Salvat, R., & Silsby, J. (2002). Sources of support and psychological distress among academically successful inner-city youth. *Adolescence, 37*(145), 161–182.

Kessler R.C., McGonagle K.A., Zhao S., Nelson C.B., Hughes M., Eshleman S., Wittchen H.U., Kendler K.S. (1994). Lifetime and 12-month prevalence of DSM-III-R psychiatric disorders in the United States. Results from the National Comorbidity Survey. *Archives of General Psychiatry*, 51(1), 8–19.

Khatib, S. (1980). Black Studies and the study of Black people: Reflections on the distinctive characteristics of Black Psychology. In R.L. Jones (Ed.) *Black Psychology* (2nd ed., pp. 48–55). New York: Harper and Row.

King, L. (1982). Suicide from a Black Reality Perspective. In B. Bass, G.E. Wyatt, and G. Powell (Eds.), *The Afro-American Family: Assessment Treatment and Research*. New York: Grune & Stratton.

King, L.M. (1978). Social and cultural influences on psychopathology. *Annual Review of Psychology, 29,* 405–433.

King, S.V., Burgess, E.O., Akinyela, M., Counts-Spriggs, M., & Parker, N. (2005). Your body is God's temple: the spiritualization of health beliefs in multigenerational African American families. *Research of Aging, 27*(4), 420–446.

King, L., Dixon, V., & Nobles, W.W. (1996). African-centered theses on mental health and a nosology of Black/African personality disorder. *Journal of Black Studies, 27*(2), 172–182.

Kipfer, B.A., and Chapman, R.L. (2003). *Roget's II New Thesaurus* (6th ed.). New York: Harper Collins.

Kluckjohn, F.R., & Strodtbeck, F.L. (1961). *Varaitions in Value Orientations.* Evanston, IL: Row, Peterson.

Knapp, R., Rhome, J., & Brown, D. (2006). National Hurricane Tropical Cyclone Report: Hurricane Katrina 23–30 August, 2005. http://www.hurricane.com/hurricanes/hurricane-katrina.php

Knox, S., Burkard, A.W., Johnson, A.J., Suzuki, L.A., & Ponterotto, J.G. (2003). African American and European American therapist experiences of addressing race in cross-racial counseling dyads. *Journal of Counseling Psychology, 50,* 466–481.

Koons-Whitt, B.A., & Schram, P.J. (2003). The prevalence and nature of violent offending by females. *The Journal of Criminal Justice, 31*(4), 361–371.

Kuhn, T.S. (1970). *The Structure of Scientific Revolutions.* Chicago: Chicago University Press.

Kunjufu, J. (1986). *Motivating and Preparing Black Youth to Work.* Chicago: African American Images.

Ladner, J. (1971). *Tomorrow's Tomorrow: The Black Woman.* Garden City: Doubleday.

Lazarus, A., & Fay, A. (1975). *I Can If I Want To.* New York: Morrow Books.

Leary, J.D. (2005). *Post Traumatic Slave Syndrome.* Milwaukie, OR: Uptone Press.

Lee, E.O., Shen, C., & Tran, T. (2009). Coping with hurricane Katrina: Psychological distress and resilience among African Americans. *Journal Of Black Psychology, 35*(1), 5–23.

Lewis, D.L. (1994). *W. E. B. Du Bois, 1868–1919: Biography of a Race.* New York; Henry Holt & Co., Inc.

Lipman, P. (2002). Making the global city, making inequality: The political economy and cultural politics of Chicago school policy. *American Educational Research Journal, 39*(2), 379–419.

Liu, R.X. (2004). Parent-youth conflict and school delinquency/cigarette use: The moderating effects of gender and associations with achievement-oriented peers. *Sociological Inquiry, 74,* 271–297.

Loo, C.M. (1998). *Chinese America: Mental Health and Quality of Life in the Inner City.* Thousand Oaks, CA: Sage Publications.

Majors, R., & Billson, J.M. (1992). *Cool Pose: The Dilemmas of Black Manhood in America.* New York: Simon & Schuster.

Manning, M.C., Cornelius, L.J., & Okundaye, J.N. (2004). Empowering African Americans through social work practice: Integrating an afrocentric perspective, ego psychology, and spirituality. *Families in Society, 85*(2), 229–235.

Mather, M., & Adams, D. (2006). *The Risk of Negative Child Outcomes in Low Income Families*. Baltimore, MD: Annie E. Casey Foundation, Population Reference Bureau.

Martin, J.A., Hamilton, B.E., Sutton, P.D., Ventura, S.J., Menacker, F., Kirmeyer, S., & Mathews, T.J. (2009). Births: Final data for 2006. *National Vital Statistics Reports 57*(7).

Mattis, J.S. (2000). African American women's definitions of spirituality and religiosity. *Journal of Black Psychology, 26*(1), 101–122.

Mattis, J.S., & Jagers, R.J. (2001). A relational framework for the study of religiosity and spirituality in the lives of African Americans. *Journal of Community Psychology,* 29(5), 519–539.

Mbiti, J.S. (1970). *African Religions and Philosophy*. Garden City, NY: Anchor Books.

Meraviglia, M. (1999). Critical analysis of spirituality and its empirical indicators. *Journal of Holistic Nursing Practice, 17*(1), 18–33.

McAdoo, H.P. (1981). *Black Families*. Beverly Hills, CA: Sage Publications.

McAdoo, H.P. (1979). Black Kinship. *Psychology Today,* May, 67–69, 79, 110.

McAdoo, H.P. (2006). *Black Families*. Thousand Oaks, CA: Sage Publications.

McCall, N. (1994). *Makes Me Wanna Holler: A Young Black Man in America*. New York: Vintage Books.

McClelland, D. (1961). *The Achieving Society*. Princeton, NJ: Van Nostrand.

McNeill, B.W., & Cervantes, J.M. (2008). *Latina/o Healing Practices*. New York, NY: Routledge.

Mead, G.H. (1934). *Mind, Self and Society*. Chicago: University of Chicago Press.

Midlo Hall, G. (2007). *Slavery and African Ethnicities in the Americas: Restoring the Links*. Chapel Hill: The University of North Carolina Press.

Midlo Hall, G. (1995). *Africans in Colonial Louisiana: The Development of Afro-Creole Culture in the Eighteenth Century*. Baton Rouge: Louisiana State University Press.

Monroe, S., & Goldman, P. (1988). *Brothers, Black and poor: A True Story of Courage and Survival*. Morrow Publishers: New York, New York.

Moodley, R., & West, W. (2005). *Integrating Traditional Healing Practices into Counseling and Psychotherapy*. Thousand Oaks, CA: Sage Publications.

Morland, J.K. (1958). Racial recognition by nursery school children. *Social Forces, 37,* 132–137.

Morton, S.G. (1839). *Crania Americana* (1839), *An Inquiry into the Distinctive Characteristics of the Aboriginal Race of America*. Philadelphia: J. Dobson.

Moses, W.J. (1988). *The Golden Age of Black Nationalism, 1850–1925*. New York: Oxford University Press.

Moses, W.J. (1989). *Alexander Crummell: A Study of Civilization and Discontent*. New York: Oxford University Press.

Moyers, B. (1986). *CBS Report: The Vanishing Family-Crisis in Black America*. *Television Documentary*. New York: Columbia Broadcasting Systems.

Moynihan, D. (1965). *The Negro Family: The Case for National Action*. Washington, DC: Office of Policy Planning and Research, U.S. Department of Labor.

Moynihan, D.P. (1976). *Social and Economic Conditions of Negroes in the United States, Bureau of Labor Statistics and Bureau of the Census, BLS Rpt. no. 332 and Current Population Reports, Series P-23, no. 24*. Washington, DC: Government Printing Office.

Muhammad, E. (1965). *Message to a Black Man.* Chicago, IL: Muhammad Mosque # 2.

Munley, P.H., Vacha-Haase, T., Busby, R.M., & Paul, B.D. (1998). The MCMI-II and race. *Journal of Personality Assessment,* 70, 183–189.

Myers, D. (2010). *Psychology* (9th ed.). New York, NY: Worth Publishing.

Myers, L.J. (1988). *Understanding the Afrocentric Worldview: Introduction to an optimal psychology.* Dubuque, IA: Kendall Hunt.

National Government Printing Office. (1996). *National Assessment of Educational Progress.* Washington, DC: Author.

National Commission on Excellence in Education (1983). *A Nation at Risk: The Imperative for Educational Reform.* Washington, DC: Government Printing Office.

National Center for Health Statistics. (2007). *Health, United States, 2007.* Hyattsville, MD: Author.

Neighbors, H.W. (1991). Mental health. In JS Jackson (Ed.), *Life in Black America* (pp. 221–237). Newbury Park, CA: Sage Publications.

Nevid, J.S. (2007). *Essentials of Psychology: Concepts and Applications.* New York: Wadsworth Publishing.

Neville, H.A., Tynes, B.M., & Utsey, S.O. (Eds.) (2009). *Handbook of African American Psychology.* Thousand Oaks, CA: Sage Publications.

Newton, P.A. (2009). *Pharmacological Considerations in the Treatment of Major Depressive Disorders.* Presentation delivered at the annual meeting of the Association Of Black Psychologist, Atlanta, GA, August.

Nickerson, K.J., Helms, J.E., & Terrell, F. (1994). Cultural mistrust, opinions about mental illness and Black student's attitudes toward seeking psychological help from White counselors. *Journal of Counseling Psychology, 41,* 378–385.

Nobles, W.W. (2008). *Ukufu Kwa Bantu & Spirit Illness: Shattered Consciousness or Fractured Identity.* Presentation delivered at the annual convention of the national Association of Black Psychologists, Oakland, CA, August.

Nobles, W.W. (1998). To be African or not to be: The question of identity or authenticity—Some preliminary thoughts. In R.L. Jones (Ed.) *African American Identity Development,* Hampton, VA: Cobb & Henry.

Nobles, W.W. (1986). *African Psychology.* Oakland, CA: Institute for Black Family Life and Culture.

Nobles, W.W. (1985). *Africanity and the Black Family.* Oakland, CA: Black Family Institute Publications.

Nobles, W.W. (1980). *African Philosophy: Foundations for a Black Psychology.* In R.L. Jones (Ed.) Black Psychology (2nd ed). New York: Harper and Row.

Nobles, W.W. (1972). *African's Philosophy: Foundation for Black Psychology.* In N.R.L. Jones (Ed.) *Black Psychology.* New York: Harper & Row.

Norton, D.G. (1983). Black family life patterns, the development of self and cognitive development of Black children. In Powell, Yavrstate, and Morales (Eds.) *The Psychosocial Development of Minority Group Children.* Larchmont, NY: Brunner/Mazel Publishers.

Obama, B. (2006). *The Audacity of Hope.* New York: Crown Publishers.

Obama, B. (2004). *Dreams from My Father: A Story of Race and Inheritance.* New York, NY: Three Rivers Press.

Obenga, T. (1996). *Icons of Maat.* Philadelphia, PA: The Source Editions.

Ogbu, J.U. (1988). Cultural diversity and human development. *New Directions for Child Development. 42,* 11–28.

Pack-Brown, S.P., Whittington-Clark, L.E., & Parker, W.M. (1998). *Images of Me: A Guide to Group Work with African American Women.* Needham Heights, MA: Allyn and Bacon.

Pack-Brown, S., Whitington-Clark, L., & Parker, M. (2007). *Afrocentric Approaches to Group Work: I Am Because We Are.* (DVD) Hanover, MA: Microtraining.

Palardy, J.M. (1969). What Teachers Believe-What Children Achieve. *Elementary School Journal, 69,* 370–374.

Parham, T.A. (1989). Cycles of psychological Nigrescence. *The Counseling Psychologists, 17*(2), 187–226.

Parham, T.A. (1993). *Psychological Storms: The African American Struggle for Identity.* Chicago, IL:African American Images

Parham, T.A. (2000). *Innovative Approaches to Working with African American Clients.* (DVD) North Amhurst, MA: Microtraining

Parham, T.A. (2002). *Counseling Persons of African Descent: Raising the Bar of Practitioner Competence.* Thousand Oaks, CA: Sage Publications.

Parham, T.A. (2004). *Building for Eternity: Solidifying Our Competence through Principled Strength.* Keynote Address delivered at the Annual Winter Roundtable Conference on Cross-Cultural Counseling and Psychotherapy, February.

Parham, T.A. (2005). *Clinical Issues in African Centered Psychology: Lessons in Competence, Proficiency, and Certification.* Presentation at the Annual Convention of the Association of Black Psychologists, Miami, FL.

Parham, T.A. (2006a). *Rediscovering the Roots of Counseling Psychology: Transforming Intellectual Commitment into Social Justice and Community Action.* Invited address at the Winter Roundtable Conference, Teachers College—Columbia University, February.

Parham, T.A. (2006b). *The Bakari Project.* Irvine, CA: KenTay Productions.

Parham, T.A. (2007). *Working with African American Clients in Therapy.* DVD Available through the American Psychological Association, Washington, DC.

Parham, T.A. (2008). *ABPsi: 40 Years in the Making.* Presentation delivered at the annual meeting of the American Psychological Association. San Francisco, CA, August.

Parham, T.A. (2009). Foundations for an African American psychology: Extending roots to an ancient Kemetic past. In H. Neville, B. Tynes, and S. Utsey (eds.) *Handbook of African American Psychology* (pp. 269–281). Thousand Oaks, CA: Sage Publications.

Parham, T.A., & Helms, J.E. (1981). The influence of black students' racial identity attitudes on preferences for counselor's race. *Journal of Counseling Psychology, 28*(3), 250–257.

Parham, T.A., & Helms, J.E. (1985). Relation of racial identity to self-actualization and affective states of Black students. *Journal of Counseling Psychology, 32*(3), 431–440.

Parham, T.A., & Howard, T. (1999). *The state of education for African American youth: An Institutional Report Card.* Unpublished document.

Parham, T.A., & Parham, W.D. (1989). The Afro-American community and the achievement of Afro-American youngsters. In G.L. Berry and J.K. Asamen (Eds.) *Black Students: Psychosocial Issues and Academic Achievement.* Newbury Park, CA: Sage Publications.

Parham, T.A., White, J.L., & Ajamu, A. (1999). *The Psychology Of Blacks: An African Centered Perspective.* Englewood Cliffs, NJ: Prentice Hall.

Pedersen, H.C. (1999). *Multiculturalism as a Fourth Force.* Philadelphia, PA. Taylor & Francis.

Peek, P. (1991). *African Divination Systems: Ways of Knowing.* Bloomington: Indiana University Press.

Pettigrew, T. (1964). *A Profile of the Negro American.* Princeton, NJ: Van Nostrand.

Phillips, F. (1990). NTU Psychotherapy: An Afrocentric Approach. *Journal of Black Psychology, 17*(1), 215–222.

Pickett, S.A., Vraniak, D.A., Cook, J.A., & Cohler, B.J. (1993). Strength in adversity: Blacks bear burden better than Whites. *Professional Psychology: Research and Practice, 24*(4), 460–467.

Pierce, C. (1988). Stress in the workplace. In A.F. Coner-Edwards and J. Spurlock (Eds.) *Black Families in Crisis: The Middle Class* (pp. 27–34). New York, NY: Brunner Mazel.

Pierce, C. (1995). Stress analogs of racism and sexism: Terrorism, torture, and disaster. In C. Willie, P. Rieker, B. Kramer, and B Brown (Eds.) *Mental Health, Racism, and Sexism* (pp. 277–293). Pittsburgh: University of Pittsburgh Press.

Piper-Mandy, E., & Rowe, D. (2010). Educating African-centered psychologists: Towards a comprehensive paradigm. *The Journal of Pan African Studies, 3*(8), 5–23.

Ponterotto, J.G., Casas, J.M., Suzuki, L.A., & Alexander, C.M. (2001). *Handbook of Multicultural Counseling* (2nd ed.). Thousand Oaks, CA. Sage Publications.

Ponterotto, J.G., Casas, J.M., Suzuki, L.A., & Alexander, C.M. (1995). *Handbook of Multicultural Counseling* (1st ed.). Thousand Oaks, CA: Sage Publications.

Pope-Davis, D.B., Coleman, H.L.K., Liu, W.M., & Toporek, R.L. (2003). *Handbook of Mulitcultural Competencies in Counseling and Psychology.* Thousand Oaks, CA: Sage Publications.

Powell, G.J. (1973). Self concept in White and Black children. In C.B. Willie, B.M. Kramer, and B.S. Brown (Eds.) *Racism and Mental Health.* Pittsburgh, PA: University of Pittsburgh Press.

Powell, G. (1985). Self-Concepts among Afro-American Students in Racially Isolated Minority Schools: Some Regional Differences. *Journal of the American Academy of Child Psychiatry, 24*(2), 142–149.

Powell, G.J., & Fuller, M. (1970). Self-concept and school desegregation. *American Journal of Orthopsychiatry, 40,* 303.

Powell-Hopson, D., & Hopson, D. (1998). *The Power of Soul.* New York: Simon and Schuster.

Price, R., & Mintz, S.W. (1992). *The Birth of African-American Culture: An Anthropological Perspective.* Boston: Beacon Press

Pugh, R. (1972). *The Psychology of the Black Experience.* Monterey, CA: Brooks/Cole.

Puzzanchera, C., Stahl, A.L., Finnegan, T.A., Tierney, N., & Snyder, H. 2004. *Juvenile Court Statistics 2000.* Pittsburgh, PA: National Center for Juvenile Justice.

Rainwater, L. (1970*). Behind Ghetto Walls: Black Families in a Federal Slum.* Chicago: Aldine Press.

Robinson, R. (2000). *The Debt: What America Owes to Blacks.* New York, NY: Dutton Press

Robins, L.N., & Regier, D.A. (Eds.) (1991). *Psychiatric disorders in America: The Epidemiologic Catchment Area Study.* New York: The Free Press.

Rogers, C. (1961). *On Becoming a Person: A Therapist's View of Psychotherapy.* London: Constable.

Rogers, M.R., Hoffman, M.A., & Wade, J. (1998). Notable Multicultural Training in APA approved counseling psychology and school psychology programs. *Cultural Diversity and Ethnic Minority Psychology, 4,* 212–226.

Rogers, M.R., Ponterotto, J.G., Conoley, J.C., & Wiese, M.J. (1992). Multicultural training in school psychology: A national survey. *School Psychology Review, 21,* 603–616.

Rosen, B. (1959). Race, ethnicity, and the achievement syndrome. *American Sociological Review, 24,* 47–60.

Rosenberg, M. (1979). *Conceiving of Self.* New York: Basic Books.

Rosenthal, R., & Jacobson, U. (1968). *Pygmalion in the Classroom.* New York: Holt, Rinehart & Winston.

Rothbart, M., Dalfen, S., & Barrett, R. (1971). Effects of teacher expectancy on student-teacher interaction. *Journal of Educational Psychology, 62,* 1, 49–54.

Rotter, J. (1966). Generalized expectancy of internal versus external control of reinforcement. *Psychological Monographs: General and Applied, 80,* 1–28.

Rowe, T.D., & Webb-Msemaji (2004). African-centered psychology in the community. In R. Jones (Ed.) *Black Psychology* (4th ed., pp. 701–721). Hampton, VA: Cobb & Henry.

Rowley, S.J., & Sellers, R.M. (1998). Nigrescence theory: Critical issues and recommendations for future revisions. In R.L. Jones (Ed.) *African American Identity Development: Theory, Research & Intervention.* Hampton, VA: Cobb & Henry.

Rubovitz, P.C., & Maehr, M.L. (1973). Pygmalion Black and White. *Journal of Personality and Social Psychology, 25*(2), 210–218.

Saint-Laurent, G.E. (2000). *Spirituality and World Religions.* Mountain View, CA: Mayfield Publishing.

Sampson, R.J., & Laub, J.H. (2003). *Shared Beginnings, Divergent Lives: Delinquent Boys to Age 70.* Cambridge, MA: Harvard University Press.

Santiago-Rivera, A.L., Arrendondo, P., & Gallardo-Cooper, M. (2002). *Counseling Latinos and la familia.* Thousand Oaks, CA: Sage Publications.

Schulte, D.L., Skinner, T.A., & Claiborn, C.D. (2002). Religion and spiritual issues in counseling psychology training. *The Counseling Psychologist, 30*(1), 118–134.

Seligman, M.E.P. (2003). Positive Psychology: Fundamental Assumptions. *Psychologist, 16,* 126–127.

Semaj, L. (1981). The Black self: Identity and models for a psychology of Black liberation. *Western Journal of Black Studies, 5*(3), 158–171.

Serlin, I. (2005). Spiritual diversity and clinical practice. In J.L. Chin (Ed.) *The Psychology of Prejudice and Discrimination: Disability, Religion, Physique, and Other Traits.* Westport, CT: Praeger Publishers.

Shakur, S. (2004). *Monster: The Autobiography of an L.A. Gang Member.* New York, NY: Grove/Atlantic Inc.

Shipp, P. (1983). Counseling Blacks: A group approach. *Personnel and Guidance Journal, 62*(2), 108–111.

Soares, A.T., & Soares, L.M. (1969). Self perception of culturally disadvantaged children. *American Education Research Journal, 6,* 31–45.

Souza, K.Z. (2002). Spirituality in counseling: What do counseling students think about it? *Counseling & Values, 46*(3), 213–217.

Speight, S.L., Blackmon, S.M., Odugu, D., & Steele, J.C. (2009). Conceptualizing mental health for African Americans. In H.A. Neville, Tynes, B.M., and Utsey, S.O. (Eds.) *Handbook of African American Psychology*. Thousand Oaks, CA: Sage Publications.

Spenser, M.B. (1995). Old issues and new theorizing about African American youth: A phenomenological variant of ecological systems theory. In R.L. Taylor (Ed.) *Black Youth: Perspectives on Their Status in the United States* (pp. 37–69). Westport, CT. Praeger Press.

Spenser, M.B. (2006). Phenomenology and ecological systems: Development of diverse groups. In W. Damon and R. Lerner (Eds.) *Handbook of Child Psychology* (6th ed., pp. 829–893). New York: John Wiley and Sons.

Spenser, M.B., & Markstrom-Adams, C. (1990). Identity process among racial and ethnic minority children in America. *Child Development, 61*(2), 290–310.

Kenneth M. Stampp. (1956). *The Peculiar Institution: Slavery in the Ante-bellum South* New York: Vintage.

Stack, C. (1974). *All Our Kin: Strategies for Survival in the Black Community*. New York: Harper and Row.

Staples, R. (1994). *The Black Family: Essays and Studies*. Belmont, CA: Wadsworth Publishing Company.

Staples, R. (1972). *Black Masculinity*. San Francisco, CA: Black Scholar Press.

Staples, R., & Boulin-Johnson, L. (1993). *Black Families at the Crossroads: Challenges and Prospects*. San Francisco, CA: Jossey-Bass.

Stevenson, H.C. (1995). Relationship of adolescent perceptions of racial socialization to racial identity. *Journal of Black Psychology, 21*(1), 49–70.

Stokes, J.E., Murray, C.B., Chavez, D., & Peacock, M.J. (1998). The Cross stage model revisited: An analysis of theoretical formulation and empirical evidence. In R.L. Jones (Ed.) *African American Identity Development*. Hampton, VA: Cobb & Henry.

Stone, J.H. (2005). *Culture and Disability: Providing Culturally Competent Service*. Thousand Oaks: Sage Publications.

Stuckey, S. (1988/1987). *Slave Culture: Nationalist Theory and the Foundations of Black America*. New York: Oxford University Press.

Sudarkasa, N. (1981). Interpreting the African heritage in Afro-American family organization. In H.P. McAdoo (Ed.) *Black Families*. Beverly Hills: Sage Publications.

Sue, D.W., Capodilupo, C.M., Torino, G., Bucceri, J.M., Holder, A.M.B., & Nadal, K.L. (2007). Racial microaggressions in everyday life: Implications for clinical practice. *The American Psychologist, 62*, 271–286.

Sue, D.W., & Sue, D. (2003). *Counseling the Culturally Diverse: Theory and Practice*. New York, NY: John Wiley & Sons.

Sue, D.W., & Sue, D. (1990), *Counseling the Culturally Different* (2nd ed.). New York: John Wiley and Sons.

Sue, D.W., Ivey, A.E., & Pedersen, P.B. (1996). *A Theory of Multicultural Counseling & Therapy*. Pacific Grove, CA: Brooks/Cole Publishing Company.

Sue, S. (1978). *Ethnic Minority Research: Trends and Directions*. Paper presented at the National Conference on Minority Group Alcohol, Drug abuse, and Mental Health. Denver, Colorado.

Sue, D.W. (2003). *Overcoming Our Racism: A journey to Liberation*. San Francisco, CA: Jossey-Bass.

Sue, D.W., Arredondo, P. & McDavis, Rj. (1992). Multicultural counseling competencies and standards: A call to the profession. *Journal of Counseling Development and Development, 70,* 477–484.

Swanson, D.P., Cunningham, M., Youngblood II, J., & Spencer, M.B. (2009). Racial identity development during childhood. In H. Neville, B. Tynes, and S. Utsey (Eds.) *Handbook of African American Psychology* (pp. 269–281). Thousand Oaks, CA, Sage Publications.

Takeuchi, D.T., Sue, S., & Yeh, M. (1998). Return rates and outcomes from ethnicity: Specific mental health programs in Los Angeles. In P. Balls Organista, K.M. Chun, and G. Marin (Eds.) *Readings in Ethnic Psychology* (pp. 324–334). New York: Routledge.

Distribution Center, Education Commission of the States. (1983). *Taskforce on Education and Economic Growth*. Denver, CO: Author.

Taylor, R., Jackson, J.S., & Chatters, L. (1997). *Family Life In Black America*. Newberry Park, CA: Sage Publications.

Taylor, R.D., & Lopez, E.I. (2005). Family management practice, school achievement, and problem behavior in African American adolescents: Mediating process. *Journal of Applied Developmental Psychology, 26*(1), 39–49.

Thomas, W. (1967). *The Thomas Self-Concept Values Test: For Children Ages 3–9*. Grand Rapids, MI: Educational Service.

Thomas, C. (1971). *Boys No More*. Beverly Hills, CA: Glenco Press.

Thomas, C. (1972). Psychologist, psychology, and the Black community. In R.L. Jones (Ed.) *Black Psychology*. New York, NY: Harper & Row.

Thomas, W.A. (2000). *Larry P Revisited: IQ Testing of African Americans*. San Francisco, CA: California Publishing Company.

Thomas, A., & Sillen, S. (1972). *Racism in Psychiatry*. Secaucus, NJ: Citadel Press.

Thompson, R.F. (1984). *Flash of the Spirit: African & Afro-American Art & Philosophy*. New York: Random House.

Thompson, C.E., & Jenal, S.T. (1994). Interracial and intraracial quasi-counseling interactions when counselors avoid discussing race. *Journal of Counseling Psychology, 41,* 484–491.

U.S. Census Bureau. (2000). *Current Population Survey and Demographics*. Washington, DC: Author.

U.S. Census Bureau. (2008). *Preliminary Estimates of Weighted Average Poverty Thresholds for 2008*. Washington, DC: Author.

U.S. Census Bureau. (2007). *Population Statistics*. Retrieved December 1, 2007, from http://www.census.gov.

U.S. Department of Education. (2009). *The Condition of Education*. Washington, DC: National Center for Educational Statistics.

U.S. Department of Education, National Center for Educational Statistics. (2006). *Digest of Educational Statistics, Data from the National Assessment of Educational Progress, various years (1980–2004)*. Washington, DC: Author.

U.S. Department of Health and Human Services. (2001). *Mental Health: Culture, Race, & Ethnicity (a supplement to the Report of the Surgeon General)*. Rockville, MD: Office of the Surgeon General.

U.S. Department of Health and Human Services. (2003). National Healthcare Disparities Report. Washington, DC: U.S. Government Printing Office.

Vandiver, B.J., Cross, W.E., Worrell, F.C., & Fhagen-Smith, P.E. (2002). Validating the Cross Racial Identity Scale. *Journal of Counseling Psychology, 49,* 71–85.

Van Sertima, I. (1976). *They Came before Columbus: The African Presence in Ancient Africa.* New York, NY: Random House.

Walker, D. (1829/1997). *David Walker's Appeal.* Baltimore: Black Classic Press.

Walker, S. (2001). *African Roots/American Cultures: Africa in the Creation of the Americas.* Lanham: Rowman & Littlefield Publishers, Inc.

Weinberg, M. (1977). Minority students: A research appraisal. Washington DC: National Institute of Education.

Wendell, R. (2003). Lived religion and family therapy: What does spirituality have to do with it? *Family Process, 42*(1), 165–179.

West, C. (1993). *Race Matters.* Boston, MA: Beacon Press.

West, C. (1999). *The Cornel West Reader.* New York, NY: Basic Cervitas Books.

Whaley, A. (2001). Cultural mistrust of White mental health clinicians among African Americans with severe mental illness. *American Journal of Orthopsychiatry, 71*(2), 252–256.

White, C. (2010). In Encyclopædia Britannica. Retrieved July 22, 2010, from Encyclopædia Britannica Online: http://www.britannica.com/EBchecked/topic/1006895/Charles-White.

White, J.L. (1972). Toward a Black psychology. In R.L. Jones (Ed.) *Black Psychology* (pp. 43–50). New York: Harper & Row.

White, J.L. (1984). *The Psychology of Blacks.* New York: Prentice Hall.

White, J.L., & Parham, T.A. (1990). *The Psychology of Blacks: An African American Perspective* (2nd ed.). Englewood Cliffs, NJ: Prentice-Hall.

White, J.L., & Henderson, S.J. (2008). *Building Multicultural Competency: Development, Training and Practice.* Lanham, MD: Rowman & Littlefield.

White, J.L., Parham, W.D., & Parham, T.A. The Afro-American tradition as a unifying force for traditional psychology. In R.L. Jones (Ed.) *Black Psychology* (2nd ed.). New York: Harper and Row.

Williams, D.R., Gonzalez, H.M., Neighbors, H., Nesse, R., Abelson, J.M., Sweetman, J. et al (2007). Prevalence and distribution of major depressive disorders in African Americans, Caribbean Blacks, and non-Hispanic Whites: Results from a national survey of American life. *Archives of General Psychiatry, 64,* 305–315.

Williams, C. (1974). *The Destruction of Black Civilization: Great Issues of a Race 4500 B.C. to 2000 A.D.* Chicago, IL: Third World Press.

Williams, R.L. (1972). Abuses and misuses of testing Black children. In R.L. Jones (Ed.) *Black Psychology.* New York, NY: Harper & Row.

Williams, R.L., & Mitchell, H. (1980). The testing game. In R.L. Jones (Ed.) *Black Psychology* (2nd Ed.) New York, NY: Harper & Row.

Wilson, A. (1993). *The Falsification of Consciousness: Eurocentric History, Psychiatry and the Politics of White Supremacy.* New York: Afrikan World Infosystems.

Wilson, A. (1978). *The Developmental Psychology of the Black Child.* New York: United Brothers Communications Systems.

Wilson, W.J. (2009). *More Than Just Race: Being Black and Poor in the Inner City*. New York: W.W. Norton and Company.

Wilson, W.J. (1990). *More Than Just Race: Being Black and Poor in the Inner City (Issues of Our Time)*. New York: W.W. Norton and Company.

Wilson, W.J. (1997). *When Work Disappears: The World of the New Urban Poor*. New York: Vintage.

Wilson, W.J. (1990). *The Truly Disadvantaged: The Inner City, the Underclass, and Public Policy*. Chicago: University of Chicago Press.

Woodson, C.G. (1933). *The Miseducation of the Negro*. Trenton, NJ: African World Press.

Wright, R. (1937). *Black Boy*. New York: Harper and Row.

Wright, R. (1964). *White Man Listen*. Garden City, NY: Doubleday Books.

Wylie, R. (1978). *The Self Concept: Theory and Research on Selected Topics,* Volume 2. Lincoln: University of Nebraska Press.

Wynn, M.D., White, K.D., & Coop, R.H. (1974). *The Black Self.* Englewood Cliffs, NJ: Prentice Hall.

Yogananda, P. (1946). *Autobiography of a Yogi*. India: The Free Press.

Zea, M.C., Quezada, T., & Belgrave, F.Z. (1997). Limitations of an acultural health psychology: Reconstructing the African influence on Latino culture and health related behaviors. In J. Garcia and M.C. Zea, (Eds.) *Psychological Interventions and Research with Latino Populations* (pp. 55–266). Boston: Allyn & Bacon.

Zhang, A.Y., & Snowden, L.R. (1999). Ethnic characteristics of mental disorders in five U.S. communities, *Cultural Diversity and Ethnic Minority Psychology 5*, 134–146.

FOOTNOTES

Chapter 4

[1]Kenneth Clark had conducted a series of doll studies that proved to be instrumental in Brown V Board of Education decision which struck down Plessy V. Ferguson 1898?

[2]See inter alia. . . . Frazier books.

[3]The Melville J. Herskovits Library of African Studies housed at Northwestern University, established in 1954, remains to this day the largest separate collection of Africana in the world.

[4]Herskovits was not the first scholar to make the argument about cultural retentions. David Walker in David Walkers Appeal (1829), Martin Delany African life and Customs (1908) and WEB Dubois had all anticipated Herskovits arguments.

[5]Talk here about DuBois' pioneering studies on the Black Family and the Philadephia Negro and about how Dubois was a mentor to Frazier.

[6]The Condition, Elevation, Emigration and Destiny of the Colored People of the United States, Politically Considered, (1852); Black Classic Press, reprint (1993); *The Voice of Anna Julia Cooper: Including A Voice From the South and Other Important Essays, Papers, and Letters* (Rowman and Littlefield, 1998). See also Moses, Wilson Jeremiah. *Alexander Crummell: A Study of Civilization and Discontent.* New York: Oxford University Press, 1989. For a more in-depth discussion of nineteenth century black nationalism, see Wilson Jeremiah Moses' *The Golden Age of Black Nationalism, 1850–1925.*

INDEX